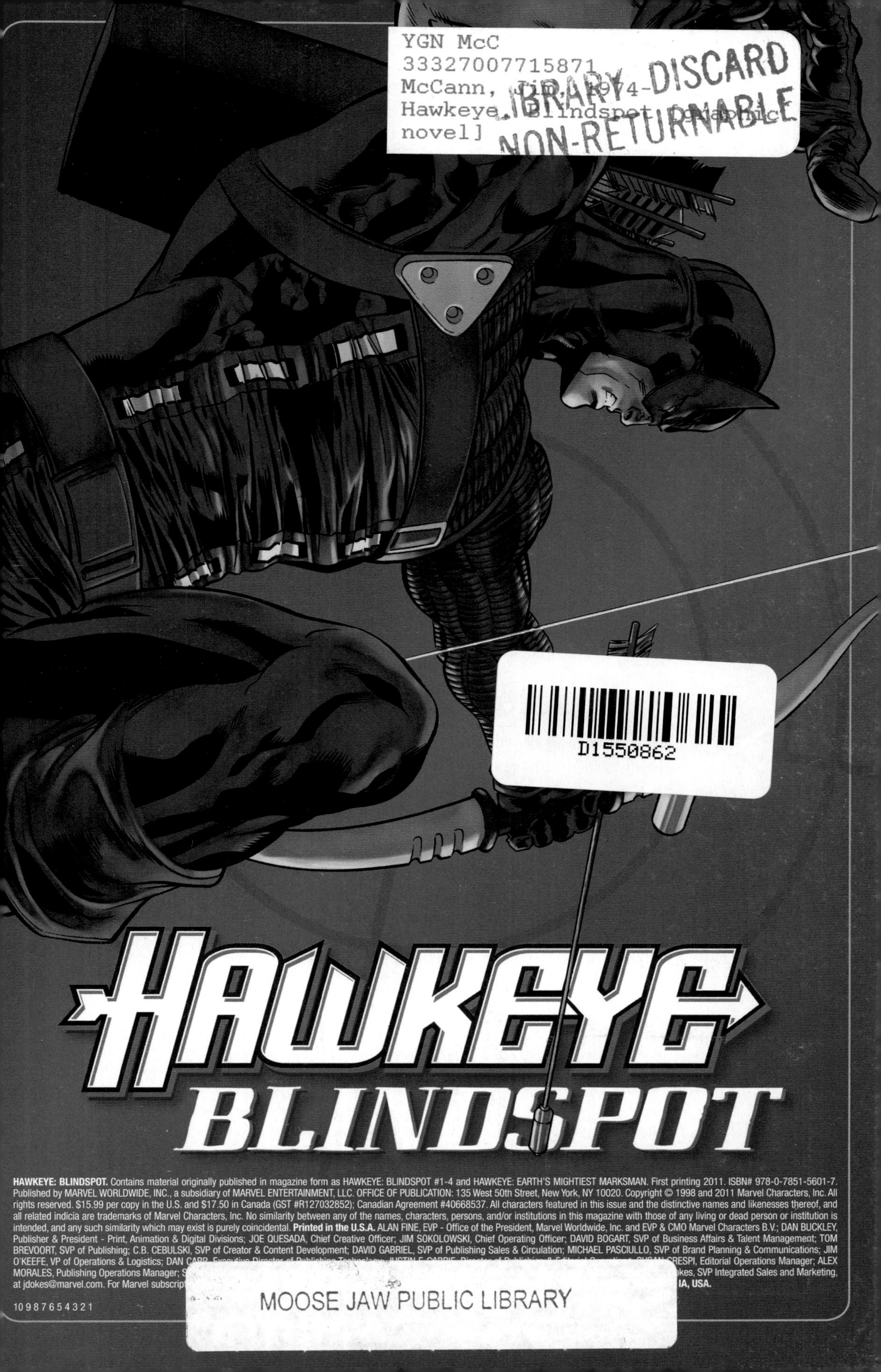

HAWKEYE
BLINDSPOT

HAWKEYE: BLINDSPOT. Contains material originally published in magazine form as HAWKEYE: BLINDSPOT #1-4 and HAWKEYE: EARTH'S MIGHTIEST MARKSMAN. First printing 2011. ISBN# 978-0-7851-5601-7. Published by MARVEL WORLDWIDE, INC., a subsidiary of MARVEL ENTERTAINMENT, LLC. OFFICE OF PUBLICATION: 135 West 50th Street, New York, NY 10020. $15.99 per copy in the U.S. and $17.50 in Canada (GST #R127032852); Canadian Agreement #40668537. **Printed in the U.S.A.** ALAN FINE, EVP - Office of the President, Marvel Worldwide, Inc. and EVP & CMO Marvel Characters B.V.; DAN BUCKLEY, Publisher & President - Print, Animation & Digital Divisions; JOE QUESADA, Chief Creative Officer; JIM SOKOLOWSKI, Chief Operating Officer; DAVID BOGART, SVP of Business Affairs & Talent Management; TOM BREVOORT, SVP of Publishing; C.B. CEBULSKI, SVP of Creator & Content Development; DAVID GABRIEL, SVP of Publishing Sales & Circulation; MICHAEL PASCIULLO, SVP of Brand Planning & Communications; JIM O'KEEFE, VP of Operations & Logistics; DAN CARR ... CRESPI, Editorial Operations Manager; ALEX MORALES, Publishing Operations Manager; S... kes, SVP Integrated Sales and Marketing, at jdokes@marvel.com. For Marvel subscript... **IA, USA.**

10 9 8 7 6 5 4 3 2 1

HAWKEYE
BLINDSPOT

Writer | JIM McCANN

Artist (modern day) | PACO DIAZ
Colorist (modern day) | TOMEU MOREY

Artists (flashbacks) | NICK DRAGOTTA (ISSUE #2)
VALENTINE DE LANDRO, LEE WEEKS & STEFANO GAUDIANO (ISSUE #3)
Colorists (flashbacks) | BRAD SIMPSON (ISSUE #2)
CHRIS SOTOMAYOR & MORRY HOLLOWELL (ISSUE #3)

Letterer | VC'S CLAYTON COWLES
Covers | MIKE PERKINS WITH MORRY HOLLOWELL & JOHN RAUCH
Assistant Editor | RACHEL PINNELAS
Editor | TOM BRENNAN

HAWKEYE: EARTH'S MIGHTIEST MARKSMAN

Writer | TOM DEFALCO
Pencilers | JEFF JOHNSON, DAVE ROSS & MARK BAGLEY

Inkers | SCOTT KOLINS, TOM WEGRZYN & AL MILGROM
Colorist | JOE ANDREANI
Letterers | JIM NOVAK & SUE CRESPI
Cover | DARICK ROBERTSON & ROB MCNABB
Editor | GLENN GREENBERG

Collection Editor | CORY LEVINE • Editorial Assistants | JAMES EMMETT & JOE HOCHSTEIN
Assistant Editors | MATT MASDEU, ALEX STARBUCK & NELSON RIBEIRO
Editors, Special Projects | JENNIFER GRÜNWALD & MARK D. BEAZLEY
Senior Editor, Special Projects | JEFF YOUNGQUIST • Senior Vice President of Sales | DAVID GABRIEL
SVP of Brand Planning & Communications | MICHAEL PASCIULLO
Book Designer | ARLENE SO

Editor in Chief | AXEL ALONSO • Chief Creative Officer | JOE QUESADA
Publisher | DAN BUCKLEY • Executive Producer | ALAN FINE

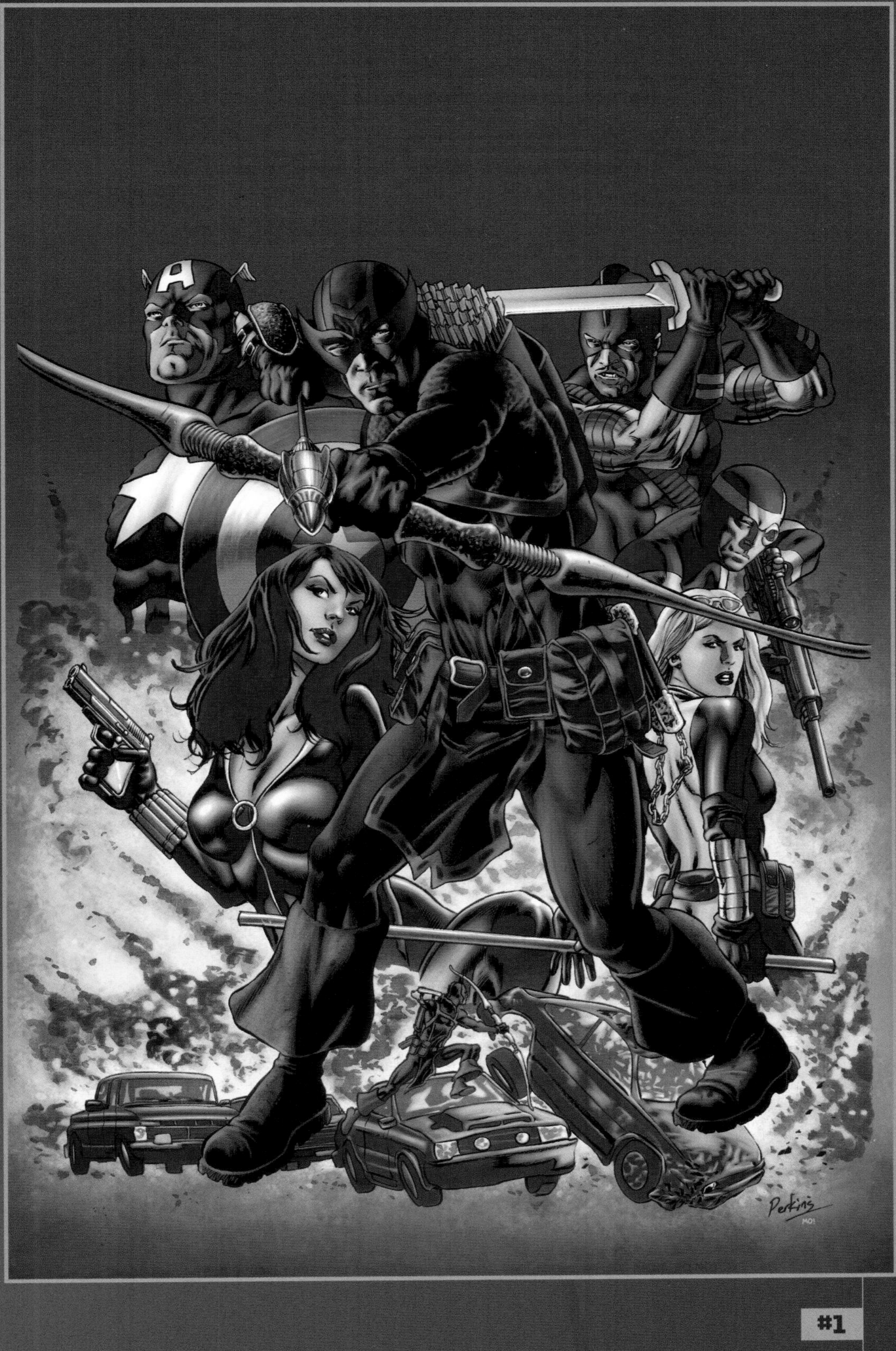
Perkins
MO1

#1

Clint Barton. Hawkeye. Marksman. Archer. Avenger.

After Norman Osborn's Dark Reign ended, Barton resumed the mantle of Hawkeye after his apparent death and subsequent stint as *"Ronin"* and rejoined the Avengers alongside Steve Rogers. He happily reunited with Bobbi Morse, a.k.a. Mockingbird, his ex-wife and fellow Avenger.

When Bobbi returned to Earth during the Skrull invasion, she put her S.H.I.E.L.D. training to use and formed the W.C.A. and recruited Hawkeye to partner with her romantically and tackling international threats.

A recent adventure took them to Russia to aid Natasha Romanova, the Black Widow, in stopping a terrorist who was not only targeting spies such as Mockingbird and Natasha, but masquerading in Clint's old Ronin costume. Their mission was victorious, but not without some damage.

Although his reputation survived unscathed, his abilities as an expert shot have taken a beating…

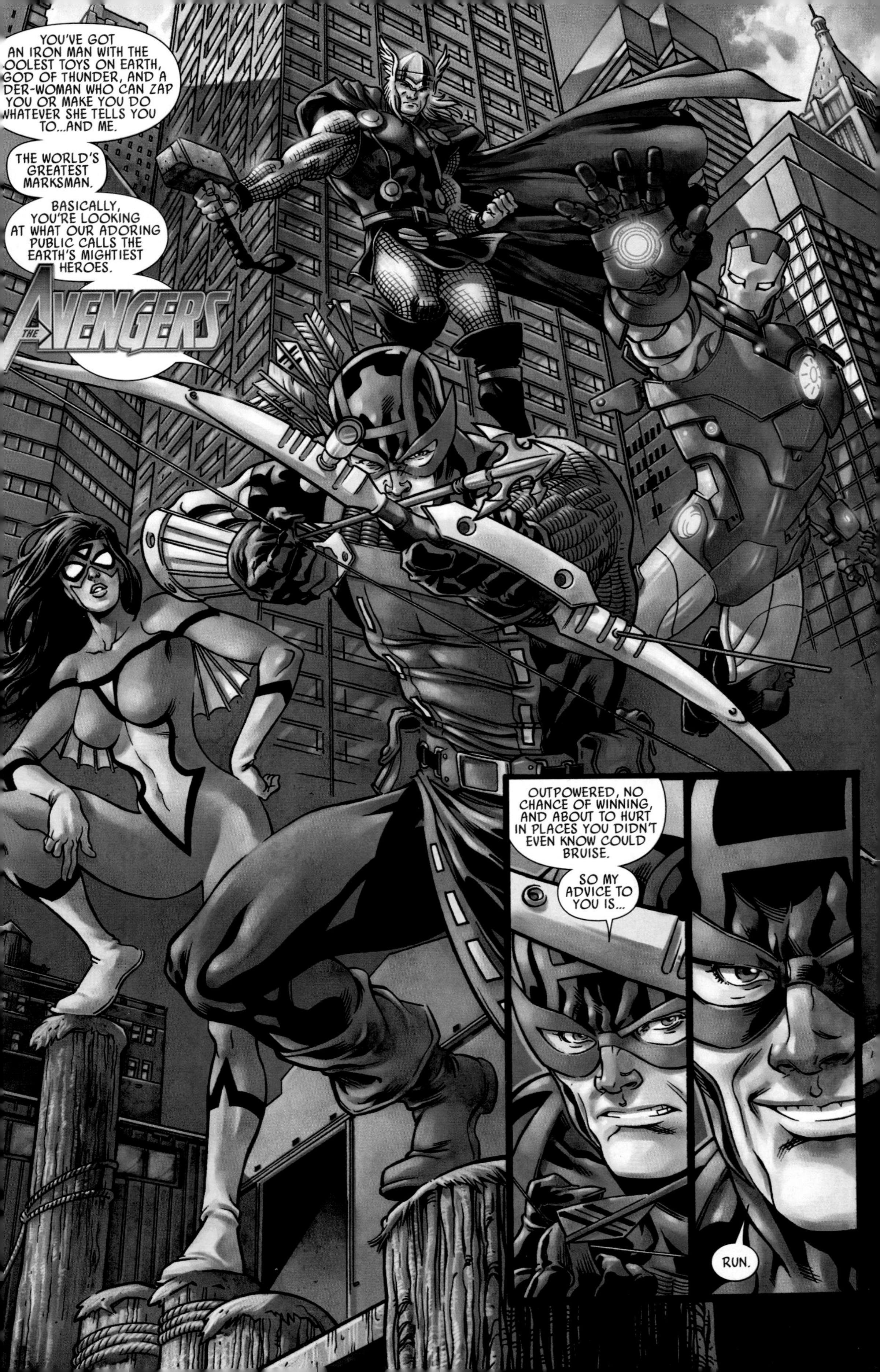
YOU'VE GOT AN IRON MAN WITH THE OOLEST TOYS ON EARTH, GOD OF THUNDER, AND A DER-WOMAN WHO CAN ZAP YOU OR MAKE YOU DO WHATEVER SHE TELLS YOU TO...AND ME.
THE WORLD'S GREATEST MARKSMAN.
BASICALLY, YOU'RE LOOKING AT WHAT OUR ADORING PUBLIC CALLS THE EARTH'S MIGHTIEST HEROES.
THE AVENGERS
OUTPOWERED, NO CHANCE OF WINNING, AND ABOUT TO HURT IN PLACES YOU DIDN'T EVEN KNOW COULD BRUISE.
SO MY ADVICE TO YOU IS...
RUN.

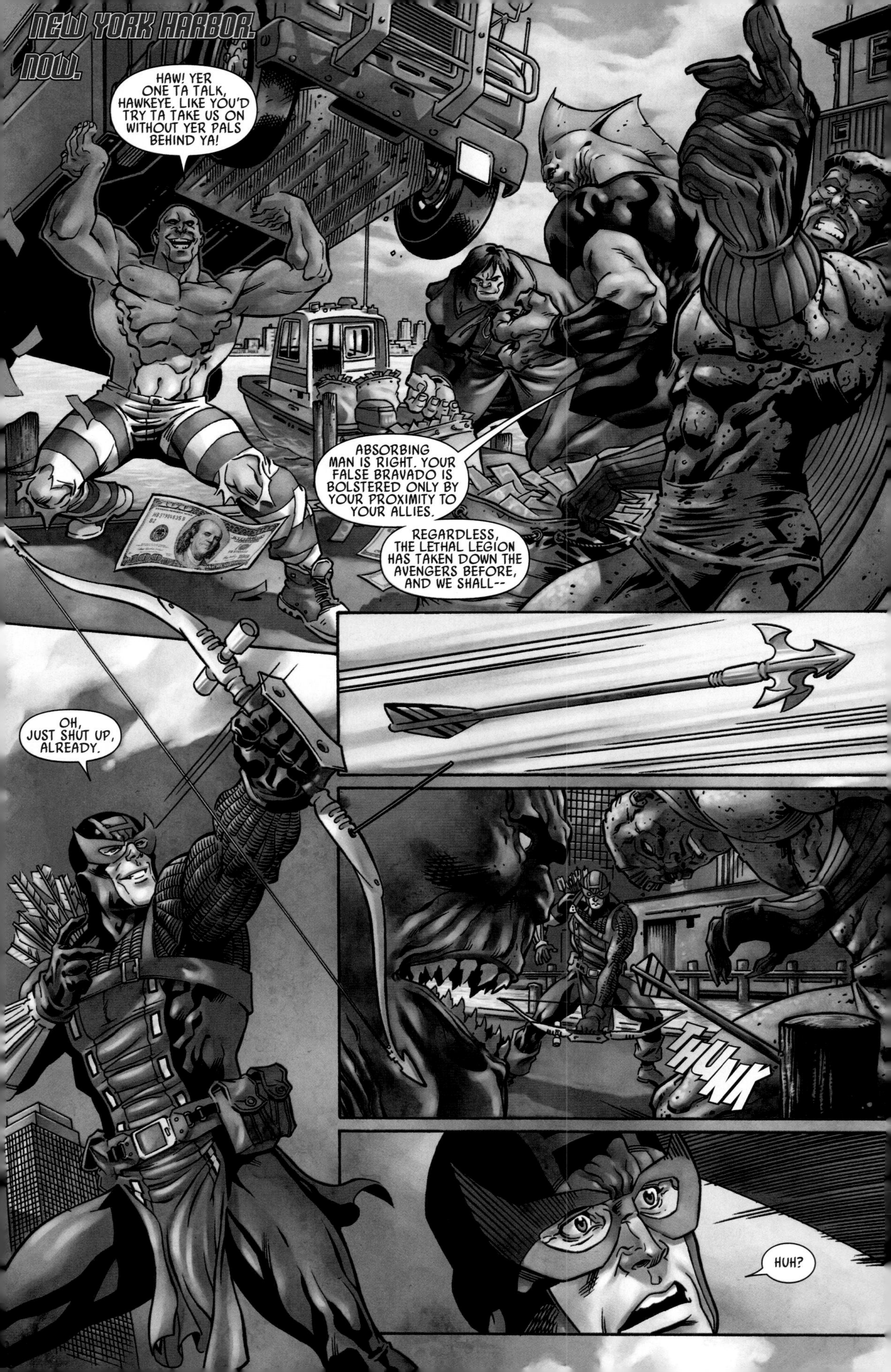
NEW YORK HARBOR. NOW.
HAW! YER ONE TA TALK, HAWKEYE. LIKE YOU'D TRY TA TAKE US ON WITHOUT YER PALS BEHIND YA!
ABSORBING MAN IS RIGHT. YOUR FALSE BRAVADO IS BOLSTERED ONLY BY YOUR PROXIMITY TO YOUR ALLIES.
REGARDLESS, THE LETHAL LEGION HAS TAKEN DOWN THE AVENGERS BEFORE, AND WE SHALL--
OH, JUST SHUT UP, ALREADY.
THUNK
HUH?

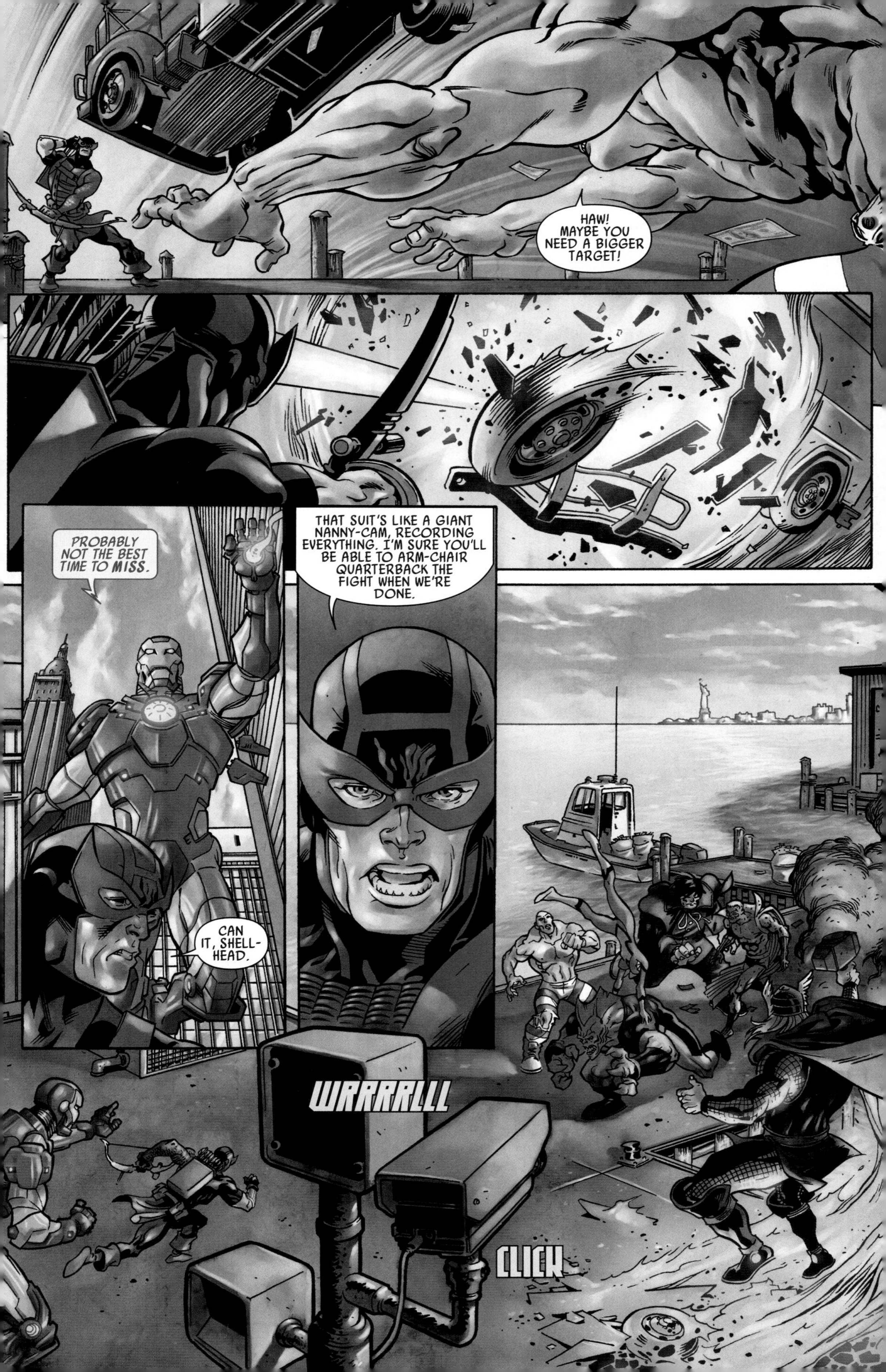
HAW! MAYBE YOU NEED A BIGGER TARGET!
PROBABLY NOT THE BEST TIME TO MISS.
THAT SUIT'S LIKE A GIANT NANNY-CAM, RECORDING EVERYTHING. I'M SURE YOU'LL BE ABLE TO ARM-CHAIR QUARTERBACK THE FIGHT WHEN WE'RE DONE.
CAN IT, SHELL-HEAD.
WRRRRLLL
CLICK

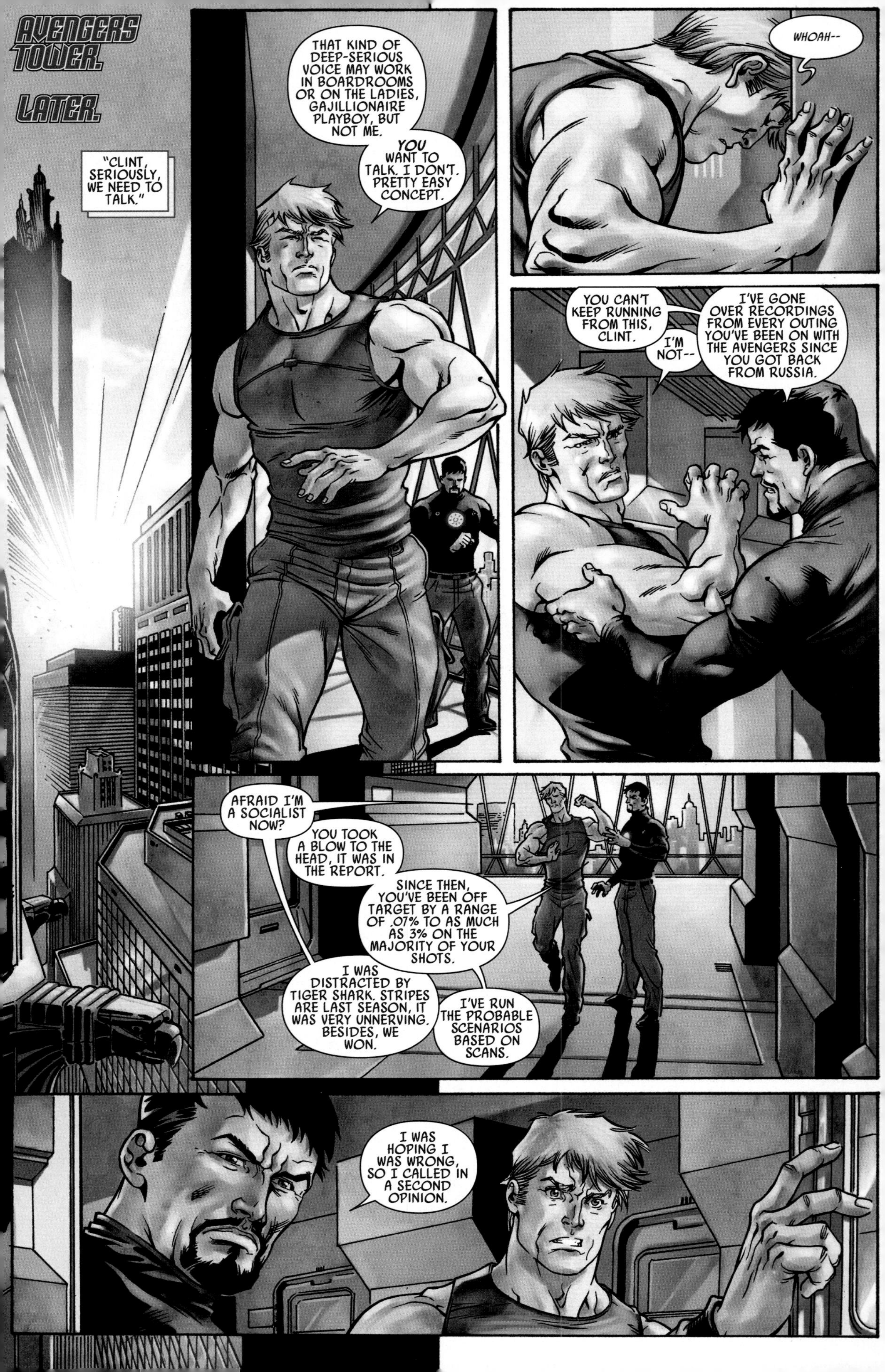
AVENGERS TOWER.
LATER.
"CLINT, SERIOUSLY, WE NEED TO TALK."
THAT KIND OF DEEP-SERIOUS VOICE MAY WORK IN BOARDROOMS OR ON THE LADIES, GAJILLIONAIRE PLAYBOY, BUT NOT ME.
YOU WANT TO TALK. I DON'T. PRETTY EASY CONCEPT.
WHOAH--
YOU CAN'T KEEP RUNNING FROM THIS, CLINT.
I'M NOT--
I'VE GONE OVER RECORDINGS FROM EVERY OUTING YOU'VE BEEN ON WITH THE AVENGERS SINCE YOU GOT BACK FROM RUSSIA.
AFRAID I'M A SOCIALIST NOW?
YOU TOOK A BLOW TO THE HEAD, IT WAS IN THE REPORT.
SINCE THEN, YOU'VE BEEN OFF TARGET BY A RANGE OF .07% TO AS MUCH AS 3% ON THE MAJORITY OF YOUR SHOTS.
I WAS DISTRACTED BY TIGER SHARK. STRIPES ARE LAST SEASON, IT WAS VERY UNNERVING. BESIDES, WE WON.
I'VE RUN THE PROBABLE SCENARIOS BASED ON SCANS.
I WAS HOPING I WAS WRONG, SO I CALLED IN A SECOND OPINION.

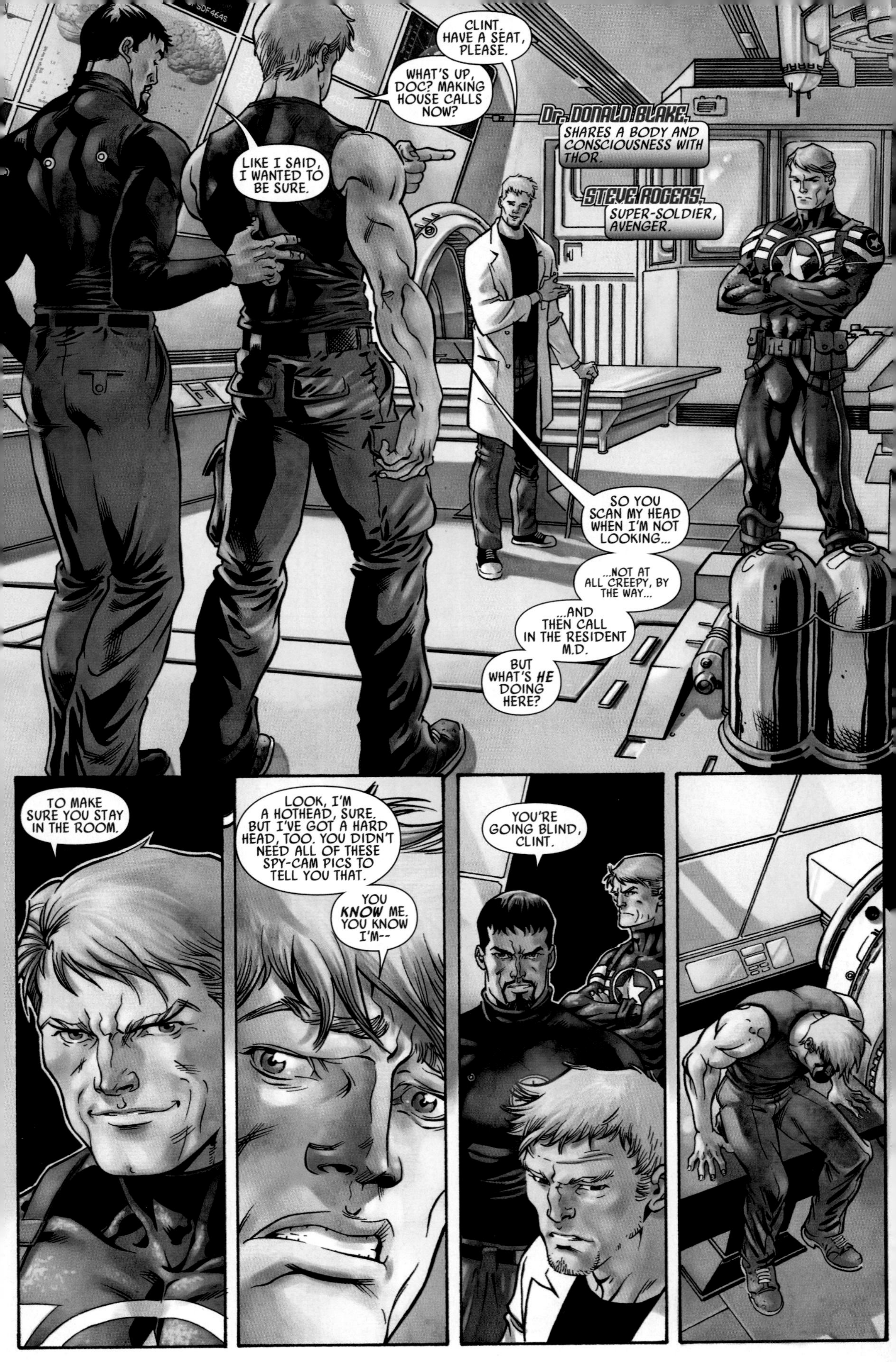
CLINT. HAVE A SEAT, PLEASE.
WHAT'S UP, DOC? MAKING HOUSE CALLS NOW?
LIKE I SAID, I WANTED TO BE SURE.
Dr. DONALD BLAKE, SHARES A BODY AND CONSCIOUSNESS WITH THOR.
STEVE ROGERS, SUPER-SOLDIER, AVENGER.
SO YOU SCAN MY HEAD WHEN I'M NOT LOOKING...
...NOT AT ALL CREEPY, BY THE WAY...
...AND THEN CALL IN THE RESIDENT M.D.
BUT WHAT'S HE DOING HERE?
TO MAKE SURE YOU STAY IN THE ROOM.
LOOK, I'M A HOTHEAD, SURE. BUT I'VE GOT A HARD HEAD, TOO. YOU DIDN'T NEED ALL OF THESE SPY-CAM PICS TO TELL YOU THAT.
YOU KNOW ME. YOU KNOW I'M--
YOU'RE GOING BLIND, CLINT.

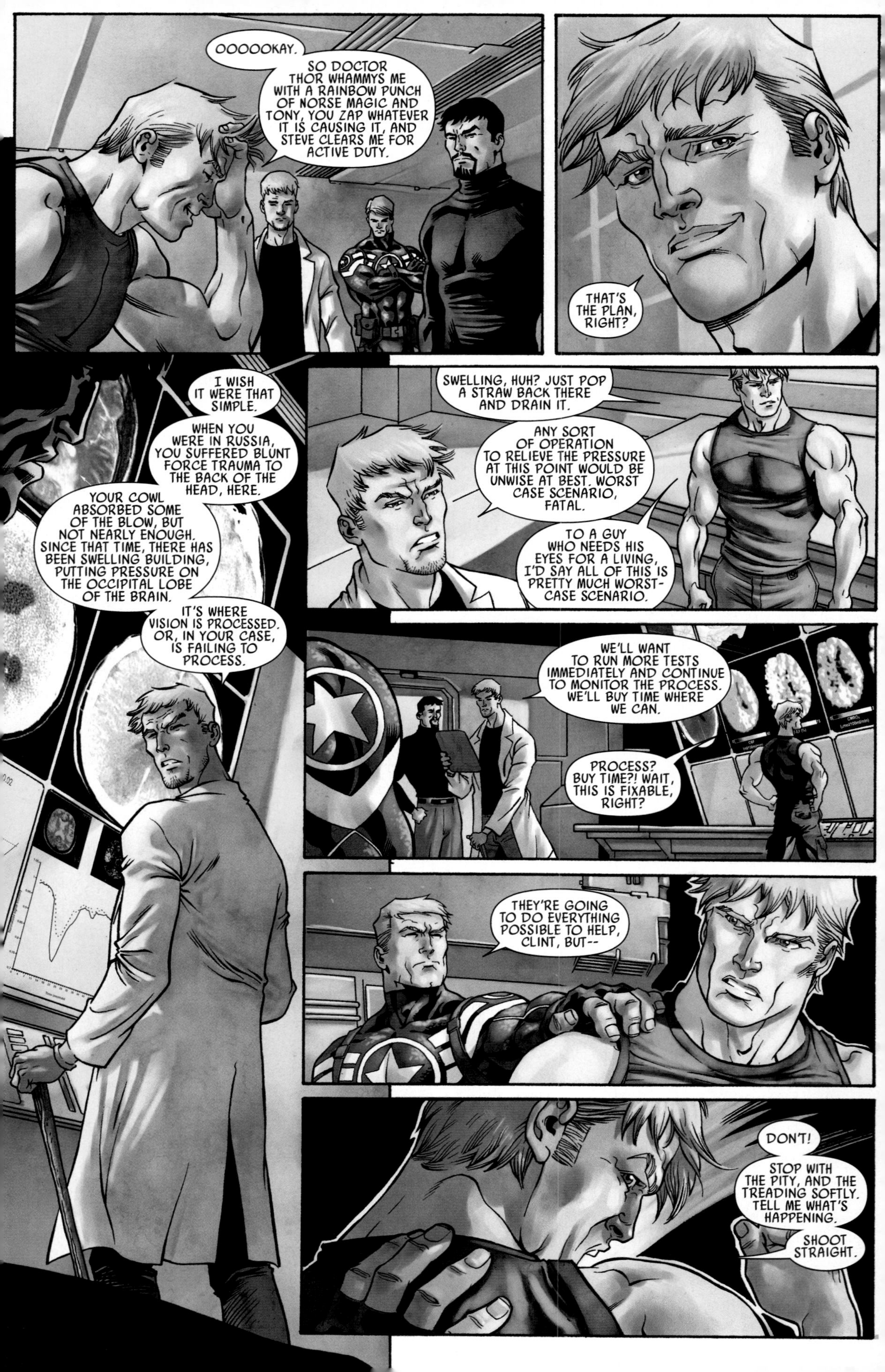
OOOOOKAY.
SO DOCTOR THOR WHAMMYS ME WITH A RAINBOW PUNCH OF NORSE MAGIC AND TONY, YOU ZAP WHATEVER IT IS CAUSING IT, AND STEVE CLEARS ME FOR ACTIVE DUTY.
THAT'S THE PLAN, RIGHT?
I WISH IT WERE THAT SIMPLE.
WHEN YOU WERE IN RUSSIA, YOU SUFFERED BLUNT FORCE TRAUMA TO THE BACK OF THE HEAD, HERE.
YOUR COWL ABSORBED SOME OF THE BLOW, BUT NOT NEARLY ENOUGH. SINCE THAT TIME, THERE HAS BEEN SWELLING BUILDING, PUTTING PRESSURE ON THE OCCIPITAL LOBE OF THE BRAIN.
IT'S WHERE VISION IS PROCESSED. OR, IN YOUR CASE, IS FAILING TO PROCESS.
SWELLING, HUH? JUST POP A STRAW BACK THERE AND DRAIN IT.
ANY SORT OF OPERATION TO RELIEVE THE PRESSURE AT THIS POINT WOULD BE UNWISE AT BEST. WORST CASE SCENARIO, FATAL.
TO A GUY WHO NEEDS HIS EYES FOR A LIVING, I'D SAY ALL OF THIS IS PRETTY MUCH WORST-CASE SCENARIO.
WE'LL WANT TO RUN MORE TESTS IMMEDIATELY AND CONTINUE TO MONITOR THE PROCESS. WE'LL BUY TIME WHERE WE CAN.
PROCESS? BUY TIME?! WAIT, THIS IS FIXABLE, RIGHT?
THEY'RE GOING TO DO EVERYTHING POSSIBLE TO HELP, CLINT, BUT--
DON'T!
STOP WITH THE PITY, AND THE TREADING SOFTLY. TELL ME WHAT'S HAPPENING.
SHOOT STRAIGHT.

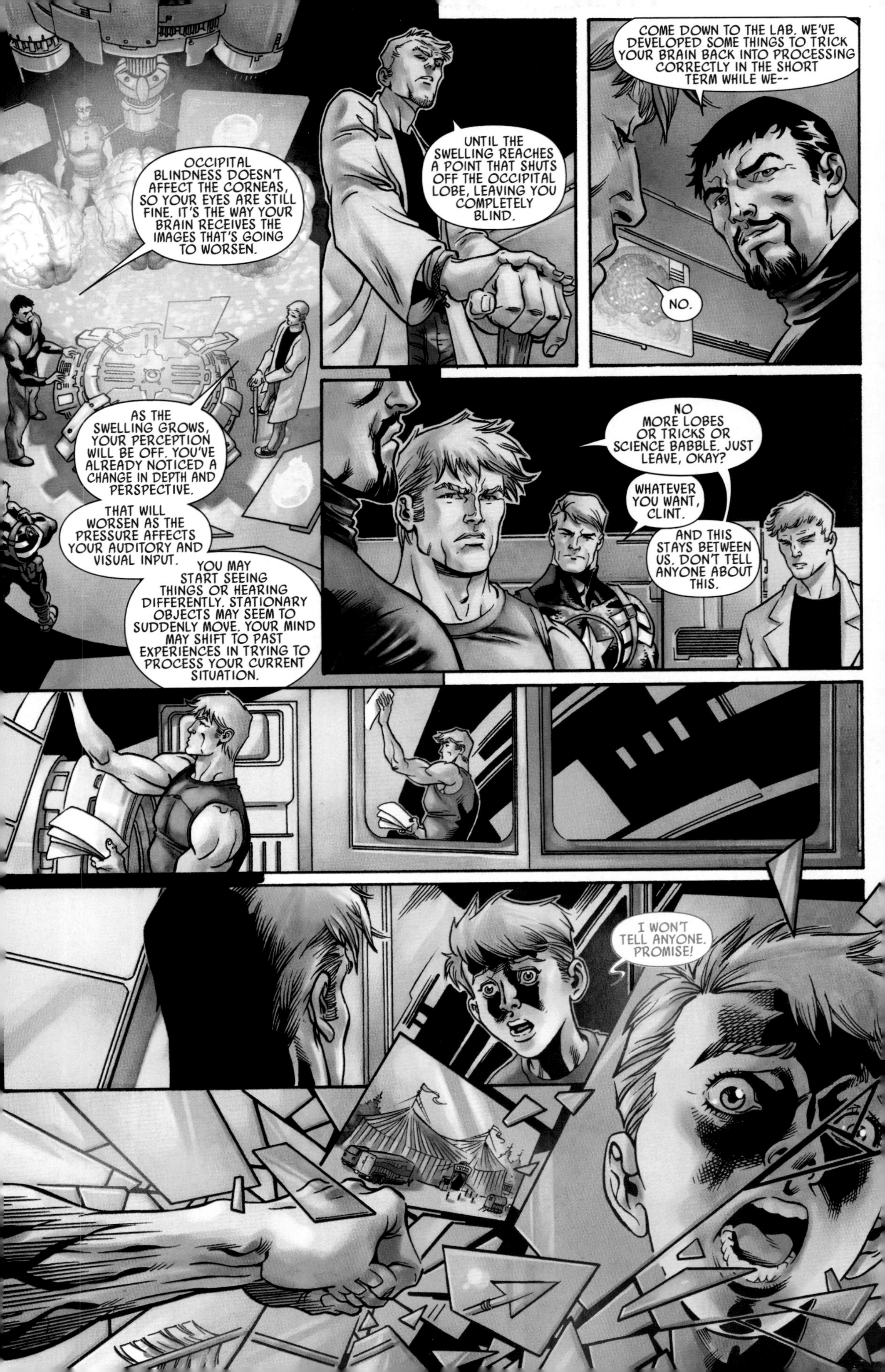
OCCIPITAL BLINDNESS DOESN'T AFFECT THE CORNEAS, SO YOUR EYES ARE STILL FINE. IT'S THE WAY YOUR BRAIN RECEIVES THE IMAGES THAT'S GOING TO WORSEN.
UNTIL THE SWELLING REACHES A POINT THAT SHUTS OFF THE OCCIPITAL LOBE, LEAVING YOU COMPLETELY BLIND.
COME DOWN TO THE LAB. WE'VE DEVELOPED SOME THINGS TO TRICK YOUR BRAIN BACK INTO PROCESSING CORRECTLY IN THE SHORT TERM WHILE WE--
NO.
AS THE SWELLING GROWS, YOUR PERCEPTION WILL BE OFF. YOU'VE ALREADY NOTICED A CHANGE IN DEPTH AND PERSPECTIVE.
THAT WILL WORSEN AS THE PRESSURE AFFECTS YOUR AUDITORY AND VISUAL INPUT.
YOU MAY START SEEING THINGS OR HEARING DIFFERENTLY. STATIONARY OBJECTS MAY SEEM TO SUDDENLY MOVE. YOUR MIND MAY SHIFT TO PAST EXPERIENCES IN TRYING TO PROCESS YOUR CURRENT SITUATION.
NO MORE LOBES OR TRICKS OR SCIENCE BABBLE. JUST LEAVE, OKAY?
WHATEVER YOU WANT, CLINT.
AND THIS STAYS BETWEEN US. DON'T TELL ANYONE ABOUT THIS.
I WON'T TELL ANYONE. PROMISE!

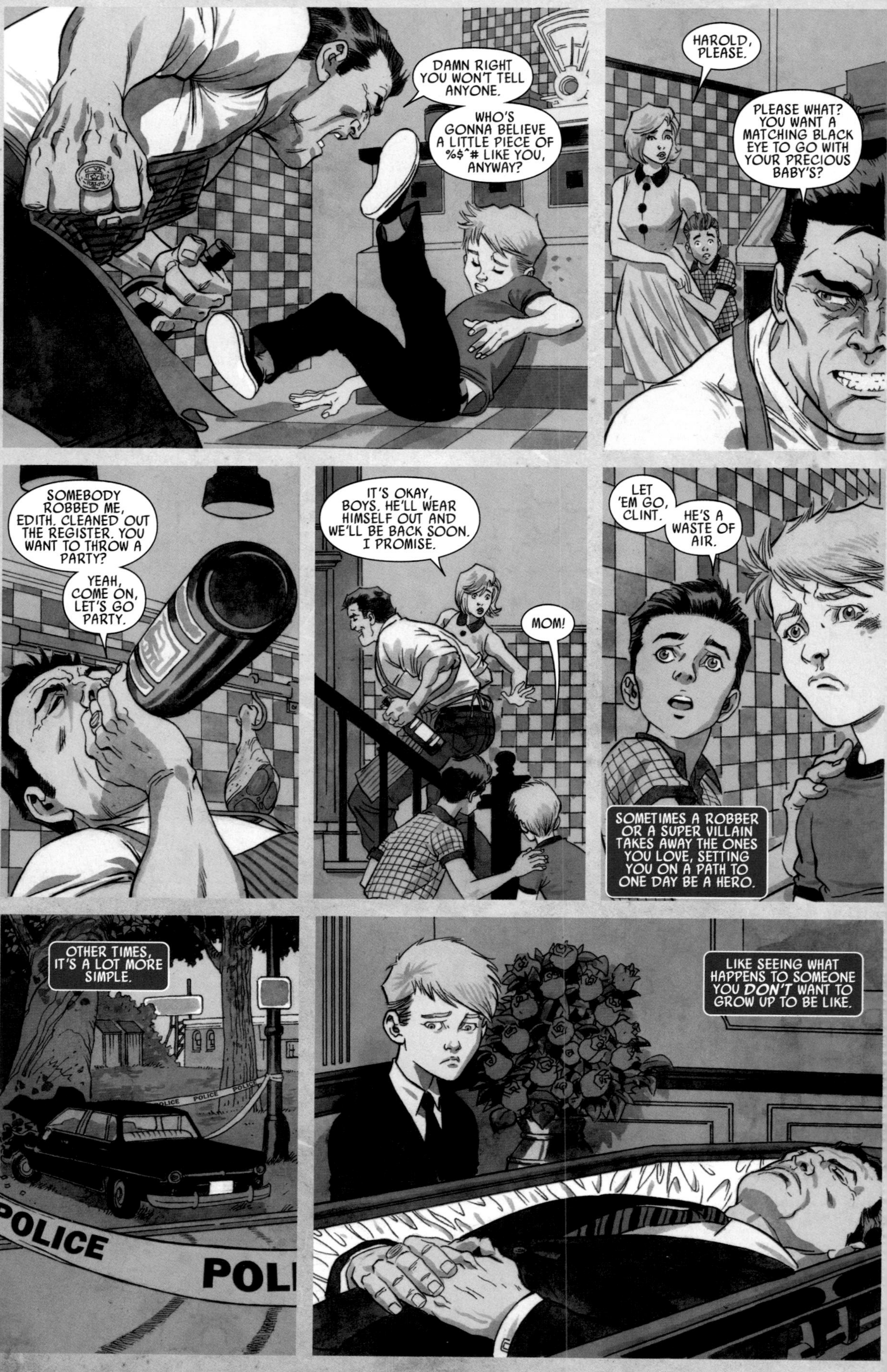
DAMN RIGHT YOU WON'T TELL ANYONE.
WHO'S GONNA BELIEVE A LITTLE PIECE OF %$^# LIKE YOU, ANYWAY?
HAROLD, PLEASE.
PLEASE WHAT? YOU WANT A MATCHING BLACK EYE TO GO WITH YOUR PRECIOUS BABY'S?
SOMEBODY ROBBED ME, EDITH. CLEANED OUT THE REGISTER. YOU WANT TO THROW A PARTY?
YEAH, COME ON, LET'S GO PARTY.
IT'S OKAY, BOYS. HE'LL WEAR HIMSELF OUT AND WE'LL BE BACK SOON. I PROMISE.
MOM!
LET 'EM GO, CLINT.
HE'S A WASTE OF AIR.
SOMETIMES A ROBBER OR A SUPER VILLAIN TAKES AWAY THE ONES YOU LOVE, SETTING YOU ON A PATH TO ONE DAY BE A HERO.
OTHER TIMES, IT'S A LOT MORE SIMPLE.
POLICE
POLICE
POLICE
POLI
LIKE SEEING WHAT HAPPENS TO SOMEONE YOU *DON'T* WANT TO GROW UP TO BE LIKE.

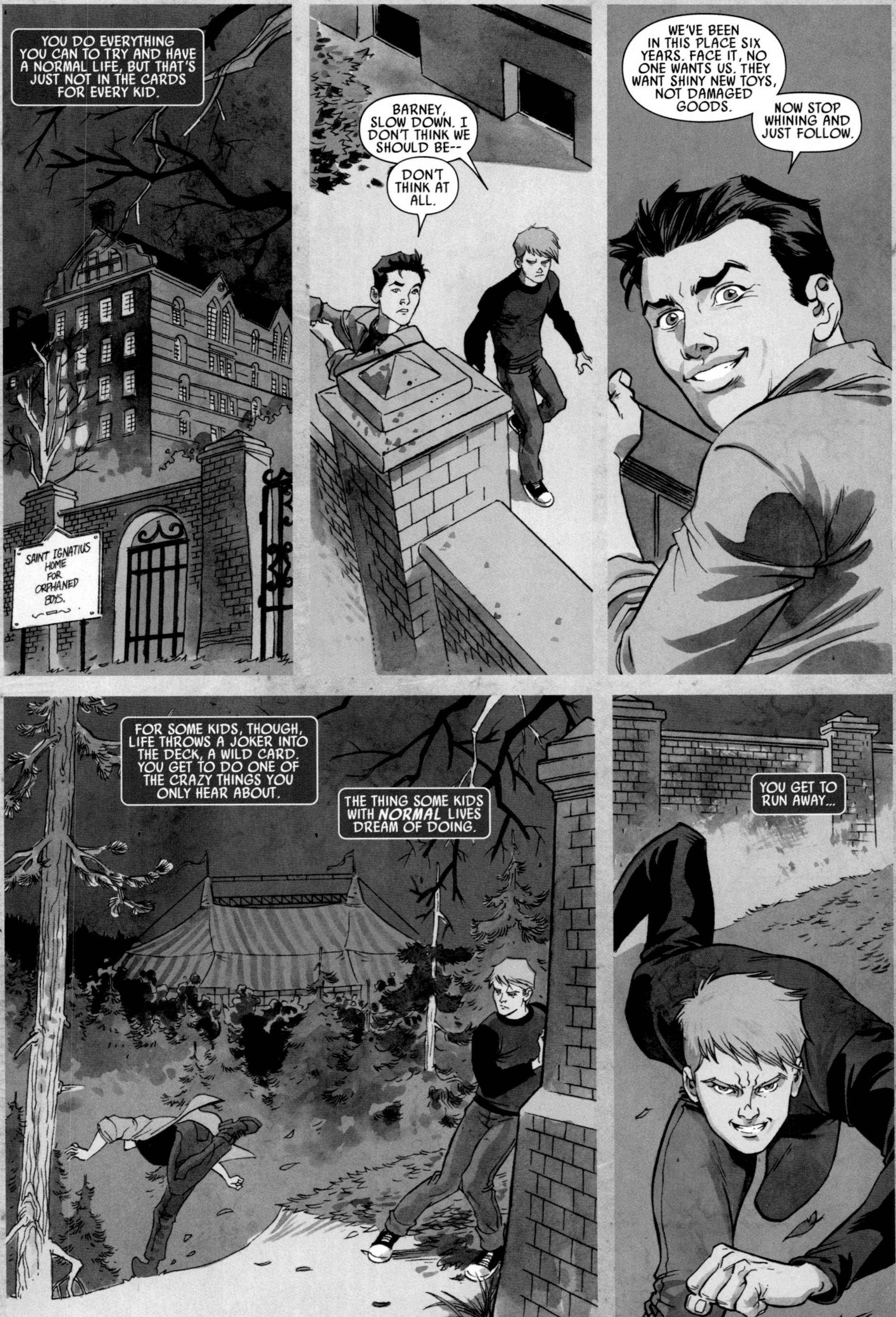

YOU DO EVERYTHING YOU CAN TO TRY AND HAVE A NORMAL LIFE, BUT THAT'S JUST NOT IN THE CARDS FOR EVERY KID.
SAINT IGNATIUS HOME FOR ORPHANED BOYS.
BARNEY, SLOW DOWN. I DON'T THINK WE SHOULD BE--
DON'T THINK AT ALL.
WE'VE BEEN IN THIS PLACE SIX YEARS. FACE IT, NO ONE WANTS US. THEY WANT SHINY NEW TOYS, NOT DAMAGED GOODS.
NOW STOP WHINING AND JUST FOLLOW.
FOR SOME KIDS, THOUGH, LIFE THROWS A JOKER INTO THE DECK, A WILD CARD. YOU GET TO DO ONE OF THE CRAZY THINGS YOU ONLY HEAR ABOUT.
THE THING SOME KIDS WITH NORMAL LIVES DREAM OF DOING.
YOU GET TO RUN AWAY...

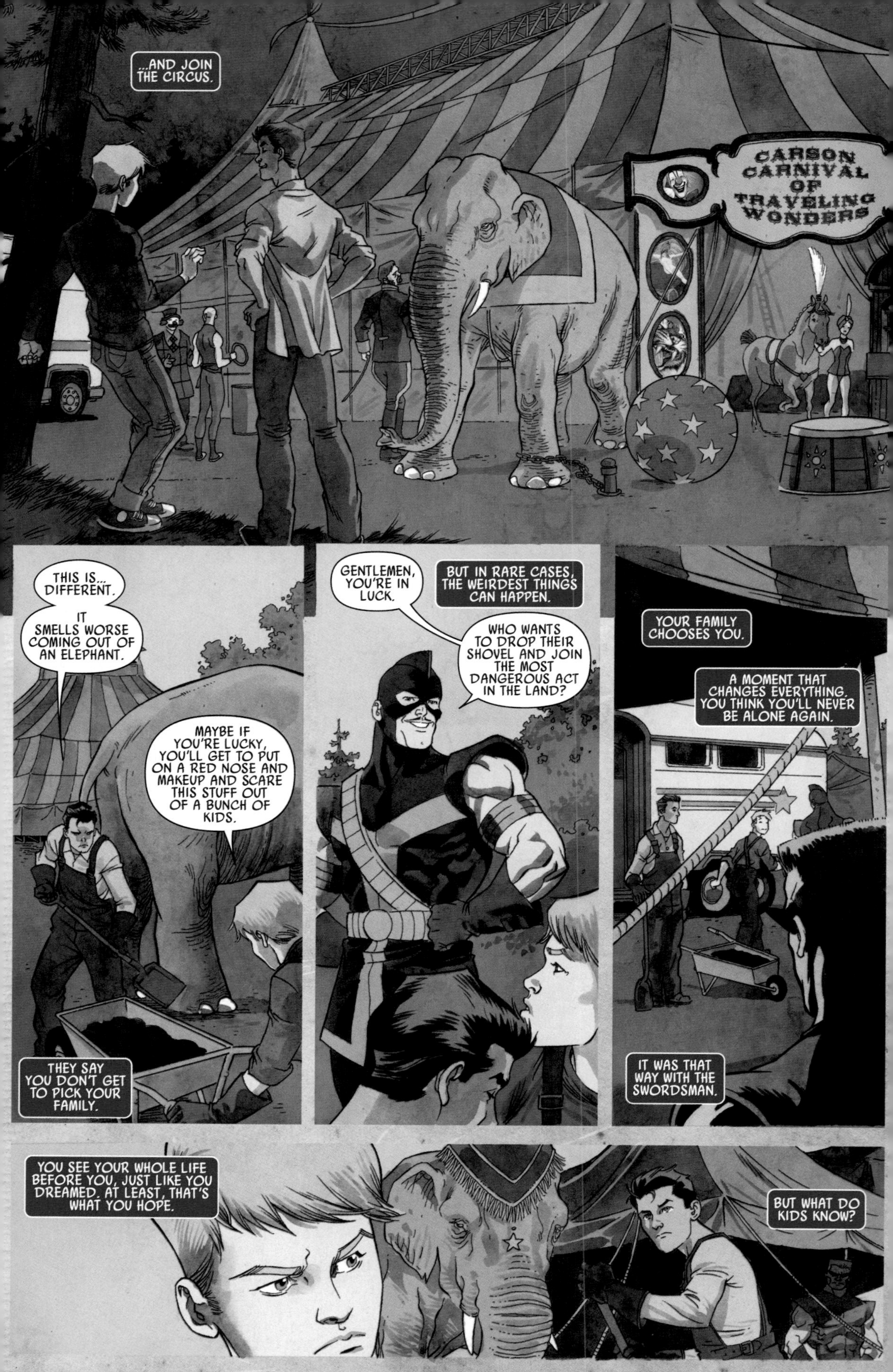
...AND JOIN THE CIRCUS.
CARSON CARNIVAL OF TRAVELING WONDERS
THIS IS... DIFFERENT.
IT SMELLS WORSE COMING OUT OF AN ELEPHANT.
MAYBE IF YOU'RE LUCKY, YOU'LL GET TO PUT ON A RED NOSE AND MAKEUP AND SCARE THIS STUFF OUT OF A BUNCH OF KIDS.
THEY SAY YOU DON'T GET TO PICK YOUR FAMILY.
GENTLEMEN, YOU'RE IN LUCK.
BUT IN RARE CASES, THE WEIRDEST THINGS CAN HAPPEN.
WHO WANTS TO DROP THEIR SHOVEL AND JOIN THE MOST DANGEROUS ACT IN THE LAND?
YOUR FAMILY CHOOSES YOU.
A MOMENT THAT CHANGES EVERYTHING. YOU THINK YOU'LL NEVER BE ALONE AGAIN.
IT WAS THAT WAY WITH THE SWORDSMAN.
YOU SEE YOUR WHOLE LIFE BEFORE YOU, JUST LIKE YOU DREAMED. AT LEAST, THAT'S WHAT YOU HOPE.
BUT WHAT DO KIDS KNOW?

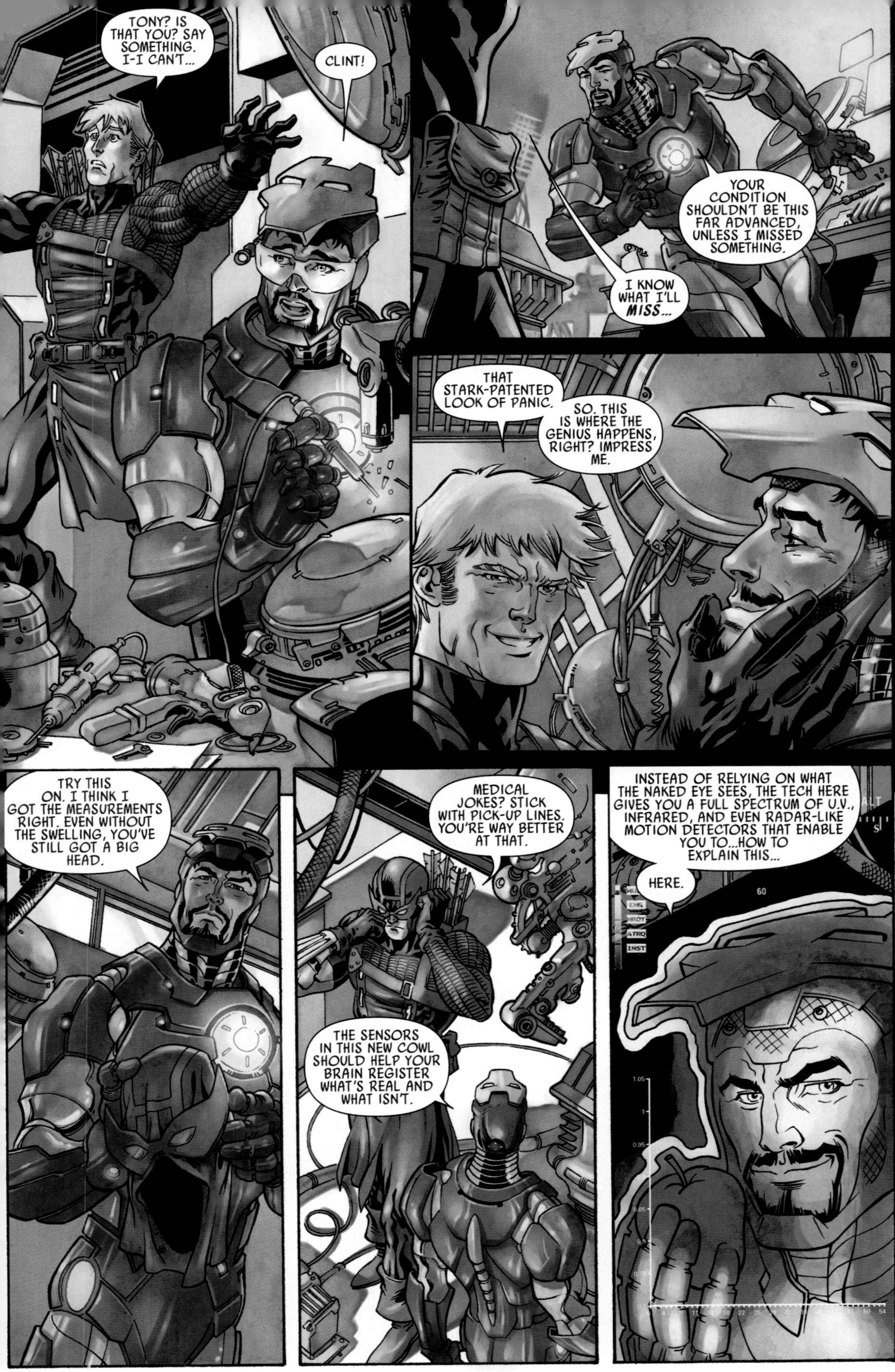
TONY? IS THAT YOU? SAY SOMETHING. I-I CAN'T...
CLINT!
YOUR CONDITION SHOULDN'T BE THIS FAR ADVANCED, UNLESS I MISSED SOMETHING.
I KNOW WHAT I'LL MISS...
THAT STARK-PATENTED LOOK OF PANIC.
SO, THIS IS WHERE THE GENIUS HAPPENS, RIGHT? IMPRESS ME.
TRY THIS ON. I THINK I GOT THE MEASUREMENTS RIGHT. EVEN WITHOUT THE SWELLING, YOU'VE STILL GOT A BIG HEAD.
MEDICAL JOKES? STICK WITH PICK-UP LINES. YOU'RE WAY BETTER AT THAT.
THE SENSORS IN THIS NEW COWL SHOULD HELP YOUR BRAIN REGISTER WHAT'S REAL AND WHAT ISN'T.
INSTEAD OF RELYING ON WHAT THE NAKED EYE SEES, THE TECH HERE GIVES YOU A FULL SPECTRUM OF U.V., INFRARED, AND EVEN RADAR-LIKE MOTION DETECTORS THAT ENABLE YOU TO...HOW TO EXPLAIN THIS...
HERE.

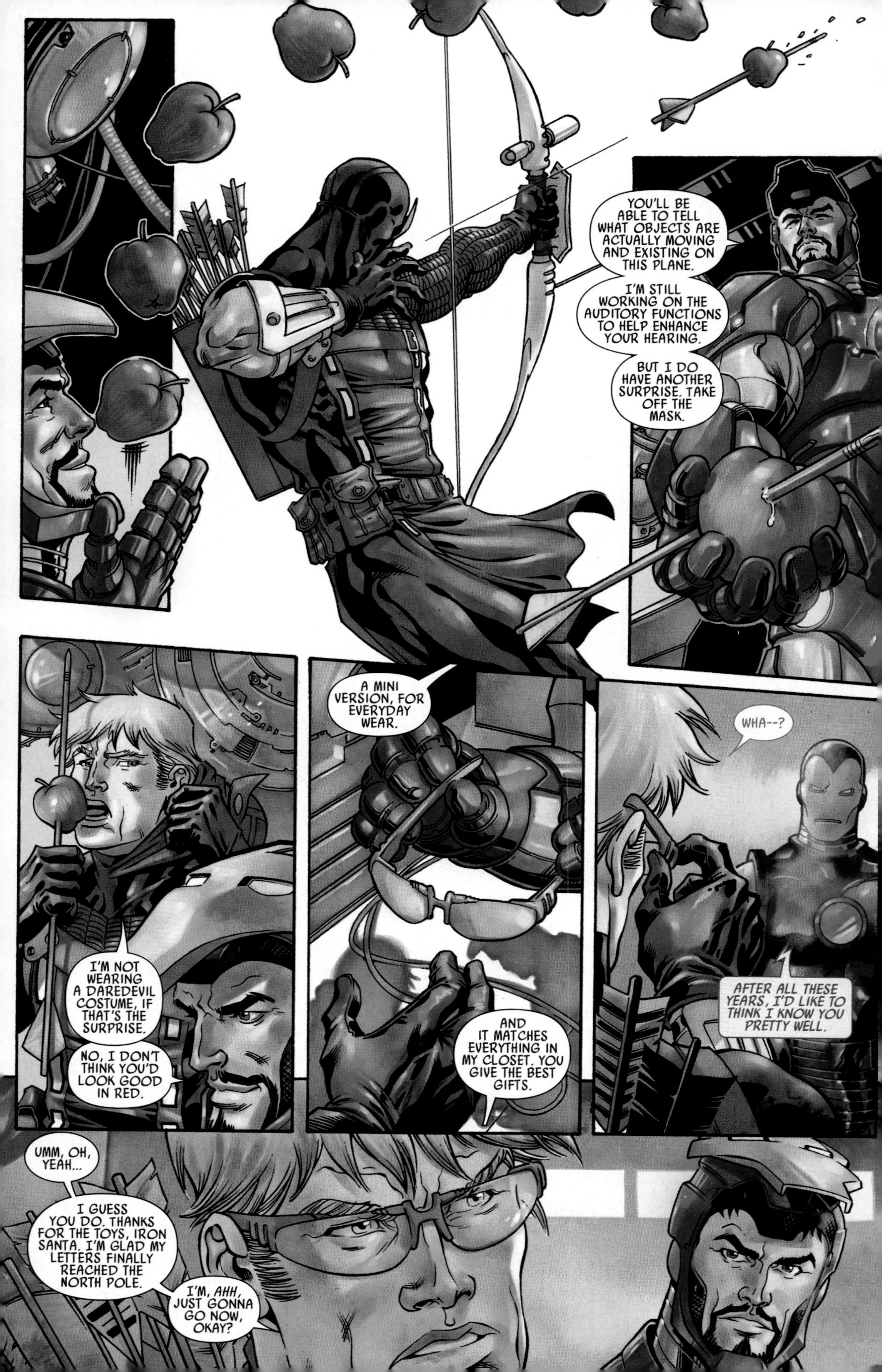

YOU'LL BE ABLE TO TELL WHAT OBJECTS ARE ACTUALLY MOVING AND EXISTING ON THIS PLANE.
I'M STILL WORKING ON THE AUDITORY FUNCTIONS TO HELP ENHANCE YOUR HEARING.
BUT I DO HAVE ANOTHER SURPRISE. TAKE OFF THE MASK.
I'M NOT WEARING A DAREDEVIL COSTUME, IF THAT'S THE SURPRISE.
NO, I DON'T THINK YOU'D LOOK GOOD IN RED.
A MINI VERSION, FOR EVERYDAY WEAR.
AND IT MATCHES EVERYTHING IN MY CLOSET. YOU GIVE THE BEST GIFTS.
WHA--?
AFTER ALL THESE YEARS, I'D LIKE TO THINK I KNOW YOU PRETTY WELL.
UMM, OH, YEAH...
I GUESS YOU DO. THANKS FOR THE TOYS, IRON SANTA. I'M GLAD MY LETTERS FINALLY REACHED THE NORTH POLE.
I'M, AHH, JUST GONNA GO NOW, OKAY?

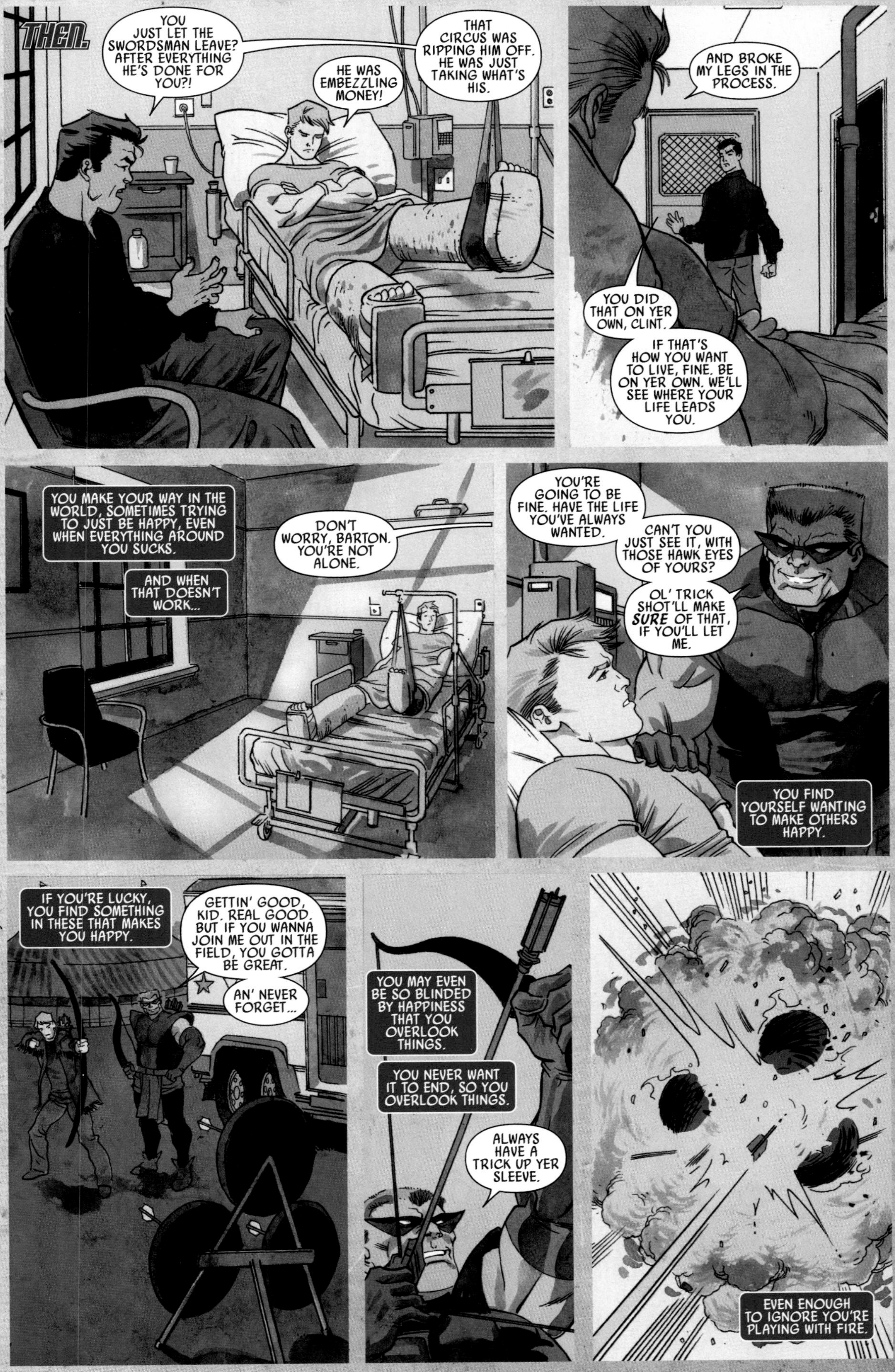
THEN.
YOU JUST LET THE SWORDSMAN LEAVE? AFTER EVERYTHING HE'S DONE FOR YOU?!
HE WAS EMBEZZLING MONEY!
THAT CIRCUS WAS RIPPING HIM OFF. HE WAS JUST TAKING WHAT'S HIS.
AND BROKE MY LEGS IN THE PROCESS.
YOU DID THAT ON YER OWN, CLINT.
IF THAT'S HOW YOU WANT TO LIVE, FINE. BE ON YER OWN. WE'LL SEE WHERE YOUR LIFE LEADS YOU.
YOU MAKE YOUR WAY IN THE WORLD, SOMETIMES TRYING TO JUST BE HAPPY, EVEN WHEN EVERYTHING AROUND YOU SUCKS.
AND WHEN THAT DOESN'T WORK...
DON'T WORRY, BARTON. YOU'RE NOT ALONE.
YOU'RE GOING TO BE FINE. HAVE THE LIFE YOU'VE ALWAYS WANTED.
CAN'T YOU JUST SEE IT, WITH THOSE HAWK EYES OF YOURS?
OL' TRICK SHOT'LL MAKE SURE OF THAT, IF YOU'LL LET ME.
YOU FIND YOURSELF WANTING TO MAKE OTHERS HAPPY.
IF YOU'RE LUCKY, YOU FIND SOMETHING IN THESE THAT MAKES YOU HAPPY.
GETTIN' GOOD, KID. REAL GOOD. BUT IF YOU WANNA JOIN ME OUT IN THE FIELD, YOU GOTTA BE GREAT.
AN' NEVER FORGET...
YOU MAY EVEN BE SO BLINDED BY HAPPINESS THAT YOU OVERLOOK THINGS.
YOU NEVER WANT IT TO END, SO YOU OVERLOOK THINGS.
ALWAYS HAVE A TRICK UP YER SLEEVE.
EVEN ENOUGH TO IGNORE YOU'RE PLAYING WITH FIRE.

YOU TURN A BLIND EYE BECAUSE YOU'RE TOO DUMB TO NOT LOOK, OR BECAUSE YOU WANT TO PROTECT YOURSELF, STAY IN THE DARK.

SNAP

TRICK! THAT YOU? WHAT'S HAPPENING--?

IT'S ROBIN HOOD! WASTE HIM!

THWAAAAANG

BUT INSTINCT EVENTUALLY TAKES OVER.

THWAAAAANG

ACTIONS REVEAL TRUE CHARACTER.

THWAAAANG

AND YOU WISH YOU COULD JUST PULL THE BLANKET BACK OVER YOUR EYES RATHER THAN FACING THE TRUTH.

C--CLINT?! YOU...SHOT ME...

BARNEY?! WHAT ARE YOU DOING RUNNING WITH THESE GUYS? THEY'RE IN THE MOB!

LEAVE HIM. WE GOT WHAT WE CAME FOR.

YOU FIND OUT, THOUGH, THE TRUTH IS ALWAYS HIDING UP SOMEONE'S SLEEVE. YOU HOPE IT'S YOURS...

IN THIS CASE, YOU'D BE WRONG.

YOU TRAINED ME, BROUGHT ME OUT "IN THE FIELD" FOR WHAT? SO YOU COULD ROB PEOPLE?!

THERE'S NO ALARMS GOING OFF, SO I GUESS YOU KILLED MARKO AND THE REST OF HIS CREW INSIDE TOO, DIDN'T YOU? *DIDN'T YOU?!*

NEVER ASKED IF YOU HAD A CONSCIENCE, KID, JUST TALENT.

THIS ISN'T WHAT I SIGNED UP FOR. MY BROTHER'S HURT BECAUSE OF MY "TALENT!" WE'RE LEAVING.

YOU WANNA STAY? FINE!

STICK AROUND!

YOU LEARN ALSO THAT LIFE HAS A SICK SENSE OF HUMOR. EVERYTHING IT GIVES YOU CAN EXPLODE IN YOUR FACE.

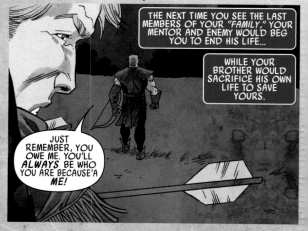

THE NEXT TIME YOU SEE THE LAST MEMBERS OF YOUR "FAMILY," YOUR MENTOR AND ENEMY WOULD BEG YOU TO END HIS LIFE...

WHILE YOUR BROTHER WOULD SACRIFICE HIS OWN LIFE TO SAVE YOURS.

JUST REMEMBER, YOU OWE ME. YOU'LL *ALWAYS* BE WHO YOU ARE BECAUSE'A *ME!*

AND LIKE THAT, YOU FIND OUT YOU CAN BE ORPHANED, OVER AND OVER AGAIN.

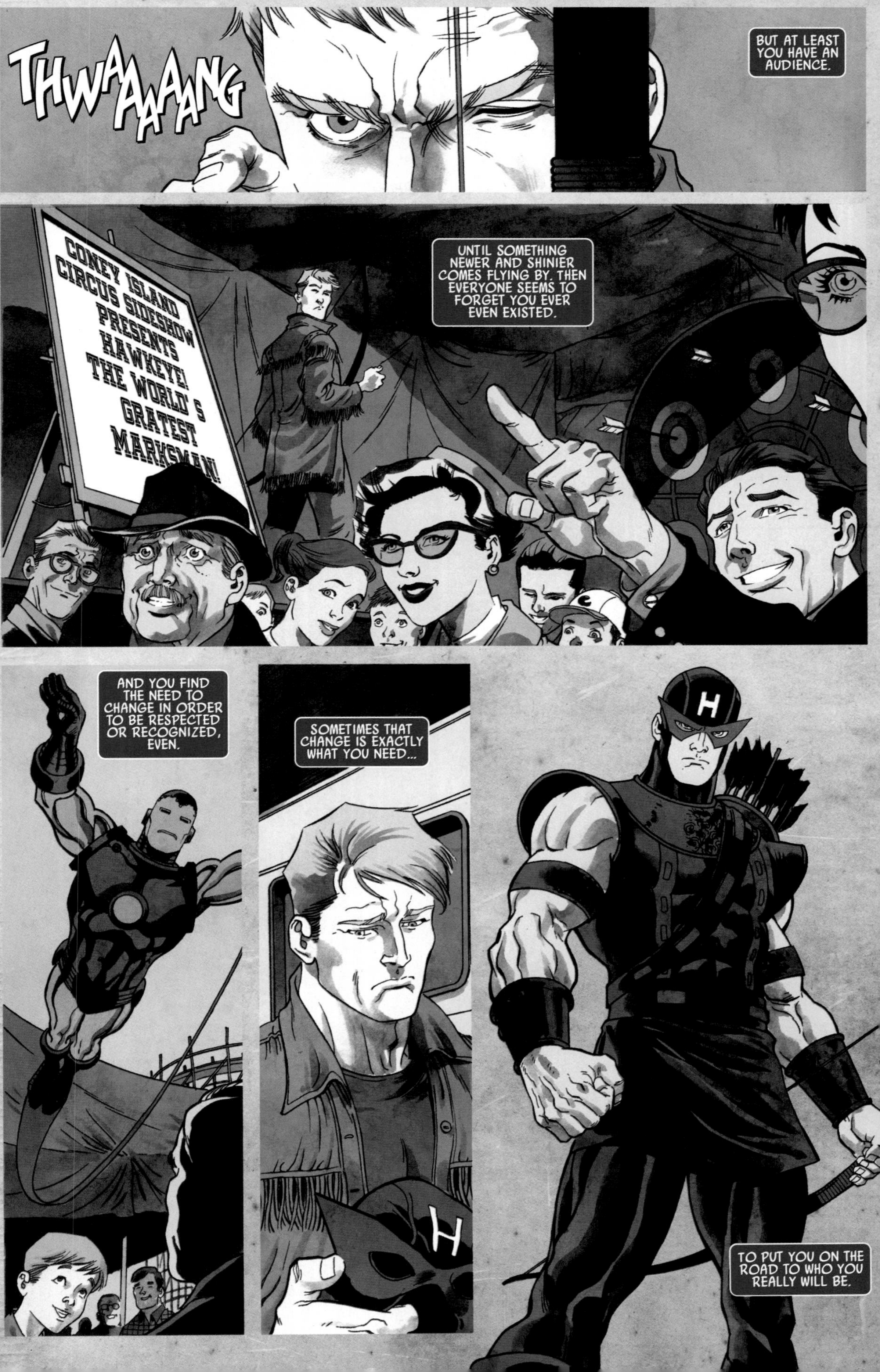
THWAAAAANG
BUT AT LEAST YOU HAVE AN AUDIENCE.
CONEY ISLAND CIRCUS SIDESHOW PRESENTS HAWKEYE! THE WORLD'S GRATEST MARKSMAN!
UNTIL SOMETHING NEWER AND SHINIER COMES FLYING BY. THEN EVERYONE SEEMS TO FORGET YOU EVER EVEN EXISTED.
AND YOU FIND THE NEED TO CHANGE IN ORDER TO BE RESPECTED OR RECOGNIZED, EVEN.
SOMETIMES THAT CHANGE IS EXACTLY WHAT YOU NEED...
TO PUT YOU ON THE ROAD TO WHO YOU REALLY WILL BE.

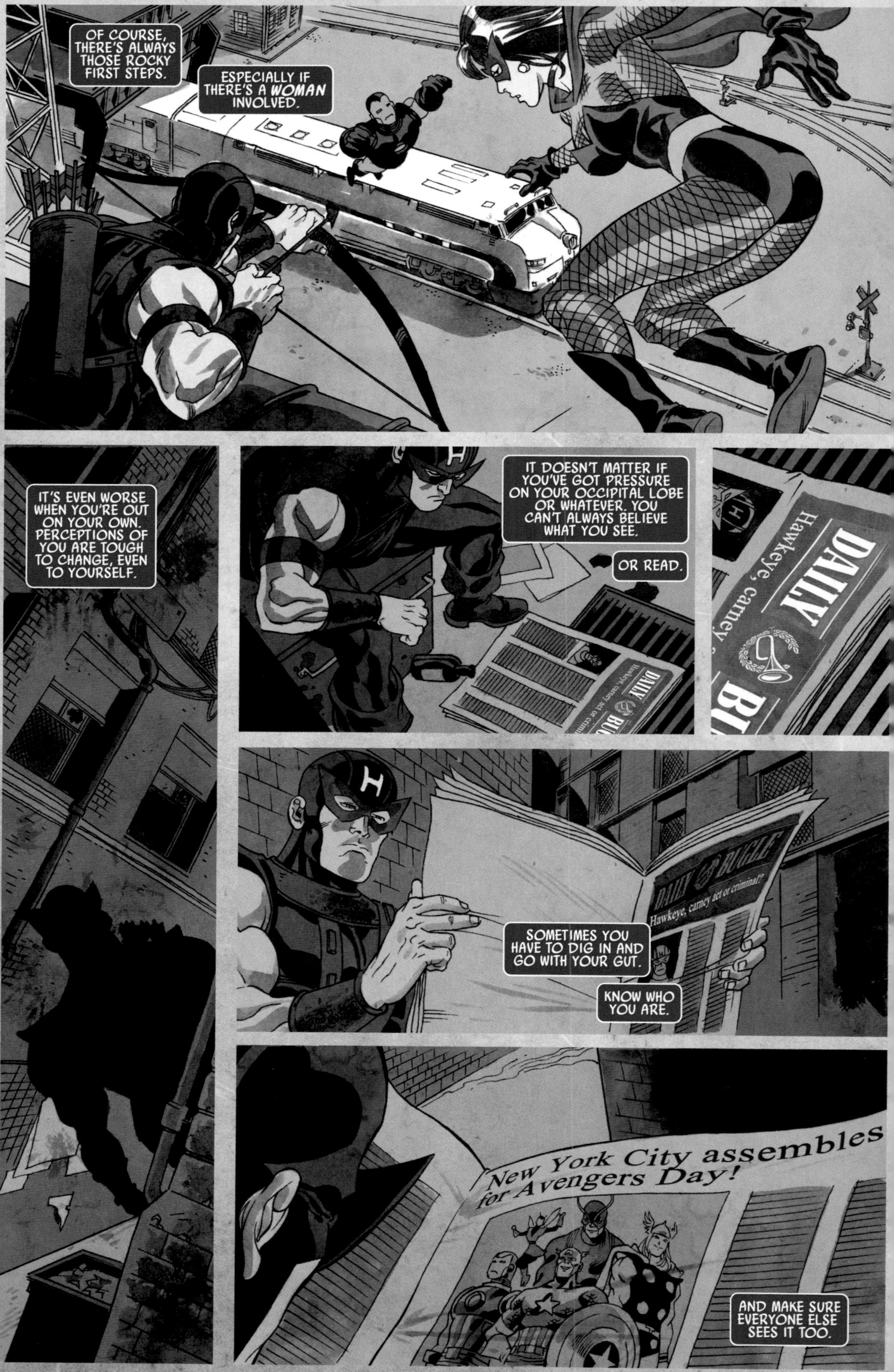
OF COURSE, THERE'S ALWAYS THOSE ROCKY FIRST STEPS.
ESPECIALLY IF THERE'S A WOMAN INVOLVED.
IT'S EVEN WORSE WHEN YOU'RE OUT ON YOUR OWN. PERCEPTIONS OF YOU ARE TOUGH TO CHANGE, EVEN TO YOURSELF.
IT DOESN'T MATTER IF YOU'VE GOT PRESSURE ON YOUR OCCIPITAL LOBE OR WHATEVER. YOU CAN'T ALWAYS BELIEVE WHAT YOU SEE.
OR READ.
DAILY
Hawkeye, carney a
DAILY BUGLE
Hawkeye, carney act or criminal?
SOMETIMES YOU HAVE TO DIG IN AND GO WITH YOUR GUT.
KNOW WHO YOU ARE.
New York City assembles for Avengers Day!
AND MAKE SURE EVERYONE ELSE SEES IT TOO.

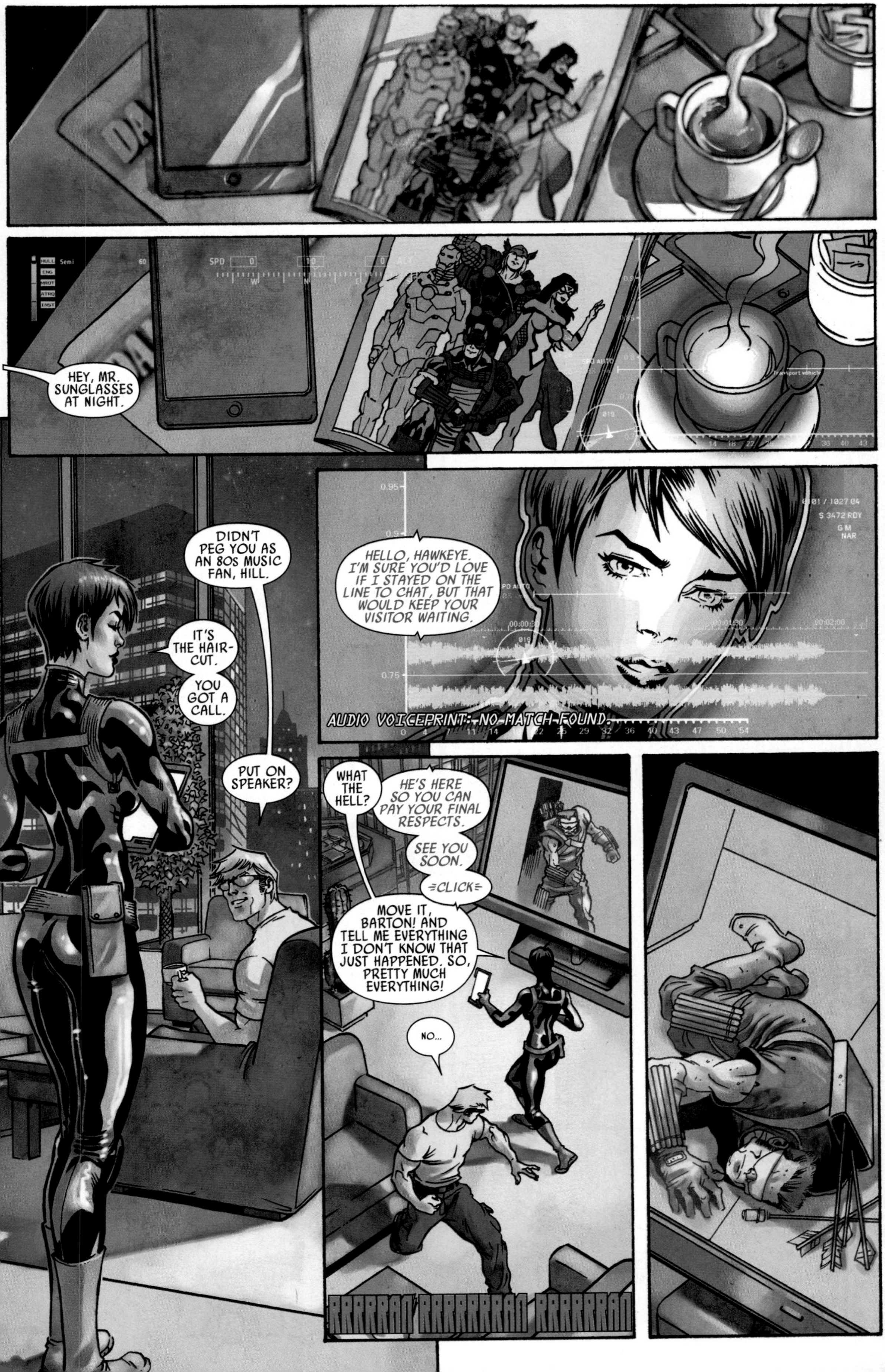

HEY, MR. SUNGLASSES AT NIGHT.
DIDN'T PEG YOU AS AN 80s MUSIC FAN, HILL.
IT'S THE HAIR-CUT.
YOU GOT A CALL.
PUT ON SPEAKER?
HELLO, HAWKEYE. I'M SURE YOU'D LOVE IF I STAYED ON THE LINE TO CHAT, BUT THAT WOULD KEEP YOUR VISITOR WAITING.
AUDIO VOICEPRINT: NO MATCH FOUND.
WHAT THE HELL?
HE'S HERE SO YOU CAN PAY YOUR FINAL RESPECTS.
SEE YOU SOON.
CLICK
MOVE IT, BARTON! AND TELL ME EVERYTHING I DON'T KNOW THAT JUST HAPPENED. SO, PRETTY MUCH EVERYTHING!
NO...
RRRRRAN RRRRRRRAN RRRRRAN

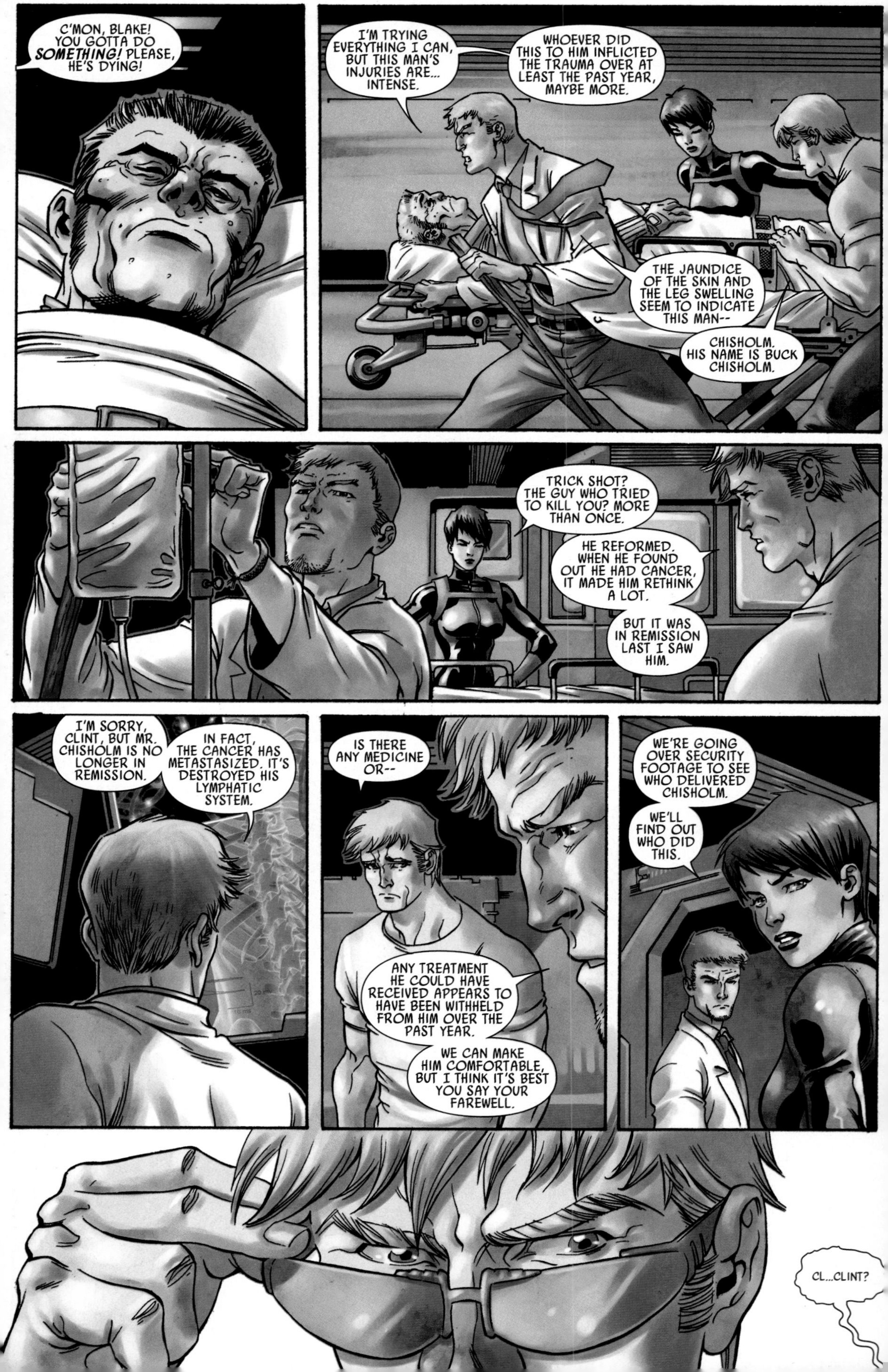
C'MON, BLAKE! YOU GOTTA DO *SOMETHING!* PLEASE, HE'S DYING!
I'M TRYING EVERYTHING I CAN, BUT THIS MAN'S INJURIES ARE... INTENSE.
WHOEVER DID THIS TO HIM INFLICTED THE TRAUMA OVER AT LEAST THE PAST YEAR, MAYBE MORE.
THE JAUNDICE OF THE SKIN AND THE LEG SWELLING SEEM TO INDICATE THIS MAN--
CHISHOLM. HIS NAME IS BUCK CHISHOLM.
TRICK SHOT? THE GUY WHO TRIED TO KILL YOU? MORE THAN ONCE.
HE REFORMED. WHEN HE FOUND OUT HE HAD CANCER, IT MADE HIM RETHINK A LOT.
BUT IT WAS IN REMISSION LAST I SAW HIM.
I'M SORRY, CLINT, BUT MR. CHISHOLM IS NO LONGER IN REMISSION.
IN FACT, THE CANCER HAS METASTASIZED. IT'S DESTROYED HIS LYMPHATIC SYSTEM.
IS THERE ANY MEDICINE OR--
ANY TREATMENT HE COULD HAVE RECEIVED APPEARS TO HAVE BEEN WITHHELD FROM HIM OVER THE PAST YEAR.
WE CAN MAKE HIM COMFORTABLE, BUT I THINK IT'S BEST YOU SAY YOUR FAREWELL.
WE'RE GOING OVER SECURITY FOOTAGE TO SEE WHO DELIVERED CHISHOLM.
WE'LL FIND OUT WHO DID THIS.
CL...CLINT?

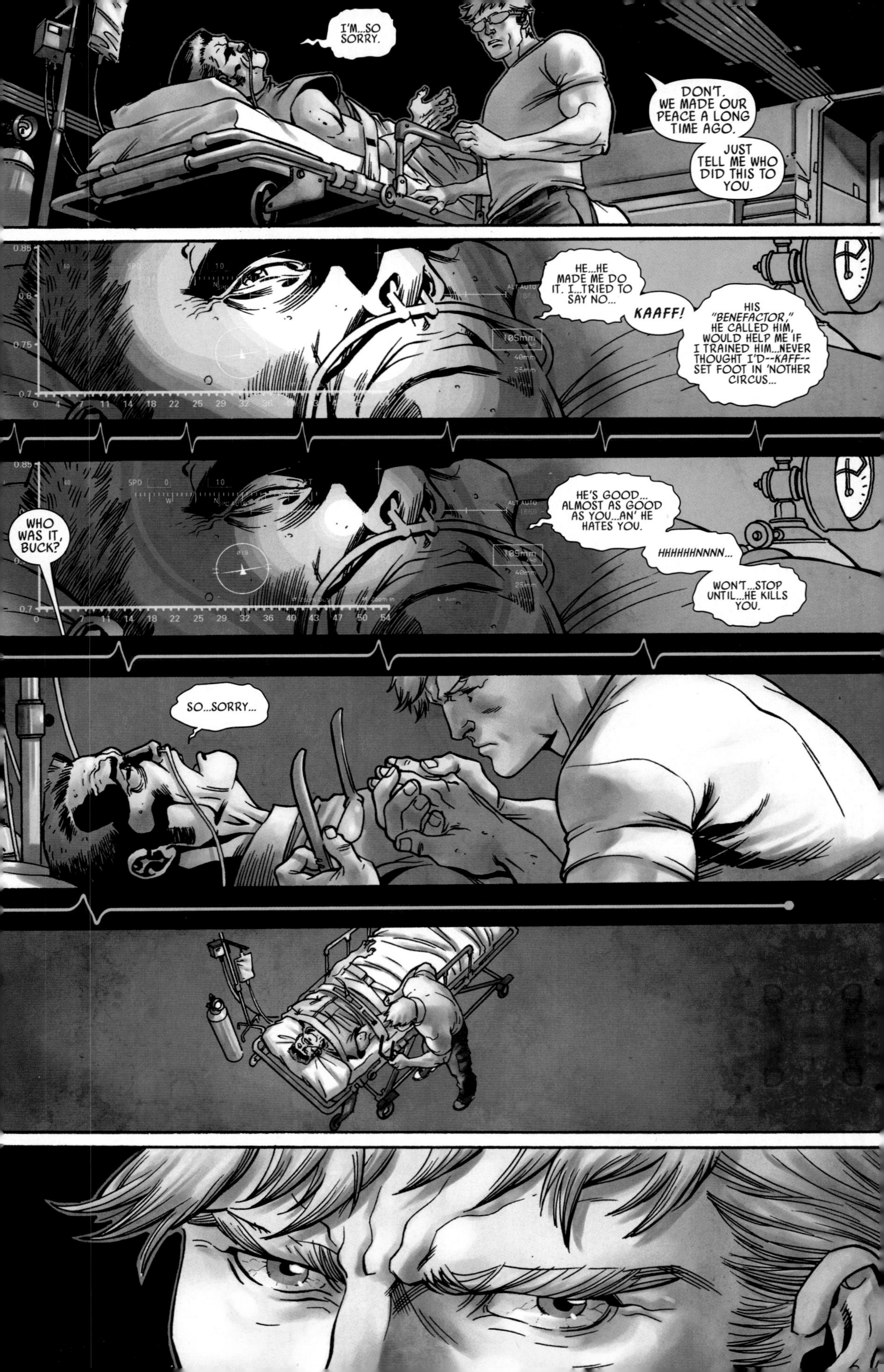
I'M...SO SORRY.
DON'T. WE MADE OUR PEACE A LONG TIME AGO.
JUST TELL ME WHO DID THIS TO YOU.
HE...HE MADE ME DO IT. I...TRIED TO SAY NO...
KAAFF!
HIS "BENEFACTOR," HE CALLED HIM, WOULD HELP ME IF I TRAINED HIM...NEVER THOUGHT I'D--KAFF--SET FOOT IN 'NOTHER CIRCUS...
WHO WAS IT, BUCK?
HE'S GOOD... ALMOST AS GOOD AS YOU...AN' HE HATES YOU.
HHHHHHNNNN...
WON'T...STOP UNTIL...HE KILLS YOU.
SO...SORRY...

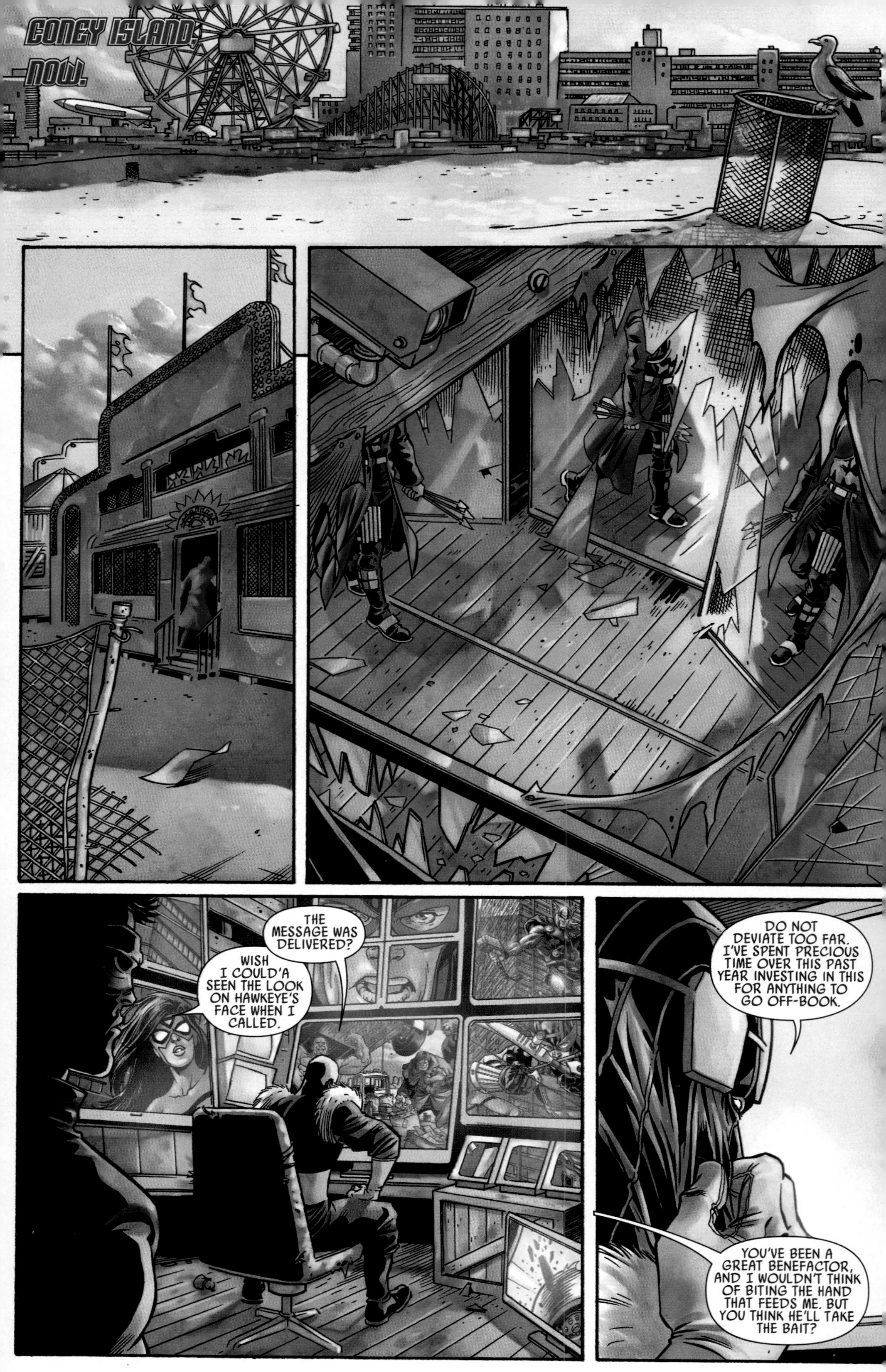
CONEY ISLAND, NOW.
THE MESSAGE WAS DELIVERED?
WISH I COULD'A SEEN THE LOOK ON HAWKEYE'S FACE WHEN I CALLED.
DO NOT DEVIATE TOO FAR. I'VE SPENT PRECIOUS TIME OVER THIS PAST YEAR INVESTING IN THIS FOR ANYTHING TO GO OFF-BOOK.
YOU'VE BEEN A GREAT BENEFACTOR, AND I WOULDN'T THINK OF BITING THE HAND THAT FEEDS ME. BUT YOU THINK HE'LL TAKE THE BAIT?

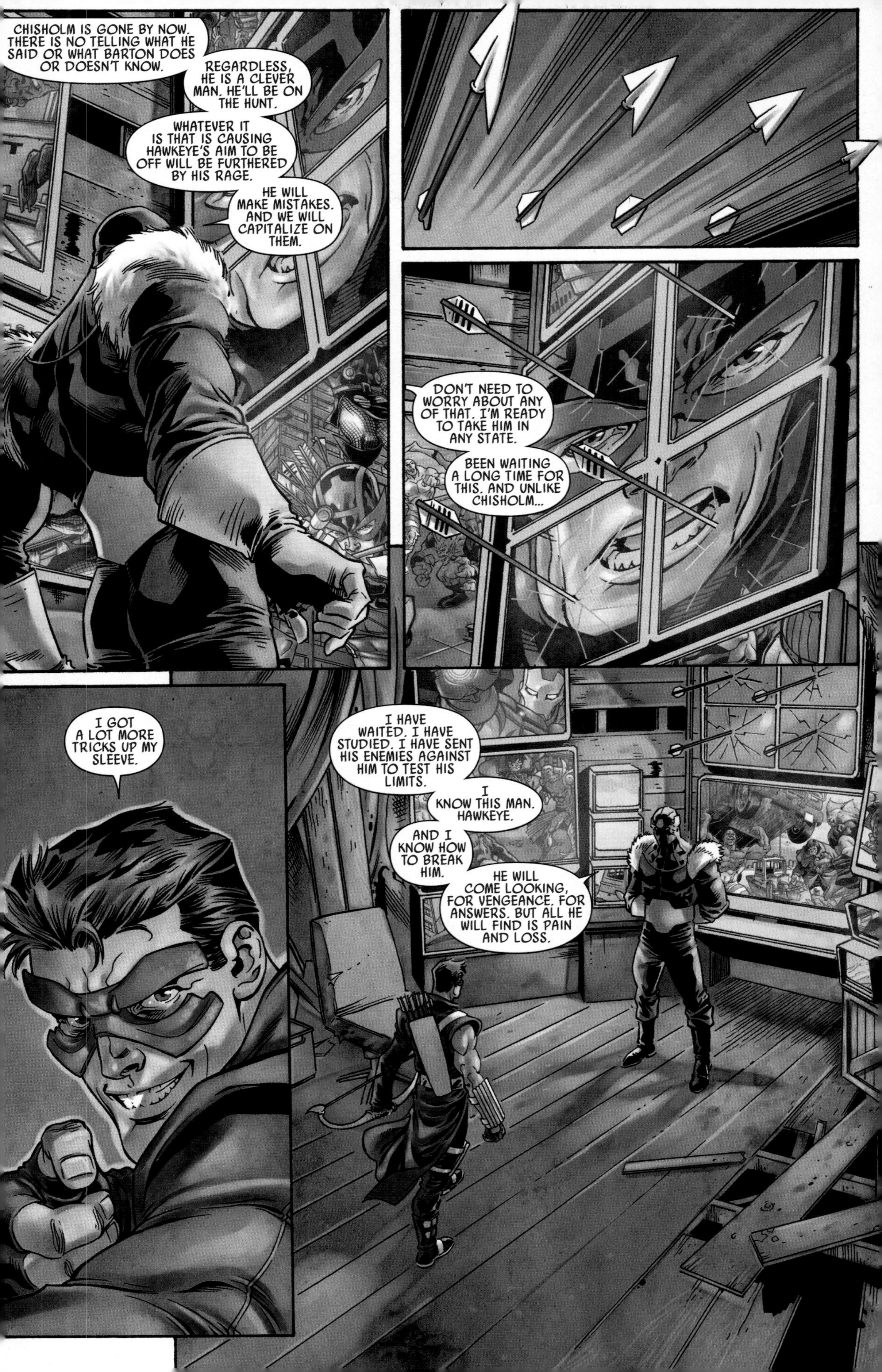
CHISHOLM IS GONE BY NOW. THERE IS NO TELLING WHAT HE SAID OR WHAT BARTON DOES OR DOESN'T KNOW.
REGARDLESS, HE IS A CLEVER MAN. HE'LL BE ON THE HUNT.
WHATEVER IT IS THAT IS CAUSING HAWKEYE'S AIM TO BE OFF WILL BE FURTHERED BY HIS RAGE.
HE WILL MAKE MISTAKES. AND WE WILL CAPITALIZE ON THEM.
DON'T NEED TO WORRY ABOUT ANY OF THAT. I'M READY TO TAKE HIM IN ANY STATE.
BEEN WAITING A LONG TIME FOR THIS. AND UNLIKE CHISHOLM...
I GOT A LOT MORE TRICKS UP MY SLEEVE.
I HAVE WAITED. I HAVE STUDIED. I HAVE SENT HIS ENEMIES AGAINST HIM TO TEST HIS LIMITS.
I KNOW THIS MAN. HAWKEYE.
AND I KNOW HOW TO BREAK HIM.
HE WILL COME LOOKING, FOR VENGEANCE. FOR ANSWERS. BUT ALL HE WILL FIND IS PAIN AND LOSS.

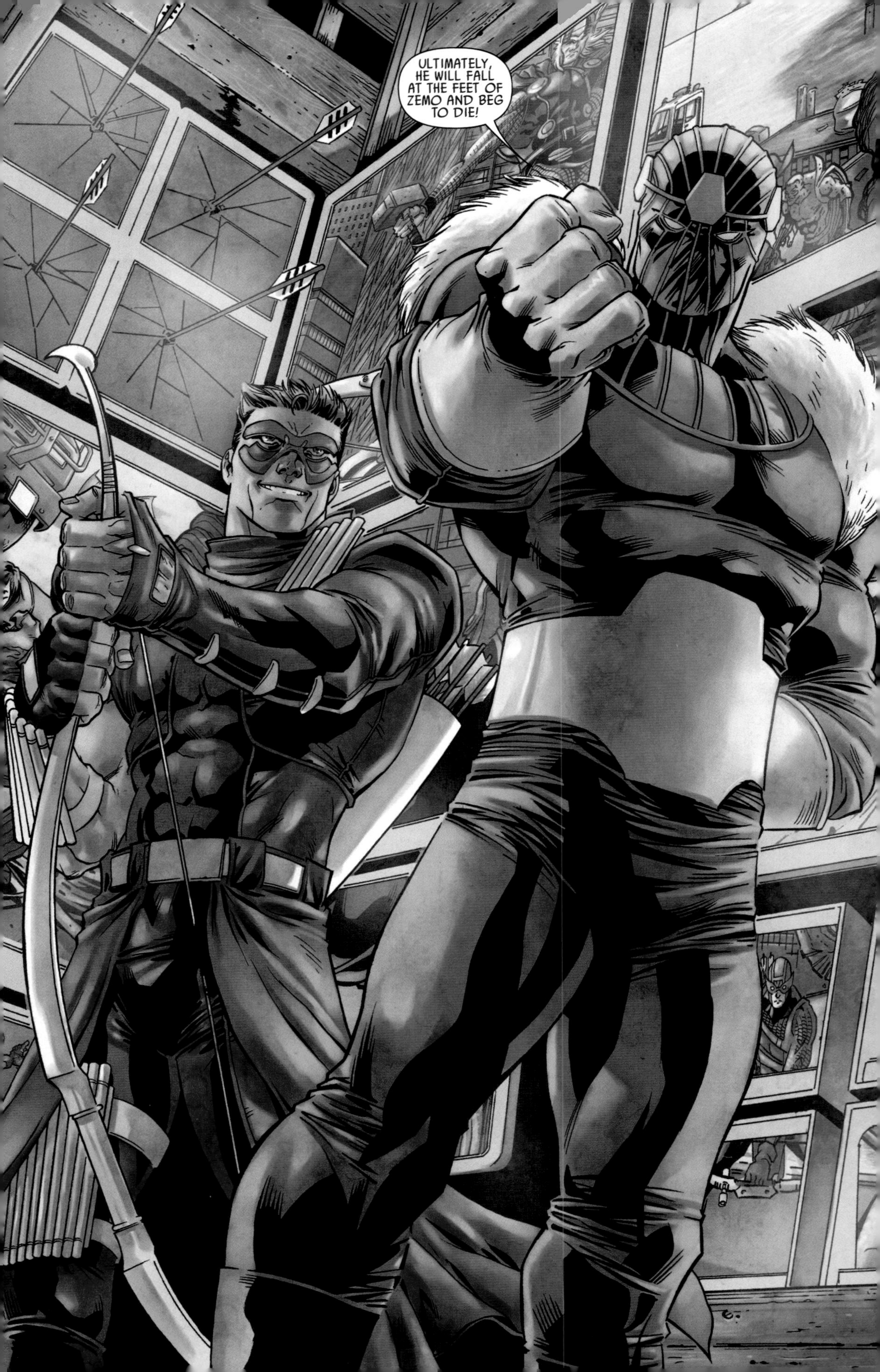
ULTIMATELY, HE WILL FALL AT THE FEET OF ZEMO AND BEG TO DIE!

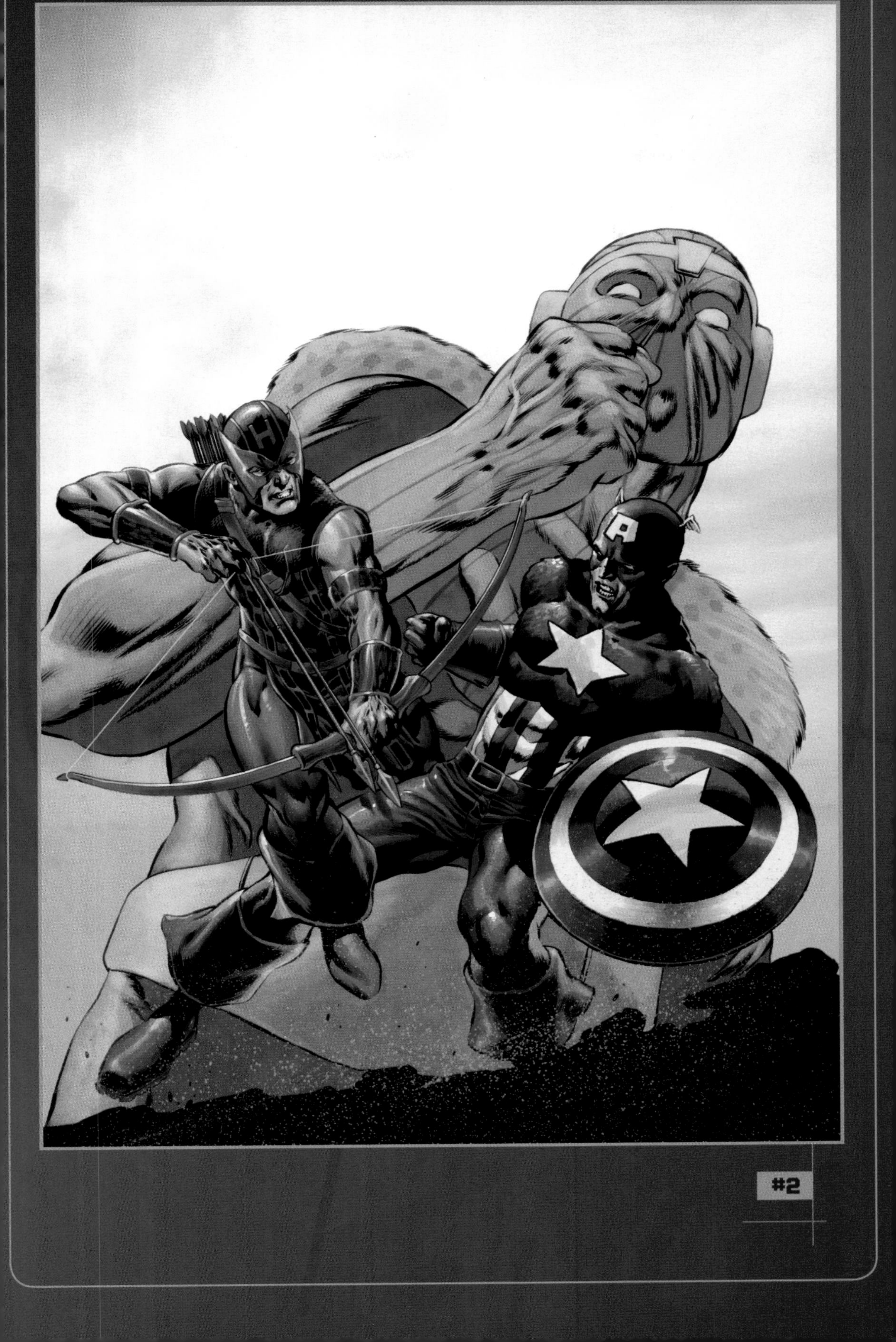

#2

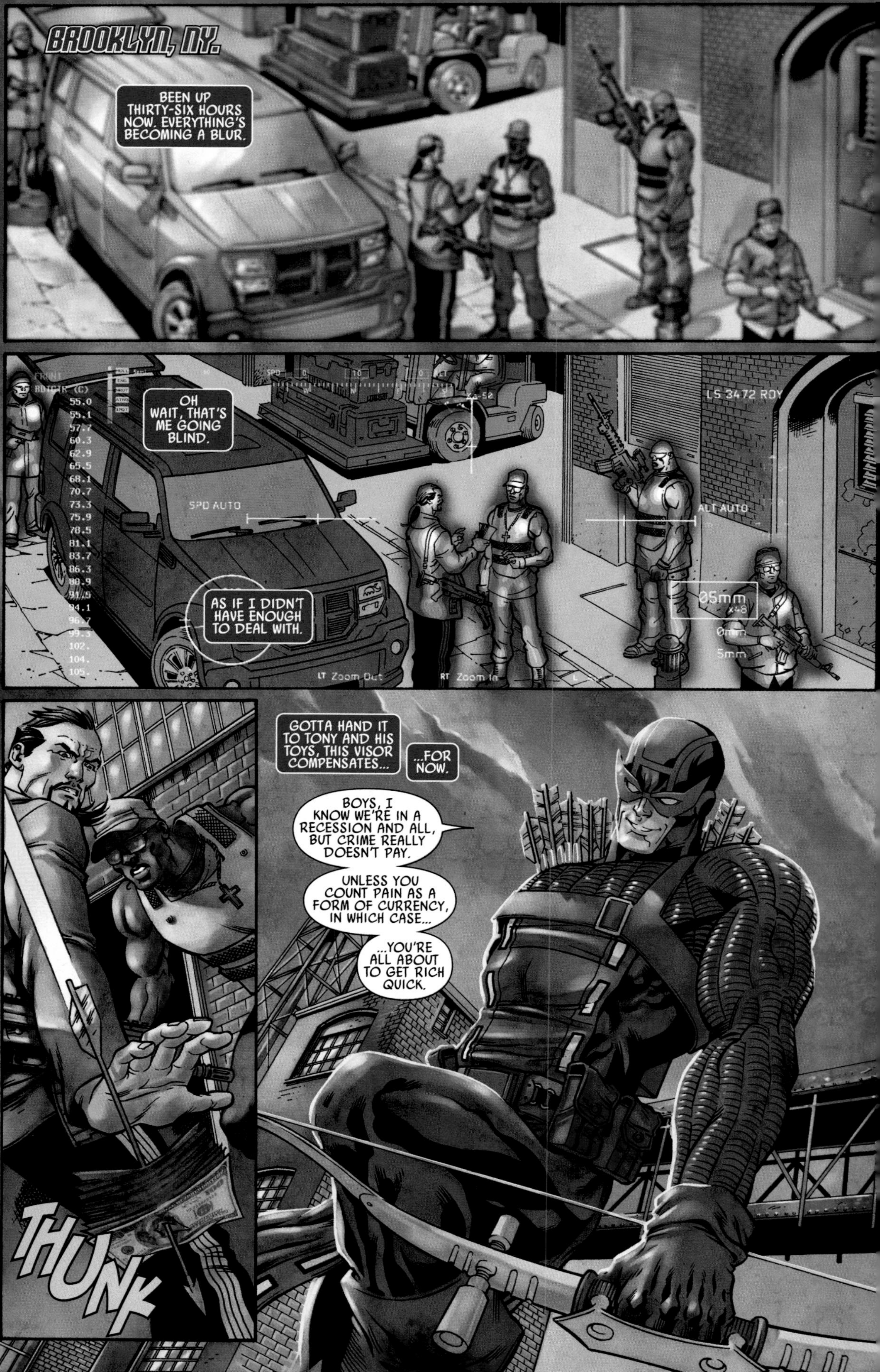
BROOKLYN, NY.
BEEN UP THIRTY-SIX HOURS NOW. EVERYTHING'S BECOMING A BLUR.
OH WAIT, THAT'S ME GOING BLIND.
AS IF I DIDN'T HAVE ENOUGH TO DEAL WITH.
SPD AUTO
ALT AUTO
LS 3472 ROY
LT Zoom Out
RT Zoom In
GOTTA HAND IT TO TONY AND HIS TOYS, THIS VISOR COMPENSATES...
...FOR NOW.
BOYS, I KNOW WE'RE IN A RECESSION AND ALL, BUT CRIME REALLY DOESN'T PAY.
UNLESS YOU COUNT PAIN AS A FORM OF CURRENCY, IN WHICH CASE...
...YOU'RE ALL ABOUT TO GET RICH QUICK.
THUNK

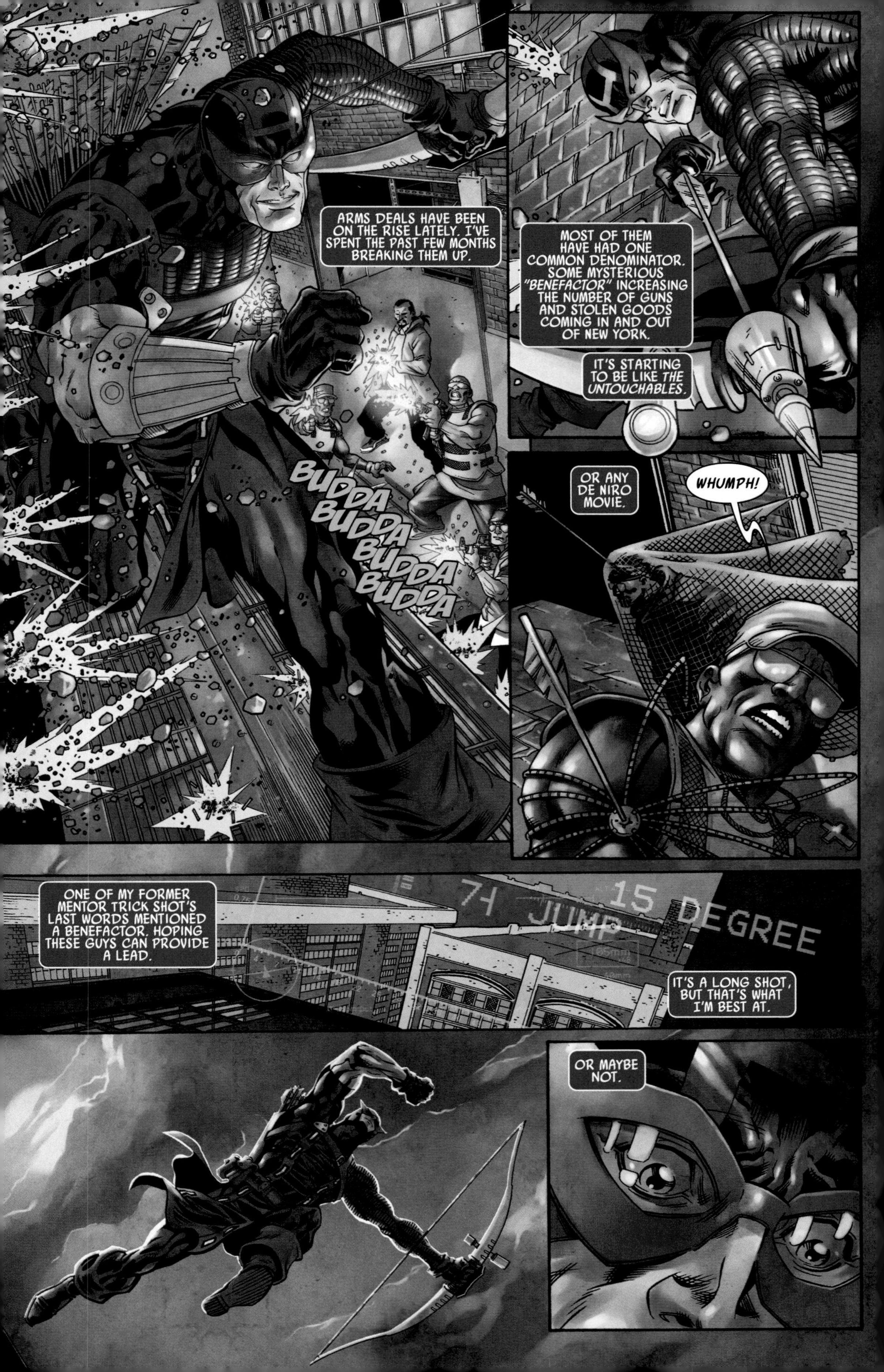

ARMS DEALS HAVE BEEN ON THE RISE LATELY. I'VE SPENT THE PAST FEW MONTHS BREAKING THEM UP.
BUDDA BUDDA BUDDA BUDDA
MOST OF THEM HAVE HAD ONE COMMON DENOMINATOR. SOME MYSTERIOUS *"BENEFACTOR"* INCREASING THE NUMBER OF GUNS AND STOLEN GOODS COMING IN AND OUT OF NEW YORK.
IT'S STARTING TO BE LIKE *THE UNTOUCHABLES.*
OR ANY DE NIRO MOVIE.
WHUMPH!
ONE OF MY FORMER MENTOR TRICK SHOT'S LAST WORDS MENTIONED A BENEFACTOR. HOPING THESE GUYS CAN PROVIDE A LEAD.
15
JUMP
DEGREE
IT'S A LONG SHOT, BUT THAT'S WHAT I'M BEST AT.
OR MAYBE NOT.

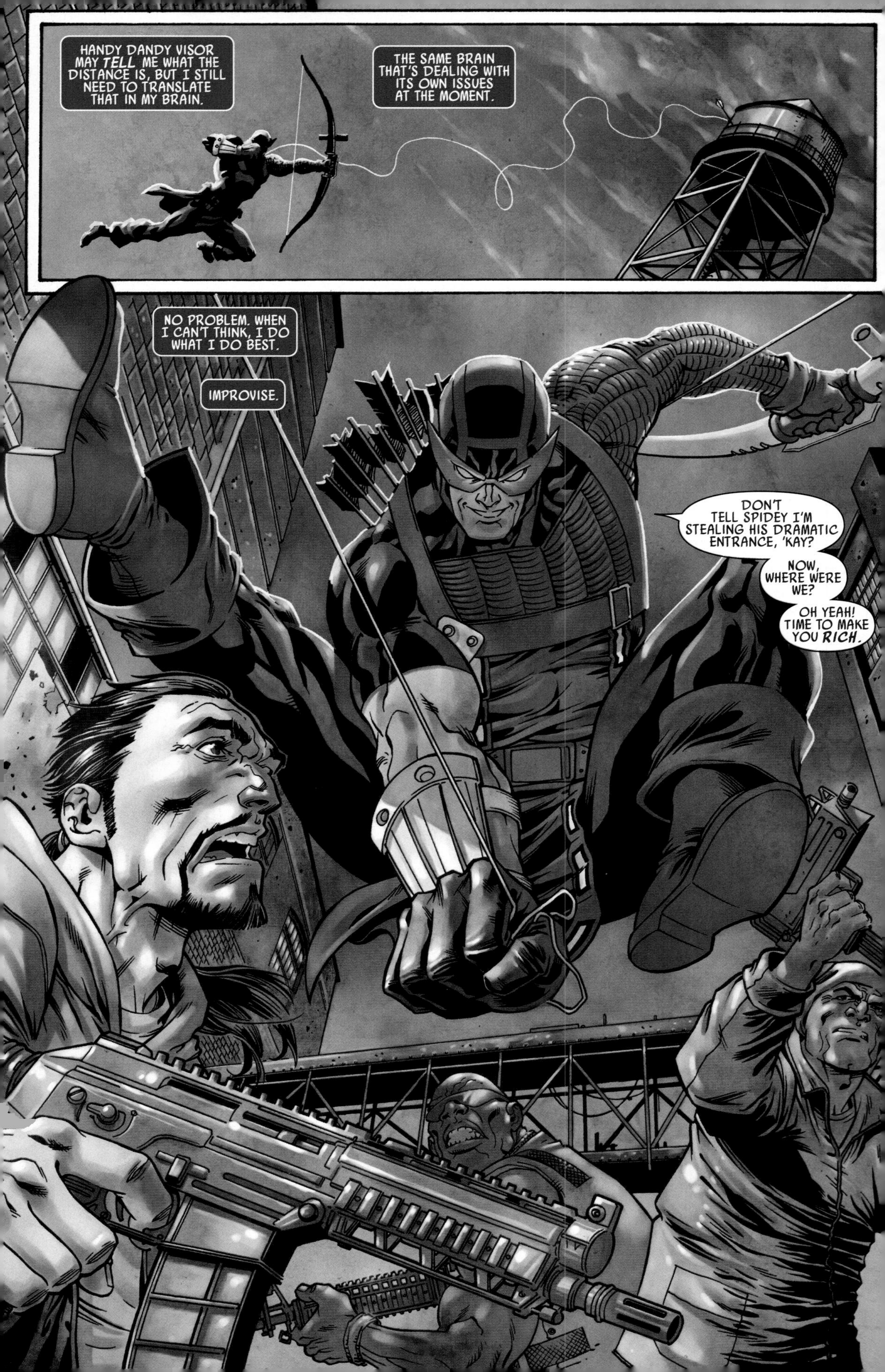
HANDY DANDY VISOR MAY TELL ME WHAT THE DISTANCE IS, BUT I STILL NEED TO TRANSLATE THAT IN MY BRAIN.
THE SAME BRAIN THAT'S DEALING WITH ITS OWN ISSUES AT THE MOMENT.
NO PROBLEM. WHEN I CAN'T THINK, I DO WHAT I DO BEST.
IMPROVISE.
DON'T TELL SPIDEY I'M STEALING HIS DRAMATIC ENTRANCE, 'KAY?
NOW, WHERE WERE WE?
OH YEAH! TIME TO MAKE YOU RICH.

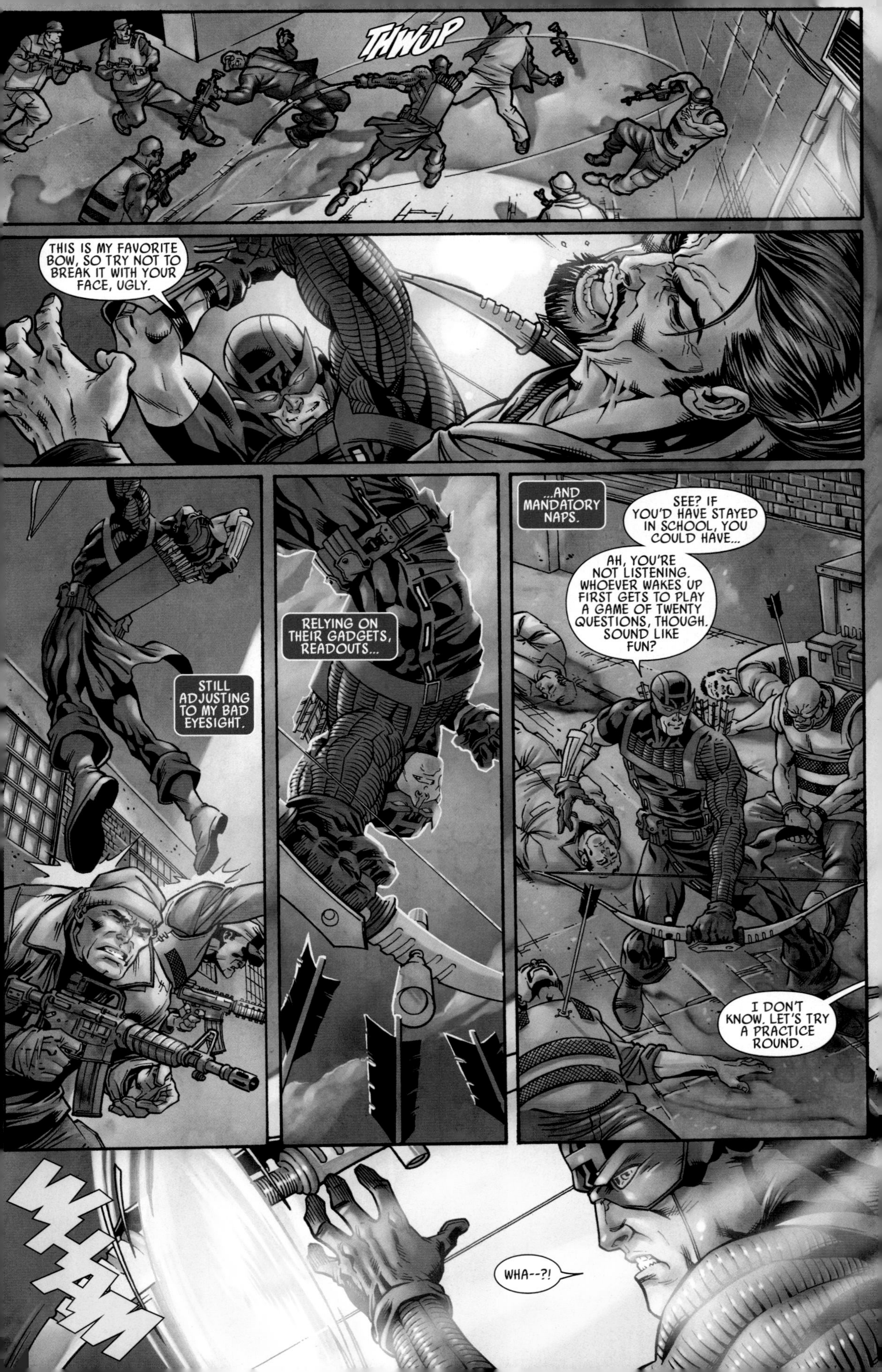
THWUP
THIS IS MY FAVORITE BOW, SO TRY NOT TO BREAK IT WITH YOUR FACE, UGLY.
STILL ADJUSTING TO MY BAD EYESIGHT.
RELYING ON THEIR GADGETS, READOUTS...
...AND MANDATORY NAPS.
SEE? IF YOU'D HAVE STAYED IN SCHOOL, YOU COULD HAVE...
AH, YOU'RE NOT LISTENING. WHOEVER WAKES UP FIRST GETS TO PLAY A GAME OF TWENTY QUESTIONS, THOUGH. SOUND LIKE FUN?
I DON'T KNOW. LET'S TRY A PRACTICE ROUND.
WHAM
WHA--?!

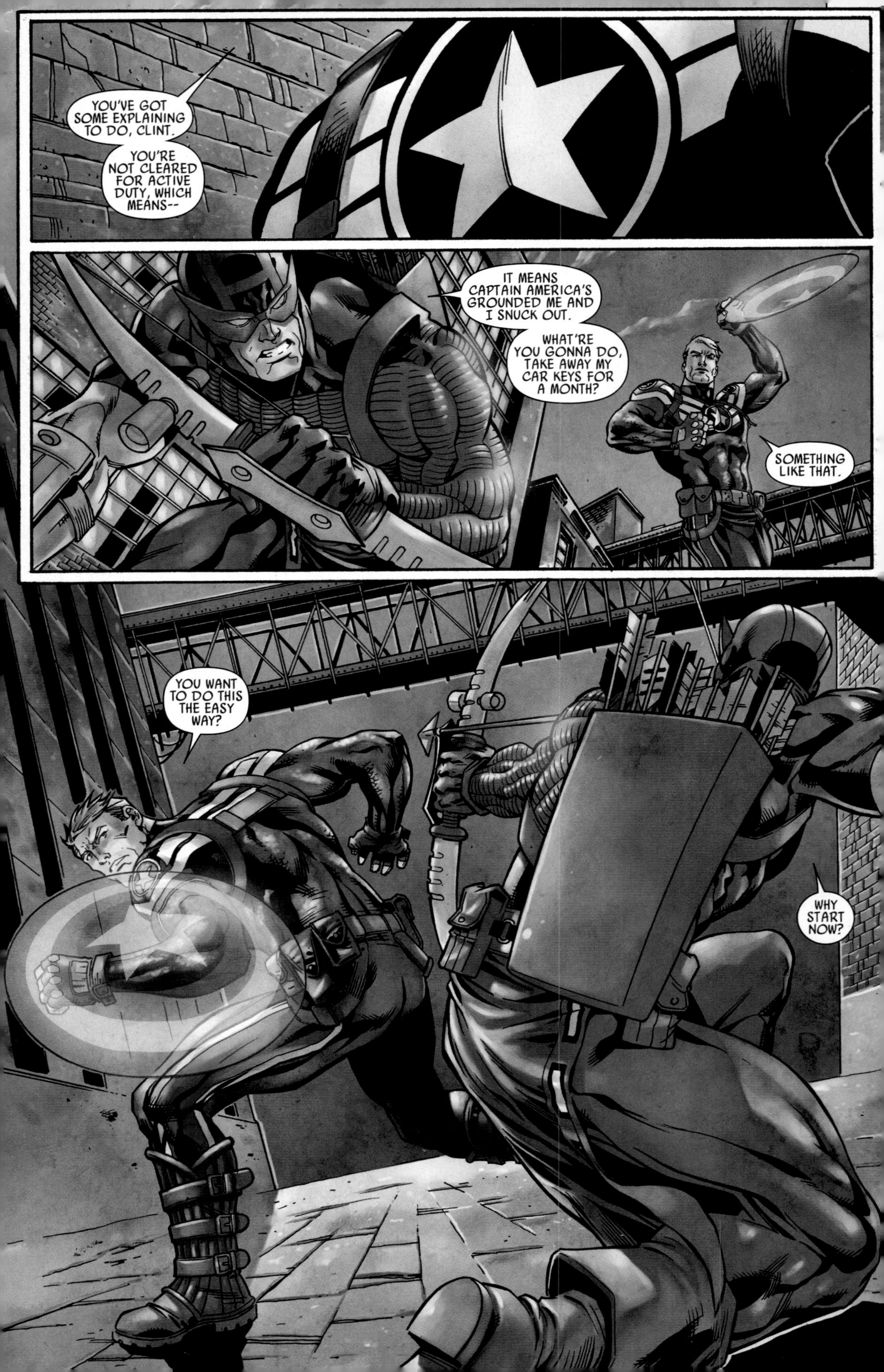
YOU'VE GOT SOME EXPLAINING TO DO, CLINT.
YOU'RE NOT CLEARED FOR ACTIVE DUTY, WHICH MEANS--
IT MEANS CAPTAIN AMERICA'S GROUNDED ME AND I SNUCK OUT.
WHAT'RE YOU GONNA DO, TAKE AWAY MY CAR KEYS FOR A MONTH?
SOMETHING LIKE THAT.
YOU WANT TO DO THIS THE EASY WAY?
WHY START NOW?

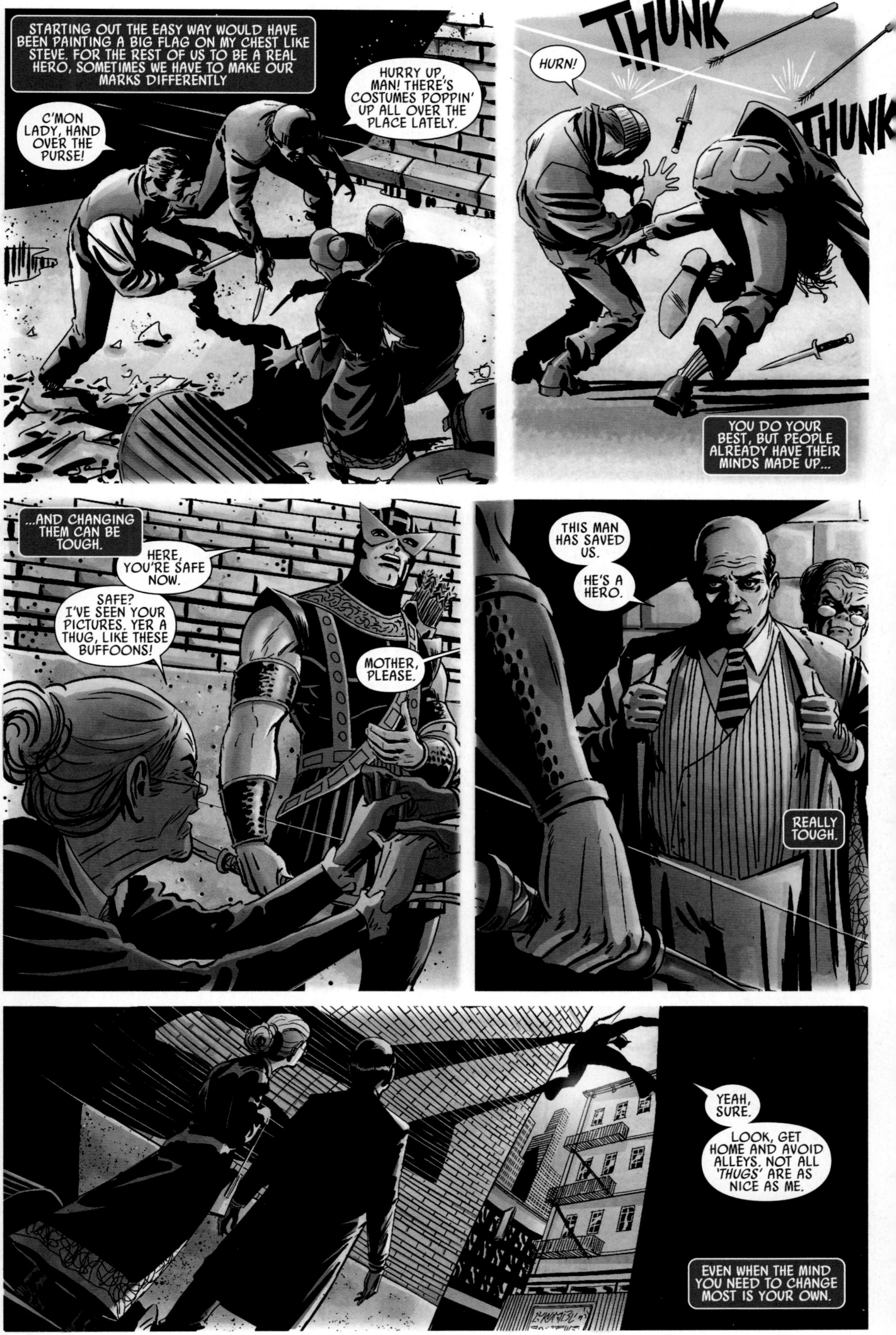

STARTING OUT THE EASY WAY WOULD HAVE BEEN PAINTING A BIG FLAG ON MY CHEST LIKE STEVE. FOR THE REST OF US TO BE A REAL HERO, SOMETIMES WE HAVE TO MAKE OUR MARKS DIFFERENTLY
C'MON LADY, HAND OVER THE PURSE!
HURRY UP, MAN! THERE'S COSTUMES POPPIN' UP ALL OVER THE PLACE LATELY.
THUNK
HURN!
THUNK
YOU DO YOUR BEST, BUT PEOPLE ALREADY HAVE THEIR MINDS MADE UP...
...AND CHANGING THEM CAN BE TOUGH.
HERE, YOU'RE SAFE NOW.
SAFE? I'VE SEEN YOUR PICTURES. YER A THUG, LIKE THESE BUFFOONS!
MOTHER, PLEASE.
THIS MAN HAS SAVED US.
HE'S A HERO.
REALLY TOUGH.
YEAH, SURE.
LOOK, GET HOME AND AVOID ALLEYS. NOT ALL *'THUGS'* ARE AS NICE AS ME.
EVEN WHEN THE MIND YOU NEED TO CHANGE MOST IS YOUR OWN.

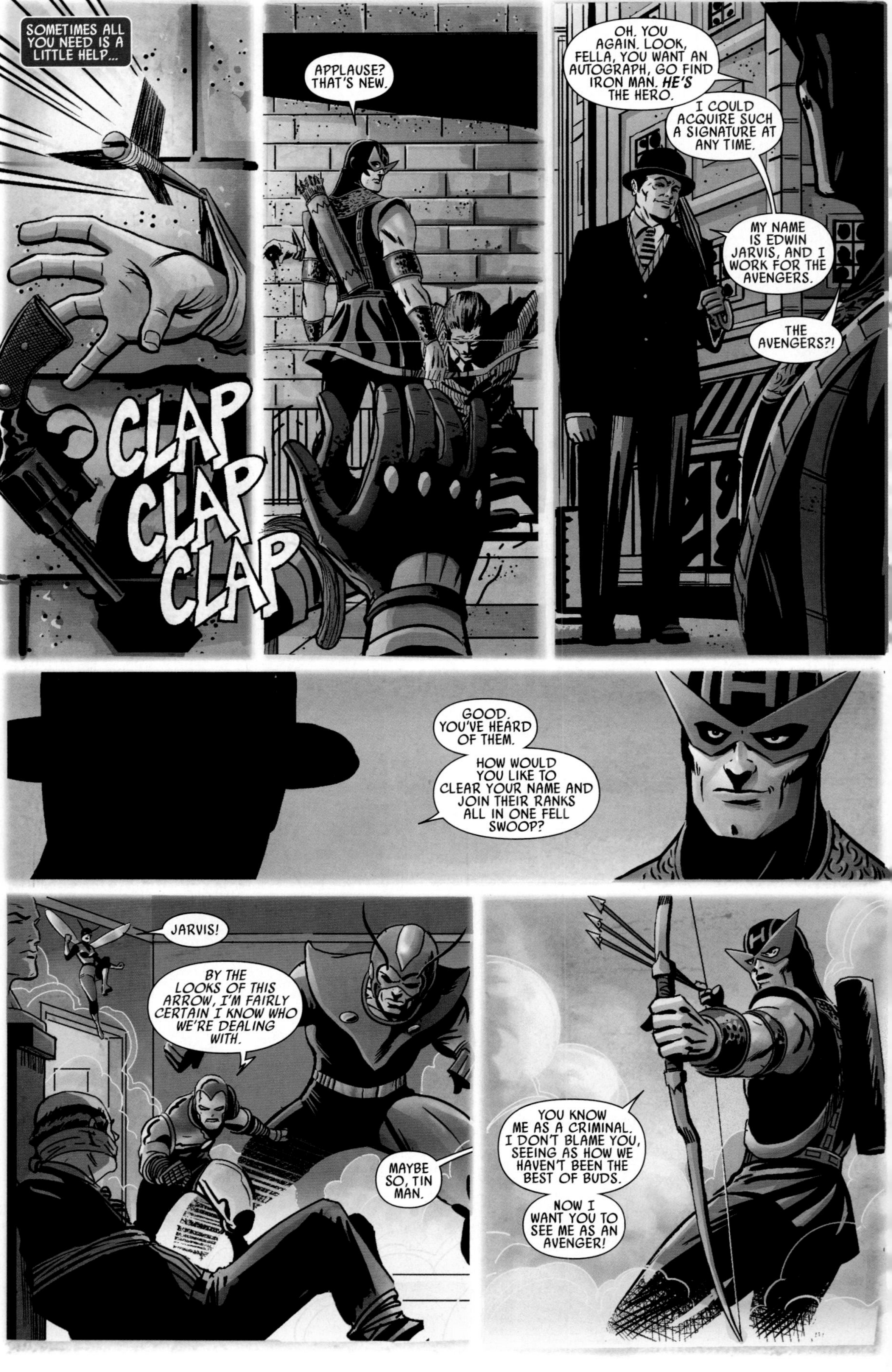
SOMETIMES ALL YOU NEED IS A LITTLE HELP...
CLAP CLAP CLAP
APPLAUSE? THAT'S NEW.
OH. YOU AGAIN. LOOK, FELLA, YOU WANT AN AUTOGRAPH, GO FIND IRON MAN. HE'S THE HERO.
I COULD ACQUIRE SUCH A SIGNATURE AT ANY TIME.
MY NAME IS EDWIN JARVIS, AND I WORK FOR THE AVENGERS.
THE AVENGERS?!
GOOD. YOU'VE HEARD OF THEM.
HOW WOULD YOU LIKE TO CLEAR YOUR NAME AND JOIN THEIR RANKS ALL IN ONE FELL SWOOP?
JARVIS!
BY THE LOOKS OF THIS ARROW, I'M FAIRLY CERTAIN I KNOW WHO WE'RE DEALING WITH.
MAYBE SO, TIN MAN.
YOU KNOW ME AS A CRIMINAL. I DON'T BLAME YOU, SEEING AS HOW WE HAVEN'T BEEN THE BEST OF BUDS.
NOW I WANT YOU TO SEE ME AS AN AVENGER!

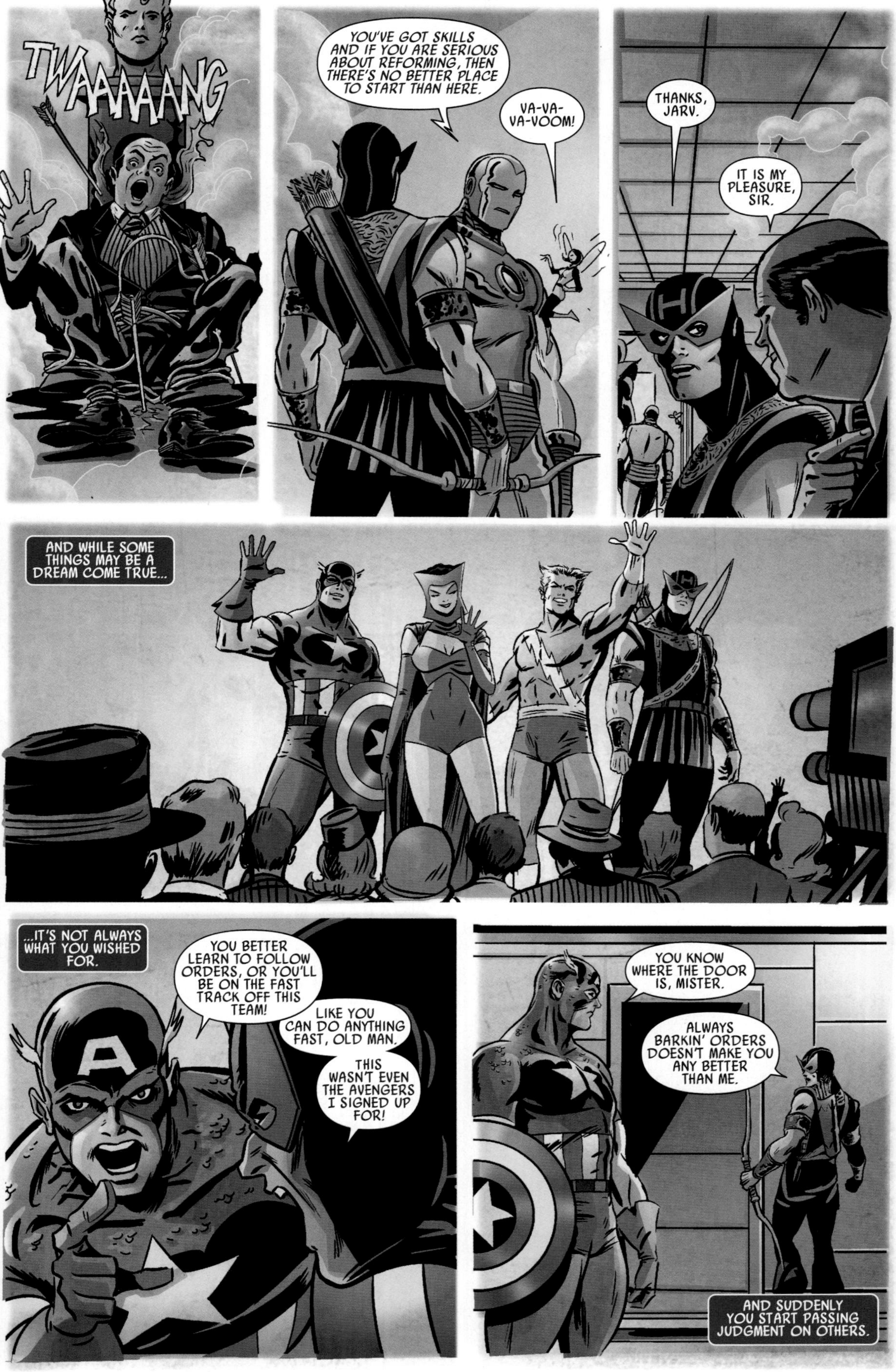
TWAAAAANG
YOU'VE GOT SKILLS AND IF YOU ARE SERIOUS ABOUT REFORMING, THEN THERE'S NO BETTER PLACE TO START THAN HERE.
VA-VA-VA-VOOM!
THANKS, JARV.
IT IS MY PLEASURE, SIR.
AND WHILE SOME THINGS MAY BE A DREAM COME TRUE...
...IT'S NOT ALWAYS WHAT YOU WISHED FOR.
YOU BETTER LEARN TO FOLLOW ORDERS, OR YOU'LL BE ON THE FAST TRACK OFF THIS TEAM!
LIKE YOU CAN DO ANYTHING FAST, OLD MAN.
THIS WASN'T EVEN THE AVENGERS I SIGNED UP FOR!
YOU KNOW WHERE THE DOOR IS, MISTER.
ALWAYS BARKIN' ORDERS DOESN'T MAKE YOU ANY BETTER THAN ME.
AND SUDDENLY YOU START PASSING JUDGMENT ON OTHERS.

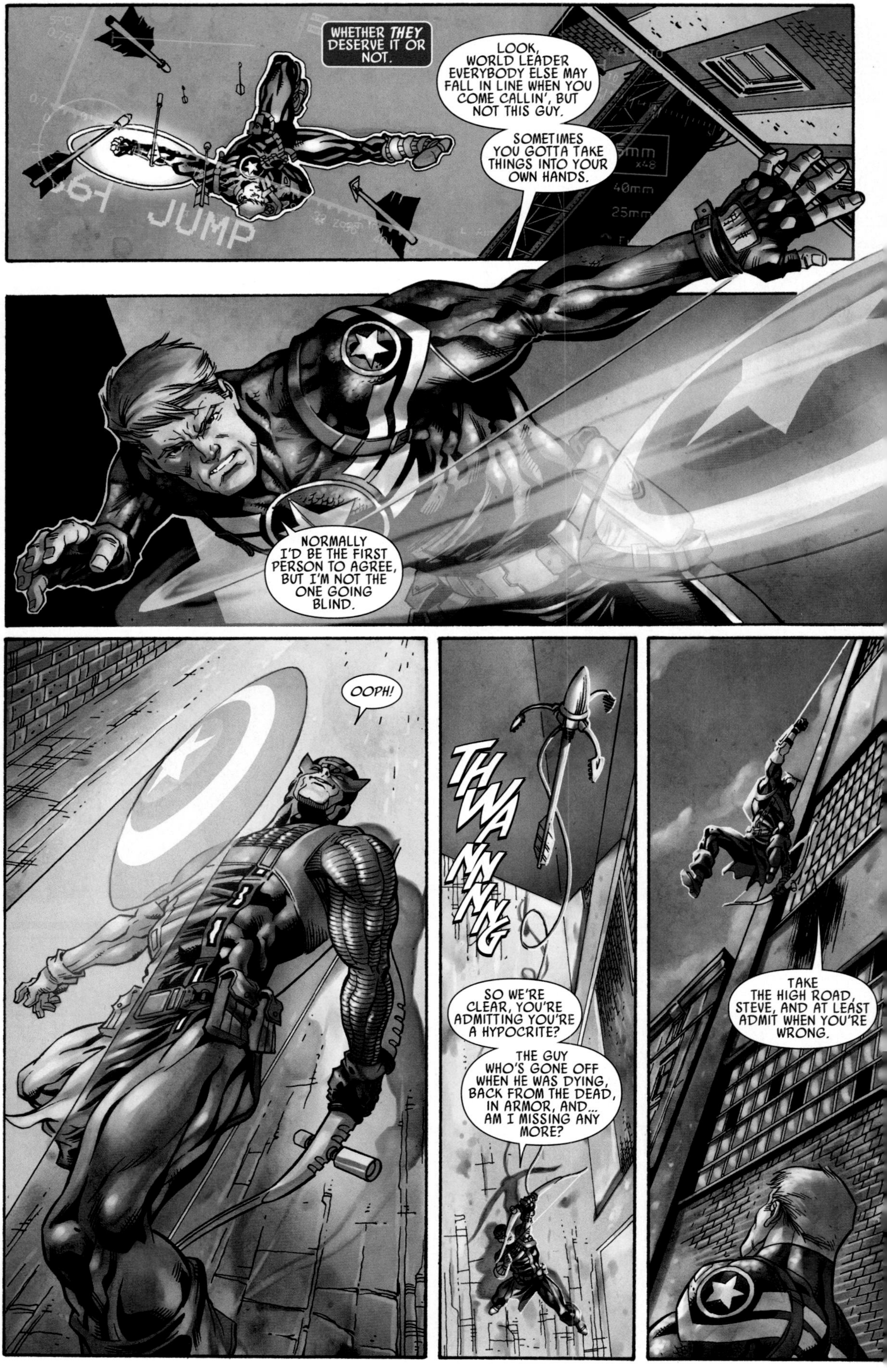
WHETHER THEY DESERVE IT OR NOT.
LOOK, WORLD LEADER EVERYBODY ELSE MAY FALL IN LINE WHEN YOU COME CALLIN', BUT NOT THIS GUY.
SOMETIMES YOU GOTTA TAKE THINGS INTO YOUR OWN HANDS.
JUMP
NORMALLY I'D BE THE FIRST PERSON TO AGREE, BUT I'M NOT THE ONE GOING BLIND.
OOPH!
THWANNNNG
SO WE'RE CLEAR, YOU'RE ADMITTING YOU'RE A HYPOCRITE?
THE GUY WHO'S GONE OFF WHEN HE WAS DYING, BACK FROM THE DEAD, IN ARMOR, AND... AM I MISSING ANY MORE?
TAKE THE HIGH ROAD, STEVE, AND AT LEAST ADMIT WHEN YOU'RE WRONG.

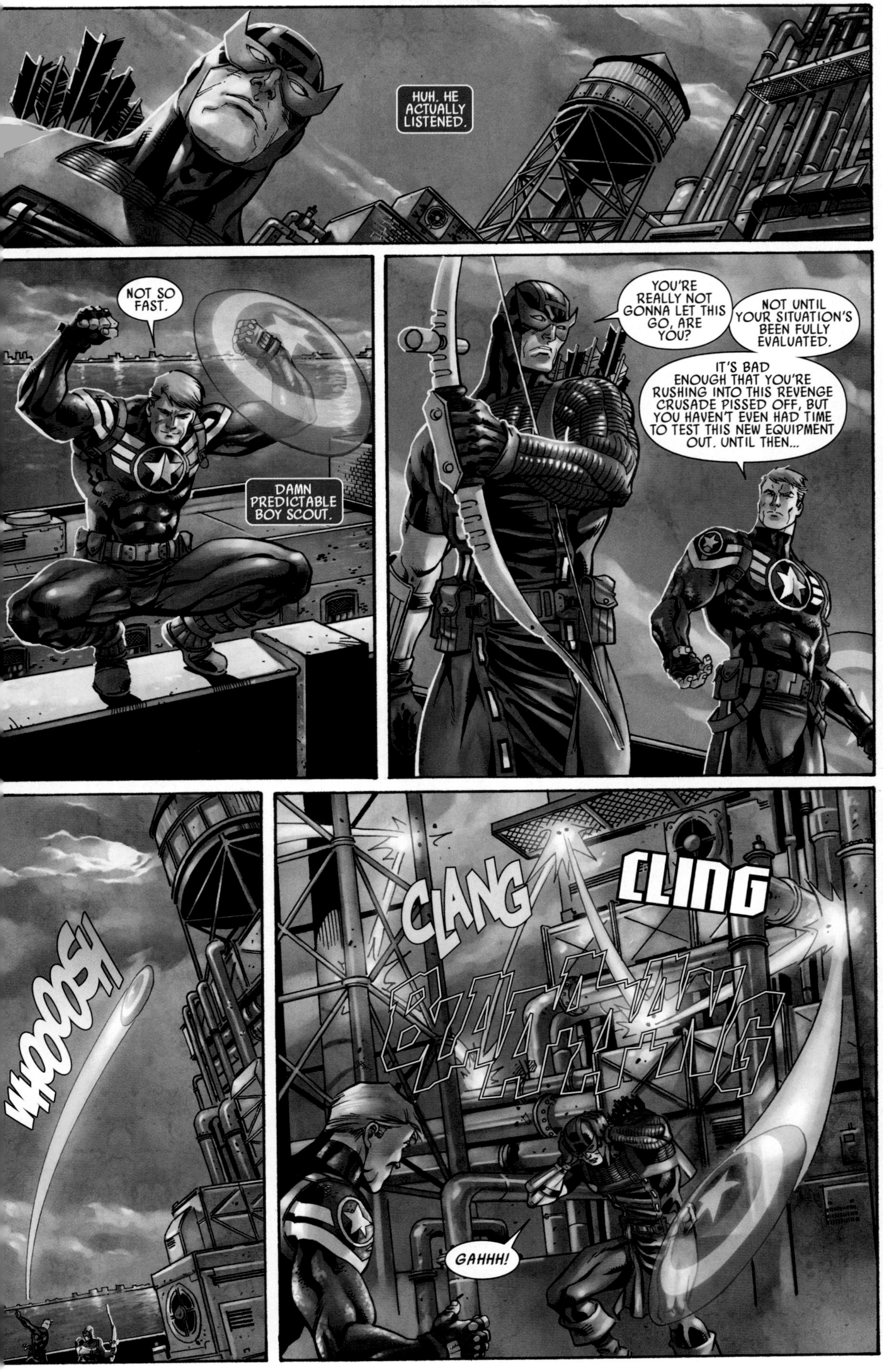
HUH. HE ACTUALLY LISTENED.
NOT SO FAST.
DAMN PREDICTABLE BOY SCOUT.
YOU'RE REALLY NOT GONNA LET THIS GO, ARE YOU?
NOT UNTIL YOUR SITUATION'S BEEN FULLY EVALUATED.
IT'S BAD ENOUGH THAT YOU'RE RUSHING INTO THIS REVENGE CRUSADE PISSED OFF, BUT YOU HAVEN'T EVEN HAD TIME TO TEST THIS NEW EQUIPMENT OUT. UNTIL THEN...
WHOOOOSH
CLANG
CLING
GAHHH!

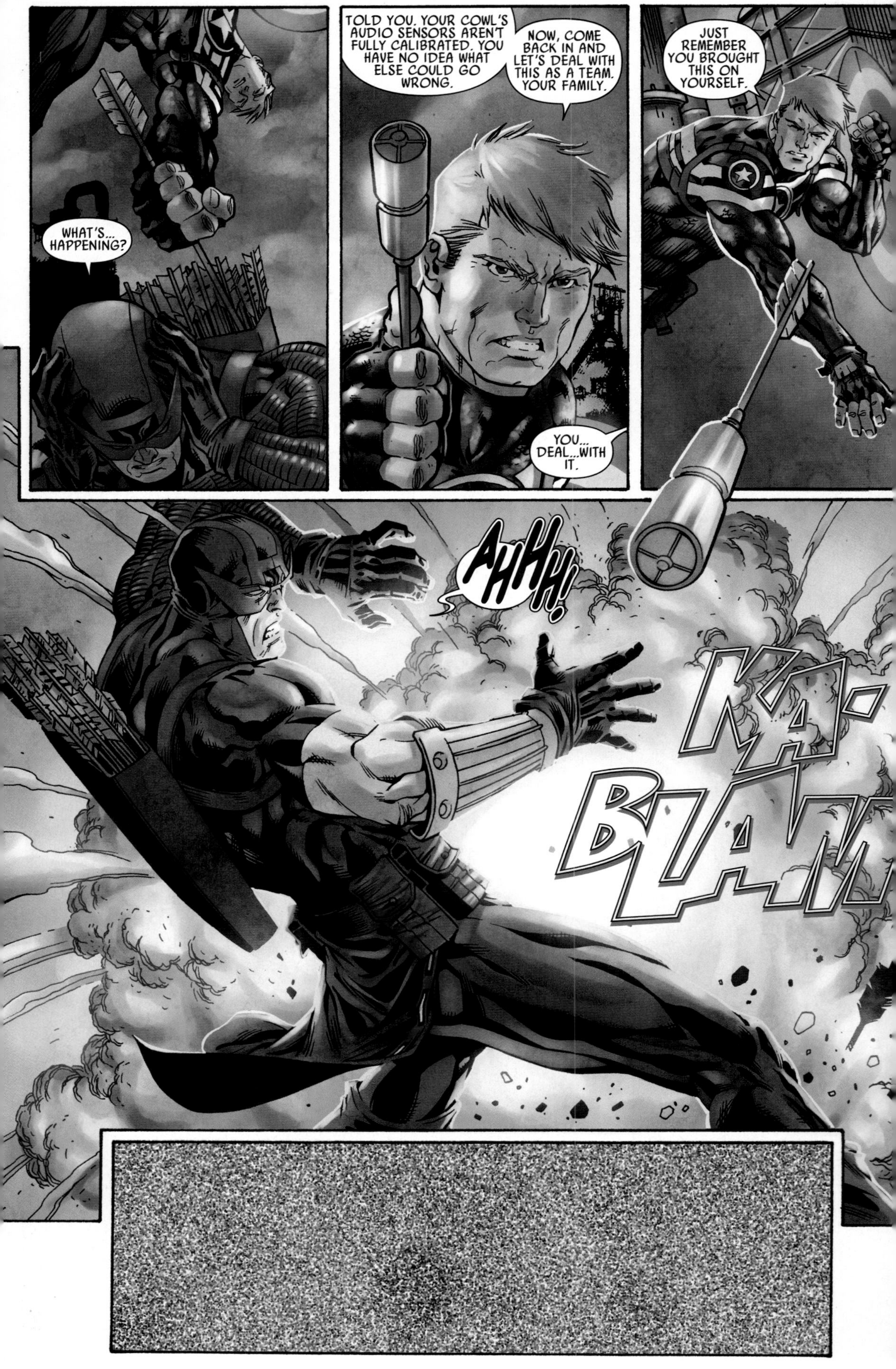
WHAT'S... HAPPENING?
TOLD YOU. YOUR COWL'S AUDIO SENSORS AREN'T FULLY CALIBRATED. YOU HAVE NO IDEA WHAT ELSE COULD GO WRONG.
NOW, COME BACK IN AND LET'S DEAL WITH THIS AS A TEAM. YOUR FAMILY.
YOU... DEAL...WITH IT.
JUST REMEMBER YOU BROUGHT THIS ON YOURSELF.
AHHH!
KA-BLAM

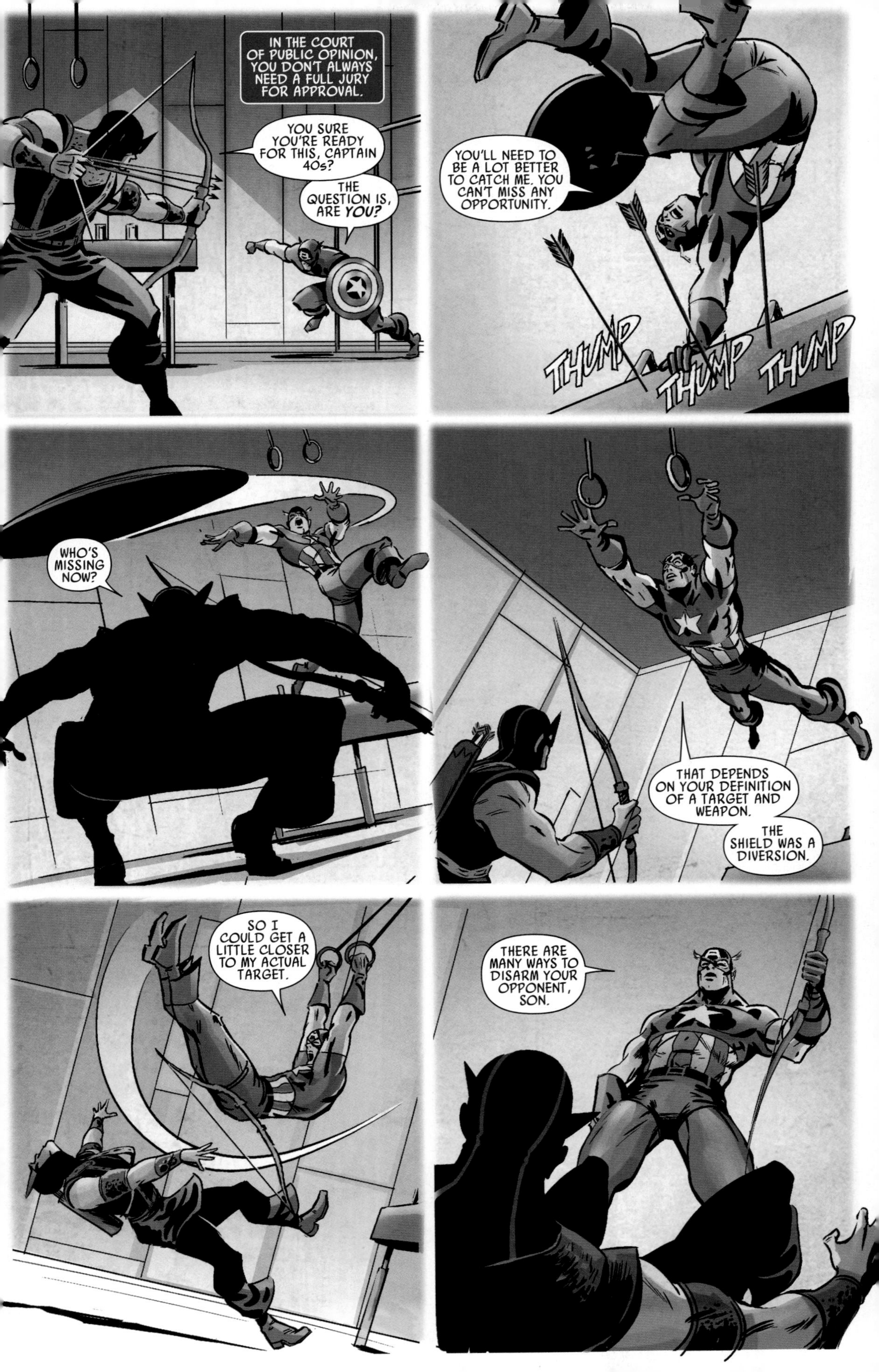
IN THE COURT OF PUBLIC OPINION, YOU DON'T ALWAYS NEED A FULL JURY FOR APPROVAL.
YOU SURE YOU'RE READY FOR THIS, CAPTAIN 40s?
THE QUESTION IS, ARE YOU?
YOU'LL NEED TO BE A LOT BETTER TO CATCH ME. YOU CAN'T MISS ANY OPPORTUNITY.
THUMP
THUMP
THUMP
WHO'S MISSING NOW?
THAT DEPENDS ON YOUR DEFINITION OF A TARGET AND WEAPON.
THE SHIELD WAS A DIVERSION.
SO I COULD GET A LITTLE CLOSER TO MY ACTUAL TARGET.
THERE ARE MANY WAYS TO DISARM YOUR OPPONENT, SON.

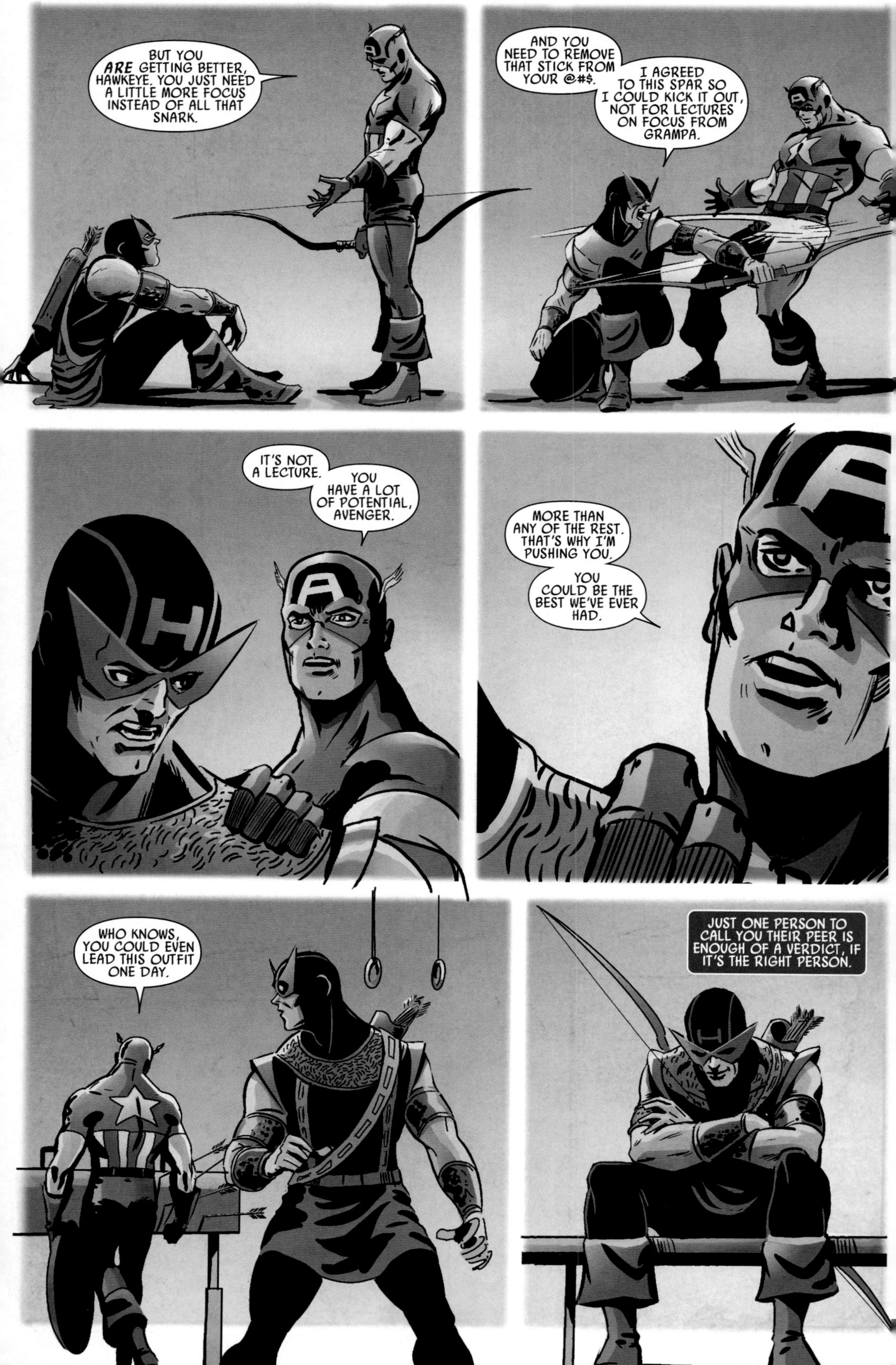

BUT YOU ARE GETTING BETTER, HAWKEYE. YOU JUST NEED A LITTLE MORE FOCUS INSTEAD OF ALL THAT SNARK.
AND YOU NEED TO REMOVE THAT STICK FROM YOUR @#$.
I AGREED TO THIS SPAR SO I COULD KICK IT OUT, NOT FOR LECTURES ON FOCUS FROM GRAMPA.
IT'S NOT A LECTURE.
YOU HAVE A LOT OF POTENTIAL, AVENGER.
MORE THAN ANY OF THE REST. THAT'S WHY I'M PUSHING YOU.
YOU COULD BE THE BEST WE'VE EVER HAD.
WHO KNOWS, YOU COULD EVEN LEAD THIS OUTFIT ONE DAY.
JUST ONE PERSON TO CALL YOU THEIR PEER IS ENOUGH OF A VERDICT, IF IT'S THE RIGHT PERSON.

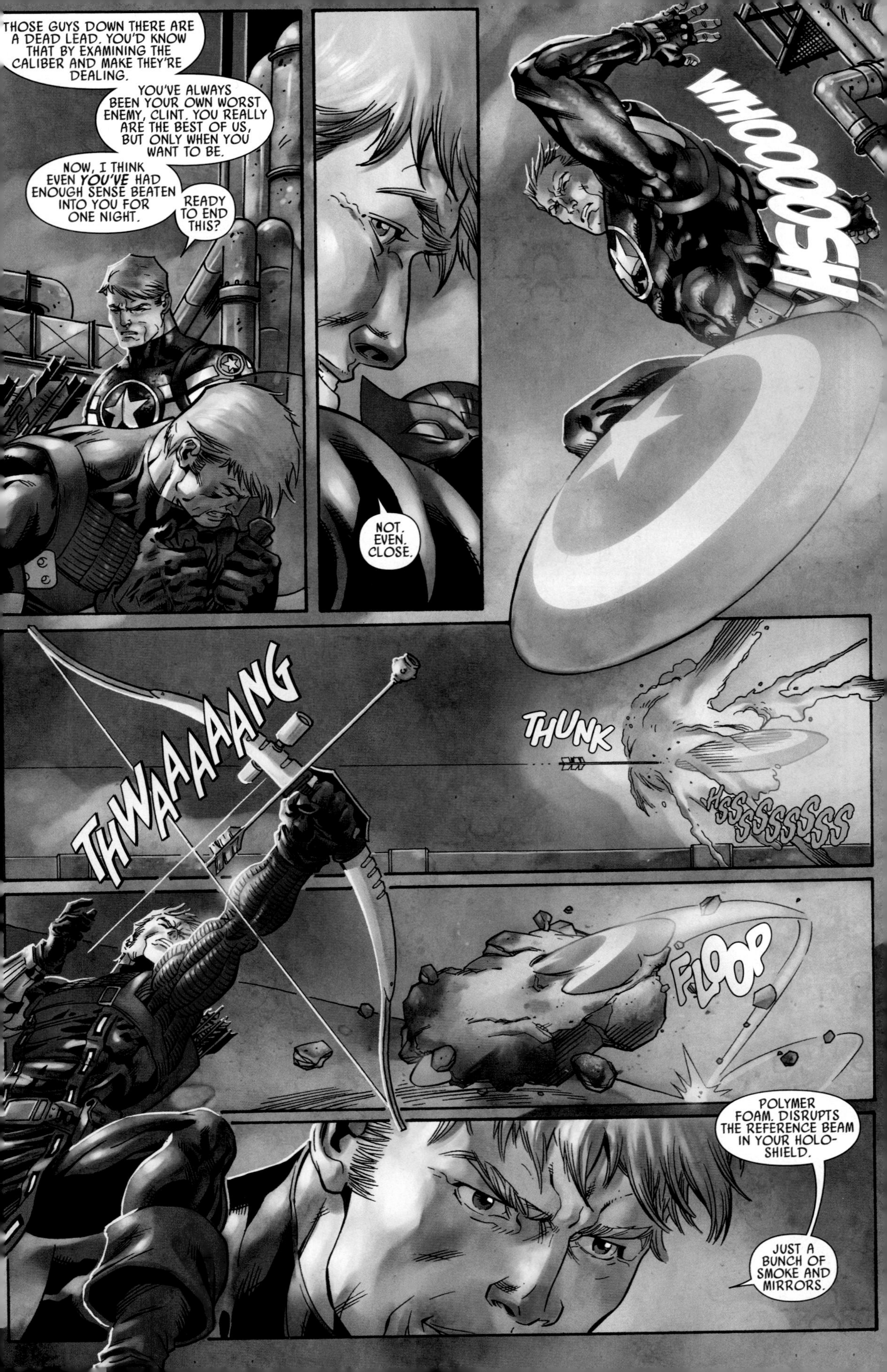
THOSE GUYS DOWN THERE ARE A DEAD LEAD. YOU'D KNOW THAT BY EXAMINING THE CALIBER AND MAKE THEY'RE DEALING.
YOU'VE ALWAYS BEEN YOUR OWN WORST ENEMY, CLINT. YOU REALLY ARE THE BEST OF US, BUT ONLY WHEN YOU WANT TO BE.
NOW, I THINK EVEN YOU'VE HAD ENOUGH SENSE BEATEN INTO YOU FOR ONE NIGHT.
READY TO END THIS?
NOT. EVEN. CLOSE.
WHOOOOOSH
THWAAAAANG
THUNK
HSSSSSSSSS
FLOOP
POLYMER FOAM. DISRUPTS THE REFERENCE BEAM IN YOUR HOLO-SHIELD.
JUST A BUNCH OF SMOKE AND MIRRORS.

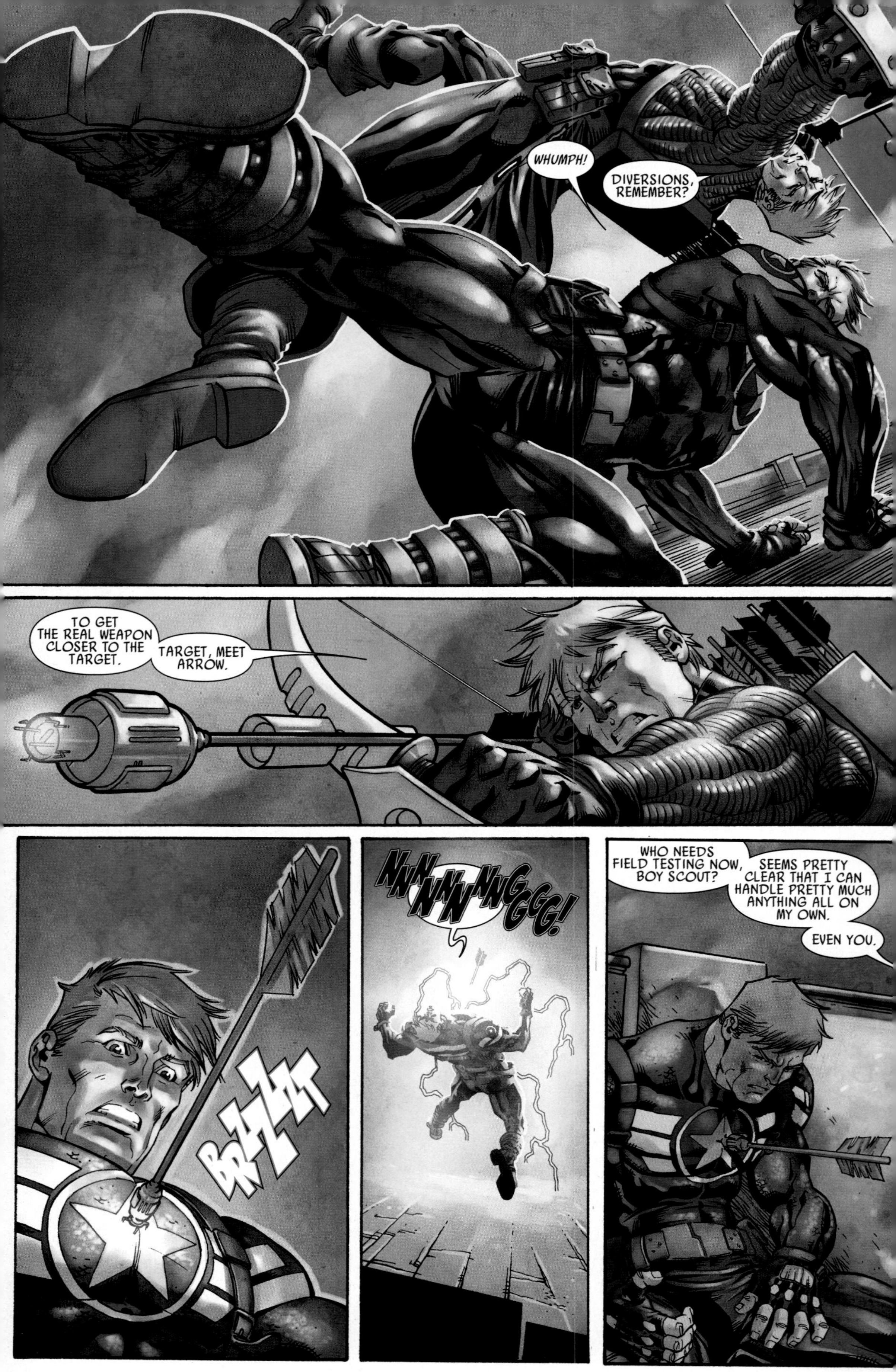
WHUMPH!
DIVERSIONS, REMEMBER?
TO GET THE REAL WEAPON CLOSER TO THE TARGET.
TARGET, MEET ARROW.
BRZZZZT
NNNNNNNGGG!
WHO NEEDS FIELD TESTING NOW, BOY SCOUT?
SEEMS PRETTY CLEAR THAT I CAN HANDLE PRETTY MUCH ANYTHING ALL ON MY OWN.
EVEN YOU.

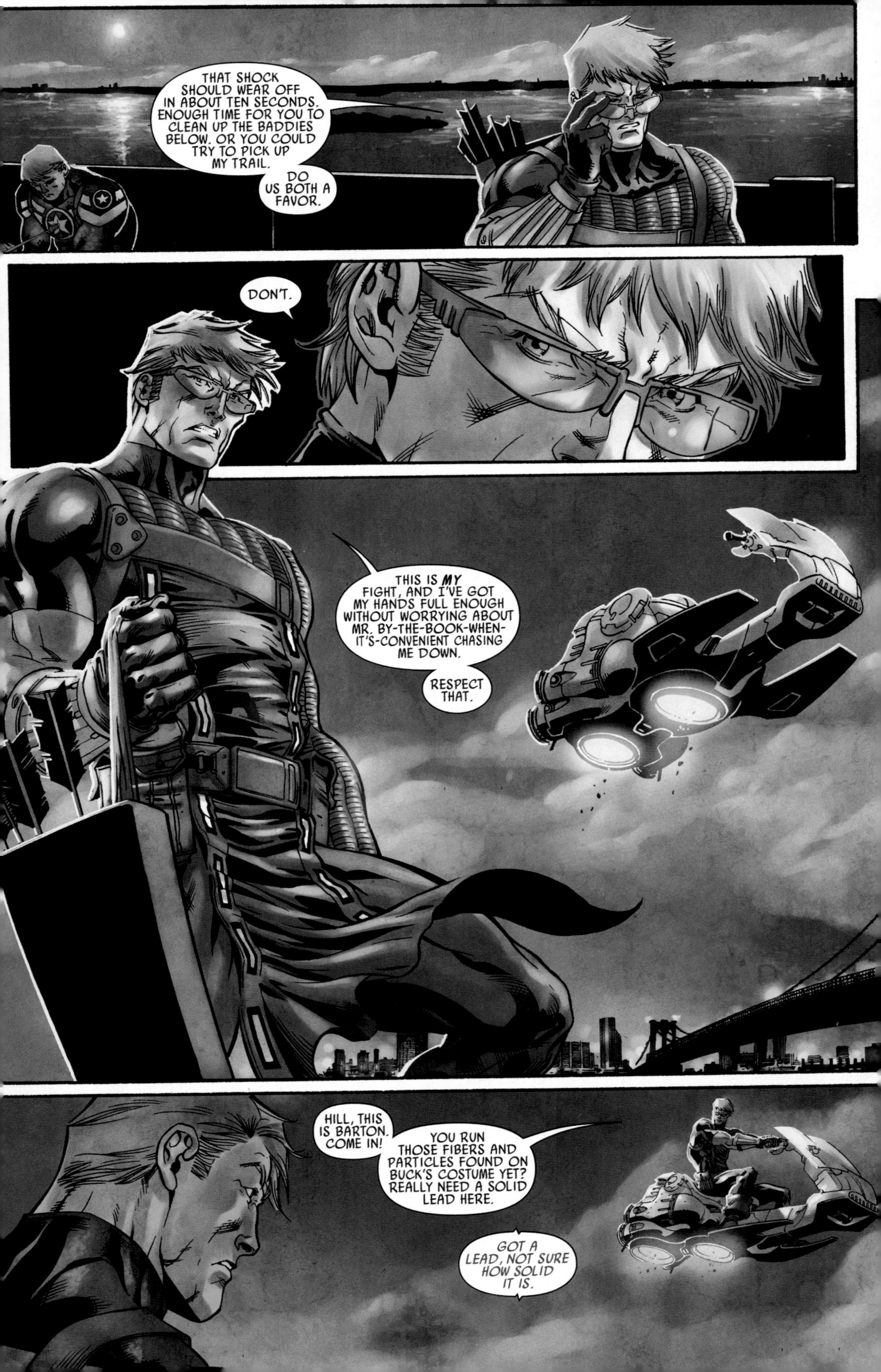
THAT SHOCK SHOULD WEAR OFF IN ABOUT TEN SECONDS. ENOUGH TIME FOR YOU TO CLEAN UP THE BADDIES BELOW. OR YOU COULD TRY TO PICK UP MY TRAIL.
DO US BOTH A FAVOR.
DON'T.
THIS IS MY FIGHT, AND I'VE GOT MY HANDS FULL ENOUGH WITHOUT WORRYING ABOUT MR. BY-THE-BOOK-WHEN-IT'S-CONVENIENT CHASING ME DOWN.
RESPECT THAT.
HILL, THIS IS BARTON. COME IN!
YOU RUN THOSE FIBERS AND PARTICLES FOUND ON BUCK'S COSTUME YET? REALLY NEED A SOLID LEAD HERE.
GOT A LEAD, NOT SURE HOW SOLID IT IS.

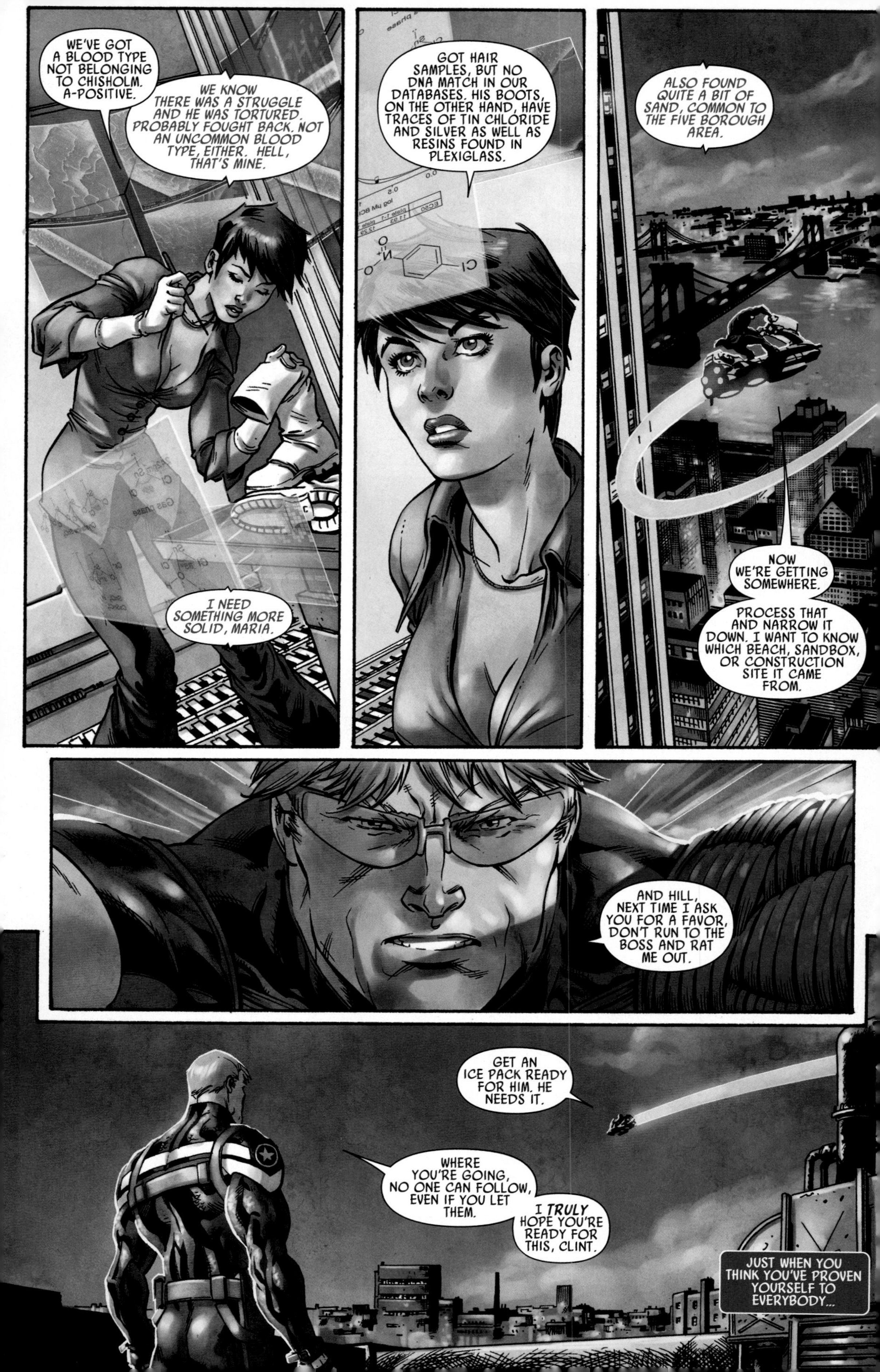
WE'VE GOT A BLOOD TYPE NOT BELONGING TO CHISHOLM. A-POSITIVE.
WE KNOW THERE WAS A STRUGGLE AND HE WAS TORTURED. PROBABLY FOUGHT BACK. NOT AN UNCOMMON BLOOD TYPE, EITHER. HELL, THAT'S MINE.
I NEED SOMETHING MORE SOLID, MARIA.
GOT HAIR SAMPLES, BUT NO DNA MATCH IN OUR DATABASES. HIS BOOTS, ON THE OTHER HAND, HAVE TRACES OF TIN CHLORIDE AND SILVER AS WELL AS RESINS FOUND IN PLEXIGLASS.
ALSO FOUND QUITE A BIT OF SAND, COMMON TO THE FIVE BOROUGH AREA.
NOW WE'RE GETTING SOMEWHERE.
PROCESS THAT AND NARROW IT DOWN. I WANT TO KNOW WHICH BEACH, SANDBOX, OR CONSTRUCTION SITE IT CAME FROM.
AND HILL, NEXT TIME I ASK YOU FOR A FAVOR, DON'T RUN TO THE BOSS AND RAT ME OUT.
GET AN ICE PACK READY FOR HIM. HE NEEDS IT.
WHERE YOU'RE GOING, NO ONE CAN FOLLOW, EVEN IF YOU LET THEM.
I TRULY HOPE YOU'RE READY FOR THIS, CLINT.
JUST WHEN YOU THINK YOU'VE PROVEN YOURSELF TO EVERYBODY...

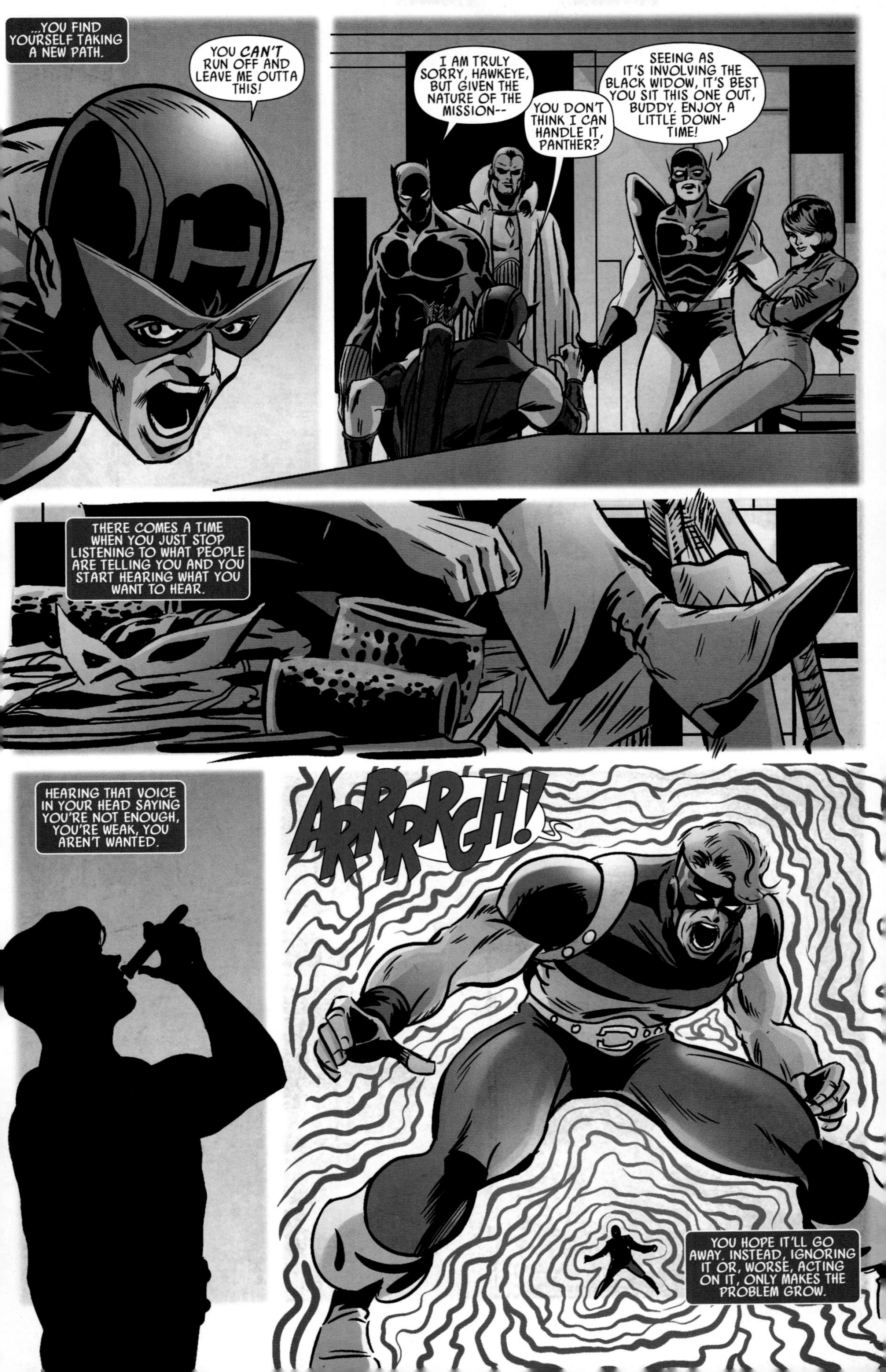

...YOU FIND YOURSELF TAKING A NEW PATH.
YOU CAN'T RUN OFF AND LEAVE ME OUTTA THIS!
I AM TRULY SORRY, HAWKEYE, BUT GIVEN THE NATURE OF THE MISSION--
YOU DON'T THINK I CAN HANDLE IT, PANTHER?
SEEING AS IT'S INVOLVING THE BLACK WIDOW, IT'S BEST YOU SIT THIS ONE OUT, BUDDY. ENJOY A LITTLE DOWN-TIME!
THERE COMES A TIME WHEN YOU JUST STOP LISTENING TO WHAT PEOPLE ARE TELLING YOU AND YOU START HEARING WHAT YOU WANT TO HEAR.
HEARING THAT VOICE IN YOUR HEAD SAYING YOU'RE NOT ENOUGH, YOU'RE WEAK, YOU AREN'T WANTED.
ARRRRGH!
YOU HOPE IT'LL GO AWAY. INSTEAD, IGNORING IT OR, WORSE, ACTING ON IT, ONLY MAKES THE PROBLEM GROW.

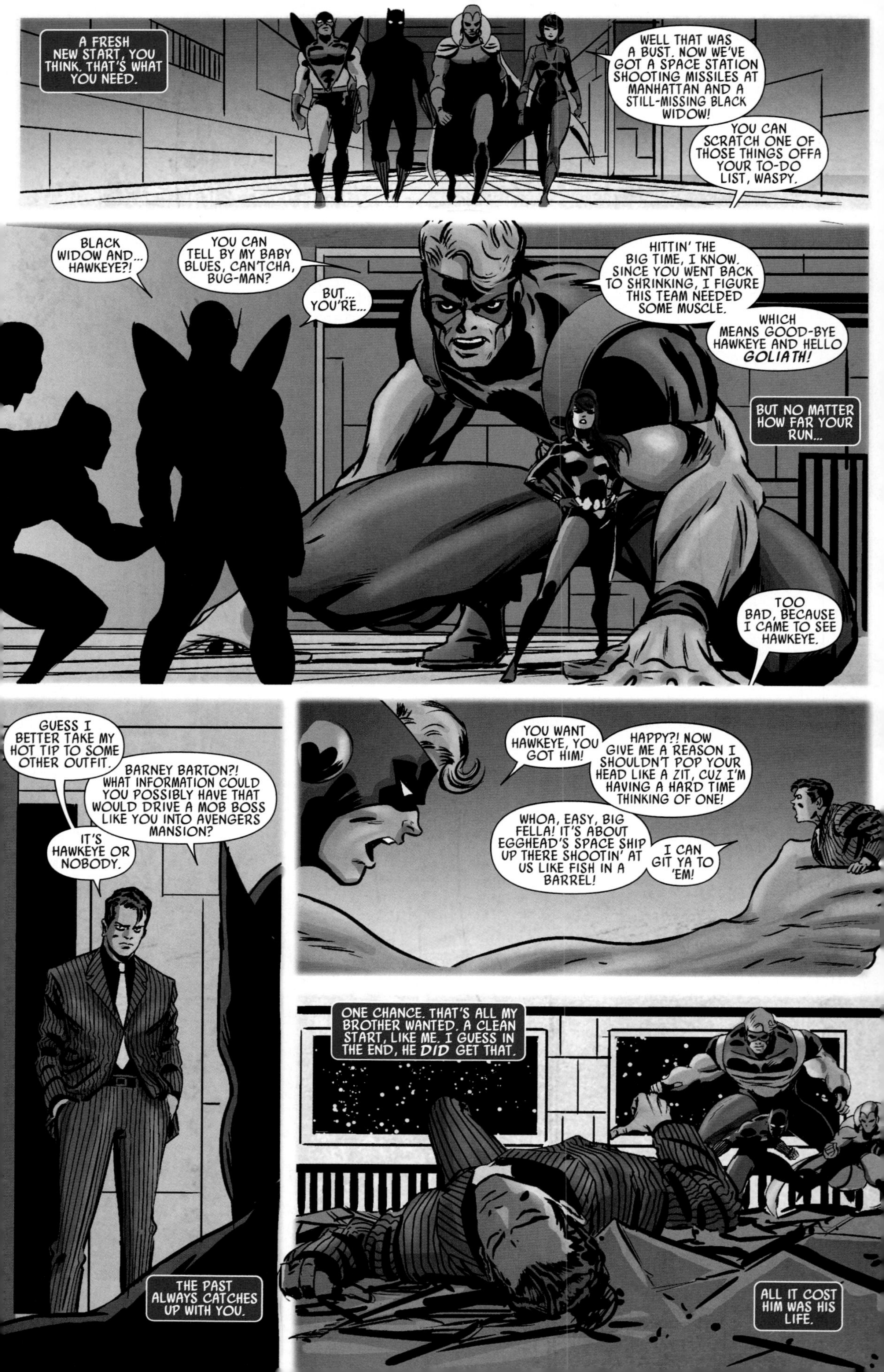
A FRESH NEW START, YOU THINK. THAT'S WHAT YOU NEED.
WELL THAT WAS A BUST. NOW WE'VE GOT A SPACE STATION SHOOTING MISSILES AT MANHATTAN AND A STILL-MISSING BLACK WIDOW!
YOU CAN SCRATCH ONE OF THOSE THINGS OFFA YOUR TO-DO LIST, WASPY.
BLACK WIDOW AND... HAWKEYE?!...
YOU CAN TELL BY MY BABY BLUES, CAN'TCHA, BUG-MAN?
BUT... YOU'RE...
HITTIN' THE BIG TIME, I KNOW. SINCE YOU WENT BACK TO SHRINKING, I FIGURE THIS TEAM NEEDED SOME MUSCLE.
WHICH MEANS GOOD-BYE HAWKEYE AND HELLO GOLIATH!
BUT NO MATTER HOW FAR YOUR RUN...
TOO BAD, BECAUSE I CAME TO SEE HAWKEYE.
GUESS I BETTER TAKE MY HOT TIP TO SOME OTHER OUTFIT.
BARNEY BARTON?! WHAT INFORMATION COULD YOU POSSIBLY HAVE THAT WOULD DRIVE A MOB BOSS LIKE YOU INTO AVENGERS MANSION?
IT'S HAWKEYE OR NOBODY.
THE PAST ALWAYS CATCHES UP WITH YOU.
YOU WANT HAWKEYE, YOU GOT HIM!
HAPPY?! NOW GIVE ME A REASON I SHOULDN'T POP YOUR HEAD LIKE A ZIT, CUZ I'M HAVING A HARD TIME THINKING OF ONE!
WHOA, EASY, BIG FELLA! IT'S ABOUT EGGHEAD'S SPACE SHIP UP THERE SHOOTIN' AT US LIKE FISH IN A BARREL!
I CAN GIT YA TO 'EM!
ONE CHANCE. THAT'S ALL MY BROTHER WANTED. A CLEAN START, LIKE ME. I GUESS IN THE END, HE DID GET THAT.
ALL IT COST HIM WAS HIS LIFE.

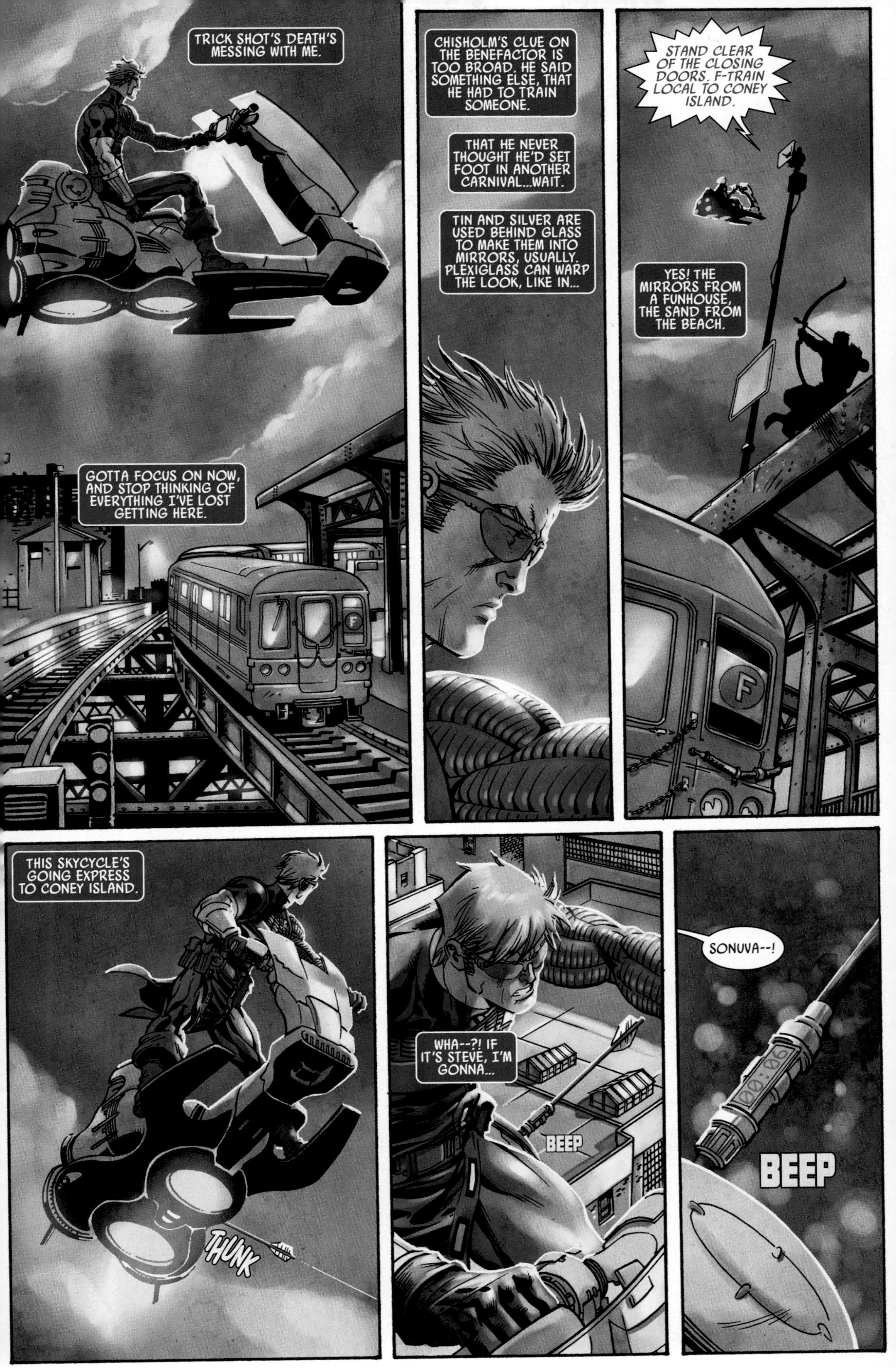
TRICK SHOT'S DEATH'S MESSING WITH ME.
GOTTA FOCUS ON NOW, AND STOP THINKING OF EVERYTHING I'VE LOST GETTING HERE.
CHISHOLM'S CLUE ON THE BENEFACTOR IS TOO BROAD. HE SAID SOMETHING ELSE, THAT HE HAD TO TRAIN SOMEONE.
THAT HE NEVER THOUGHT HE'D SET FOOT IN ANOTHER CARNIVAL...WAIT.
TIN AND SILVER ARE USED BEHIND GLASS TO MAKE THEM INTO MIRRORS, USUALLY. PLEXIGLASS CAN WARP THE LOOK, LIKE IN...
STAND CLEAR OF THE CLOSING DOORS. F-TRAIN LOCAL TO CONEY ISLAND.
YES! THE MIRRORS FROM A FUNHOUSE, THE SAND FROM THE BEACH.
THIS SKYCYCLE'S GOING EXPRESS TO CONEY ISLAND.
THUNK
WHA--?! IF IT'S STEVE, I'M GONNA...
BEEP
SONUVA--!
00:06
BEEP

GOTTA MAKE THIS QUICK, NO TIME TO THINK.

GRAB BACK-UP SUPPLIES AND FLY AS HIGH AS YOU CAN BEFORE...

00:03

BEEP

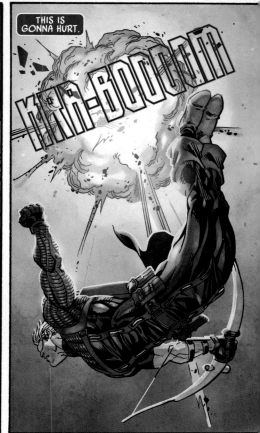

THIS IS GONNA HURT.

KAR-BOOOOM

WHUMP!

THUNK

THAT HURT.

NUTS! NOW I GOTTA TELL TONY I BROKE MY NEW GLASSES. ON THE FIRST DAY.

AFTER I FIGURE OUT WHO TRIED TO BLOW ME UP.

HEADIN' TO CONEY ISLAND WITHOUT ME? I SHOULD BE HURT.

NO...

A'COURSE, I'M KINDA MORE HURT IT TOOK YA THIS LONG TO FIGURE IT OUT.

AFTER ALL, YOU WERE ALWAYS THE SMART ONE, AND ME THE TRICKY ONE.

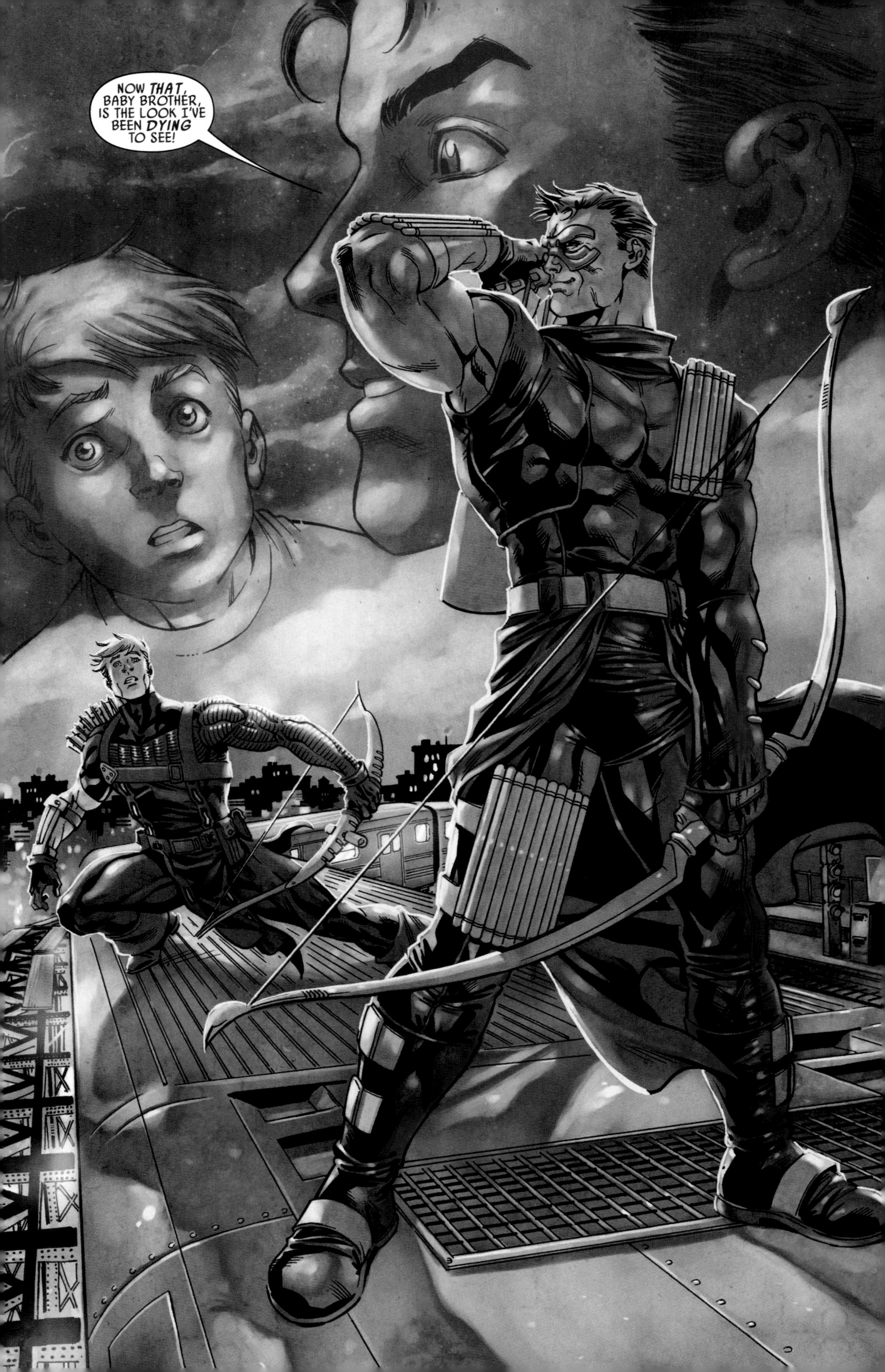
NOW *THAT*, BABY BROTHER, IS THE LOOK I'VE BEEN *DYING* TO SEE!

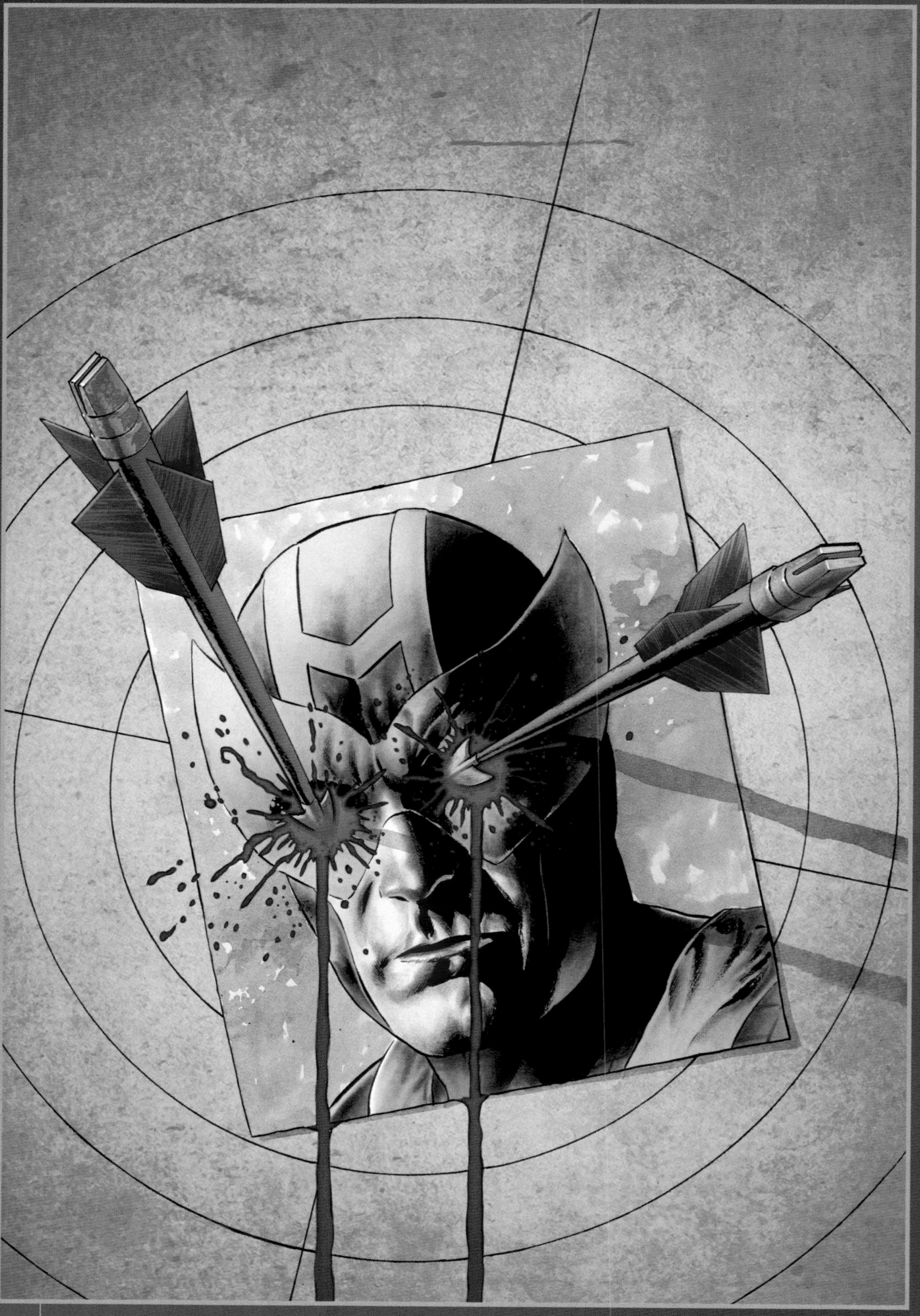

#3

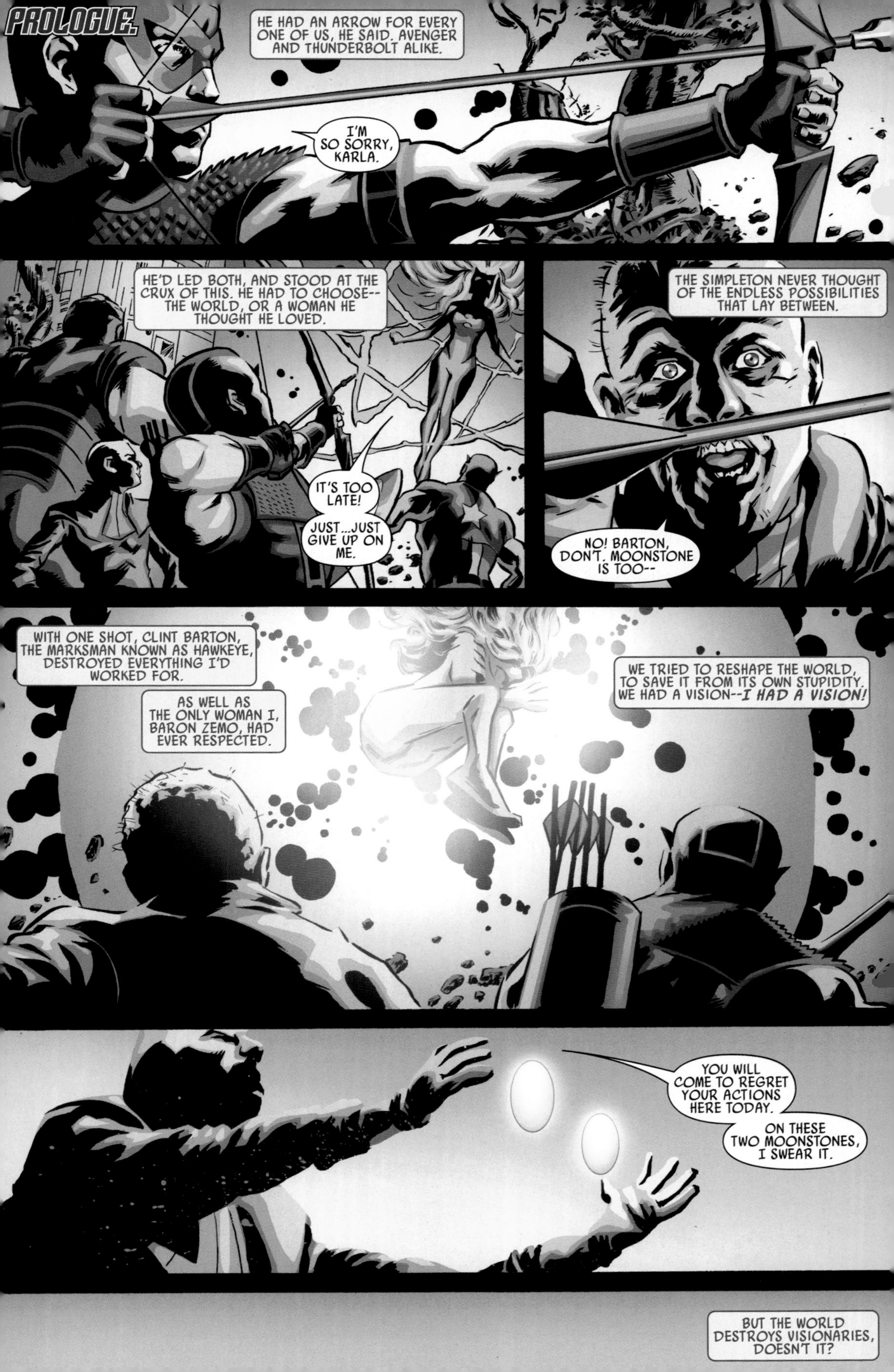
PROLOGUE.
HE HAD AN ARROW FOR EVERY ONE OF US, HE SAID. AVENGER AND THUNDERBOLT ALIKE.
I'M SO SORRY, KARLA.
HE'D LED BOTH, AND STOOD AT THE CRUX OF THIS. HE HAD TO CHOOSE-- THE WORLD, OR A WOMAN HE THOUGHT HE LOVED.
IT'S TOO LATE!
JUST...JUST GIVE UP ON ME.
THE SIMPLETON NEVER THOUGHT OF THE ENDLESS POSSIBILITIES THAT LAY BETWEEN.
NO! BARTON, DON'T. MOONSTONE IS TOO--
WITH ONE SHOT, CLINT BARTON, THE MARKSMAN KNOWN AS HAWKEYE, DESTROYED EVERYTHING I'D WORKED FOR.
AS WELL AS THE ONLY WOMAN I, BARON ZEMO, HAD EVER RESPECTED.
WE TRIED TO RESHAPE THE WORLD, TO SAVE IT FROM ITS OWN STUPIDITY. WE HAD A VISION--*I HAD A VISION!*
YOU WILL COME TO REGRET YOUR ACTIONS HERE TODAY.
ON THESE TWO MOONSTONES, I SWEAR IT.
BUT THE WORLD DESTROYS VISIONARIES, DOESN'T IT?

I HAD LOST EVERYTHING, WHICH ALLOWED FOR A FRESH START.

A BLANK CANVAS ON WHICH TO PAINT A NEW WORLD.

NEW ALLIES TO BE FOUND.

KARLA OFTEN SPOKE TO ME OF HER EARLIER DAYS WITH EGGHEAD AND *HIS* MASTERS OF EVIL, AND OF THE SCIENTIFIC BREAKTHROUGHS HE'D ACCOMPLISHED

I WANDERED THE EARTH, WITH THE MOONSTONES AS MY GUIDE, UNTIL I CAME ACROSS A LONG-ABANDONED SAFE HOUSE.

THE MAN WAS A GENIUS. ALMOST AS BRILLIANT AS ME.

A PITY HIS TIME ON THIS WORLD WAS CUT SHORT, ANOTHER VICTIM OF HAWKEYE.

BUT HE KEPT METICULOUS RECORDS.

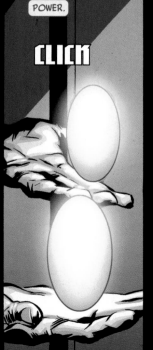

I THOUGHT HIS WORK MIGHT YIELD SOME FRUIT, STILL ON THE VINE.

TRUE VENGEANCE TAKES TIME.

PLANNING.

POWER.

CLICK

HSSSSSSSSSSSSS

MEIN GOTT...

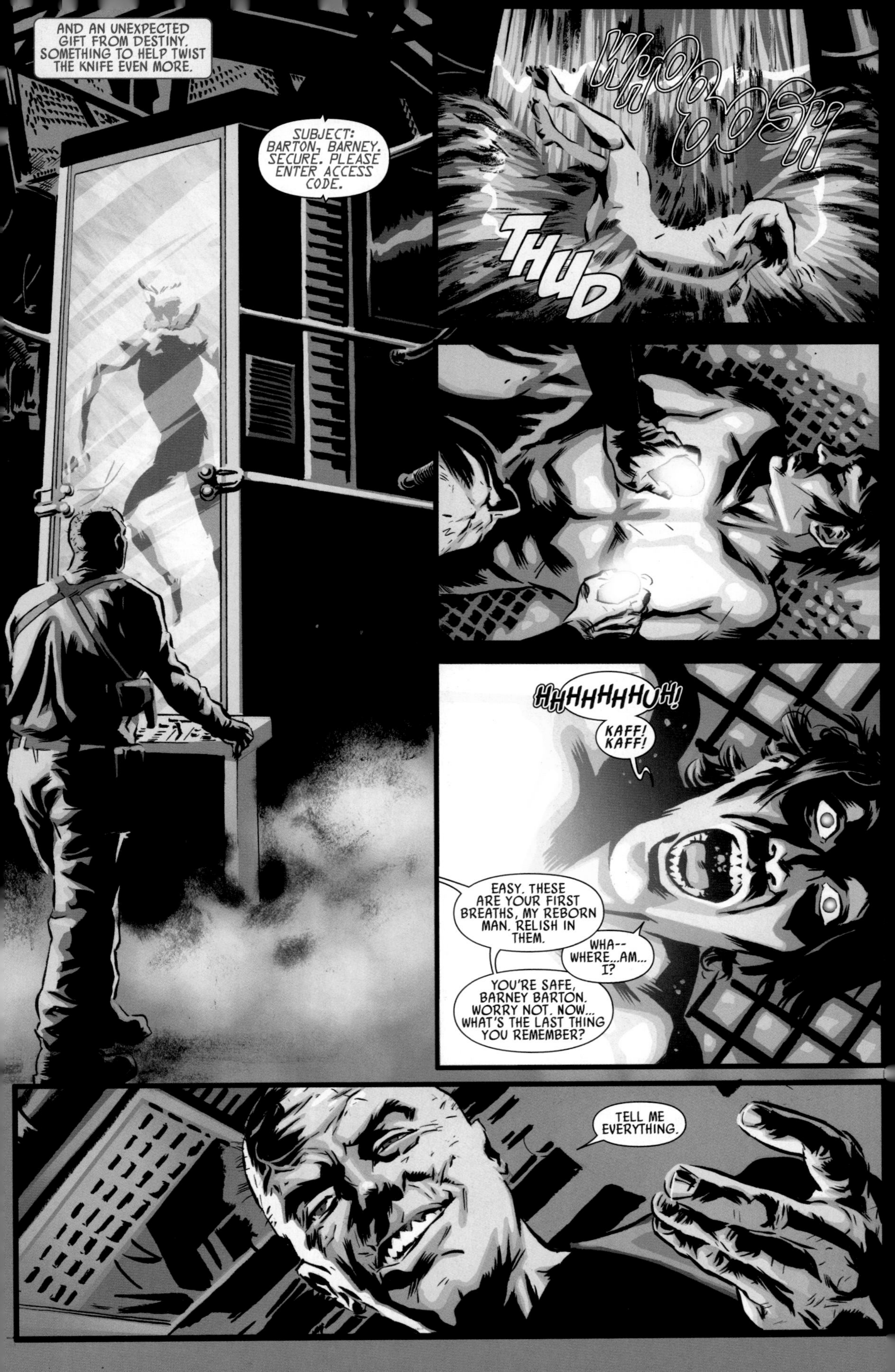
AND AN UNEXPECTED GIFT FROM DESTINY. SOMETHING TO HELP TWIST THE KNIFE EVEN MORE.
SUBJECT: BARTON, BARNEY. SECURE. PLEASE ENTER ACCESS CODE.
WHOOOOSH
THUD
HHHHHHHUH!
KAFF! KAFF!
EASY. THESE ARE YOUR FIRST BREATHS, MY REBORN MAN. RELISH IN THEM.
WHA-- WHERE...AM... I?
YOU'RE SAFE, BARNEY BARTON. WORRY NOT. NOW... WHAT'S THE LAST THING YOU REMEMBER?
TELL ME EVERYTHING.

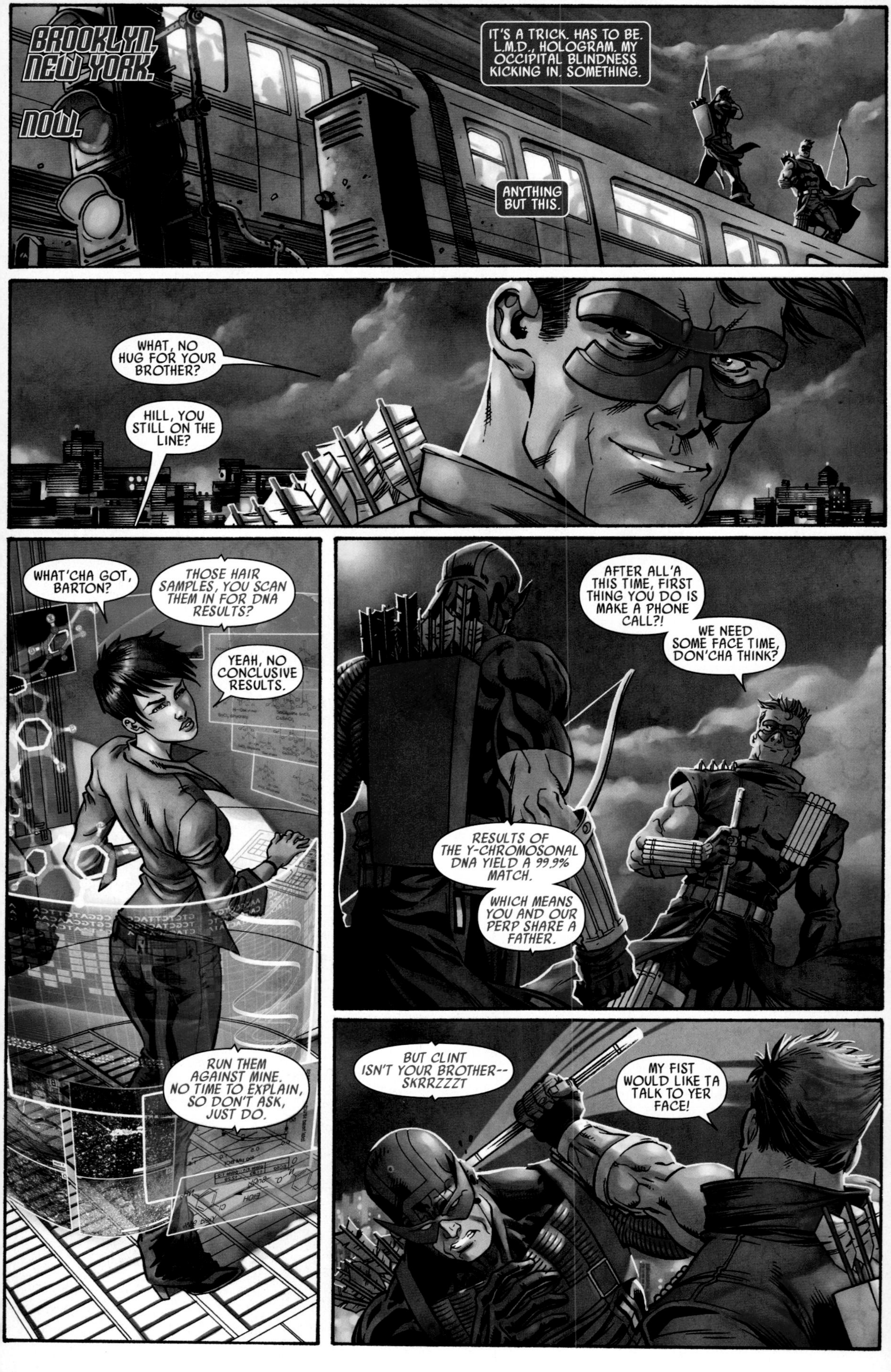
BROOKLYN, NEW YORK.
NOW.
IT'S A TRICK. HAS TO BE. L.M.D., HOLOGRAM. MY OCCIPITAL BLINDNESS KICKING IN. SOMETHING.
ANYTHING BUT THIS.
WHAT, NO HUG FOR YOUR BROTHER?
HILL, YOU STILL ON THE LINE?
WHAT'CHA GOT, BARTON?
THOSE HAIR SAMPLES, YOU SCAN THEM IN FOR DNA RESULTS?
YEAH, NO CONCLUSIVE RESULTS.
RUN THEM AGAINST MINE. NO TIME TO EXPLAIN, SO DON'T ASK, JUST DO.
AFTER ALL'A THIS TIME, FIRST THING YOU DO IS MAKE A PHONE CALL?!
WE NEED SOME FACE TIME, DON'CHA THINK?
RESULTS OF THE Y-CHROMOSONAL DNA YIELD A 99.9% MATCH.
WHICH MEANS YOU AND OUR PERP SHARE A FATHER.
BUT CLINT ISN'T YOUR BROTHER-- SKRRZZZT
MY FIST WOULD LIKE TA TALK TO YER FACE!

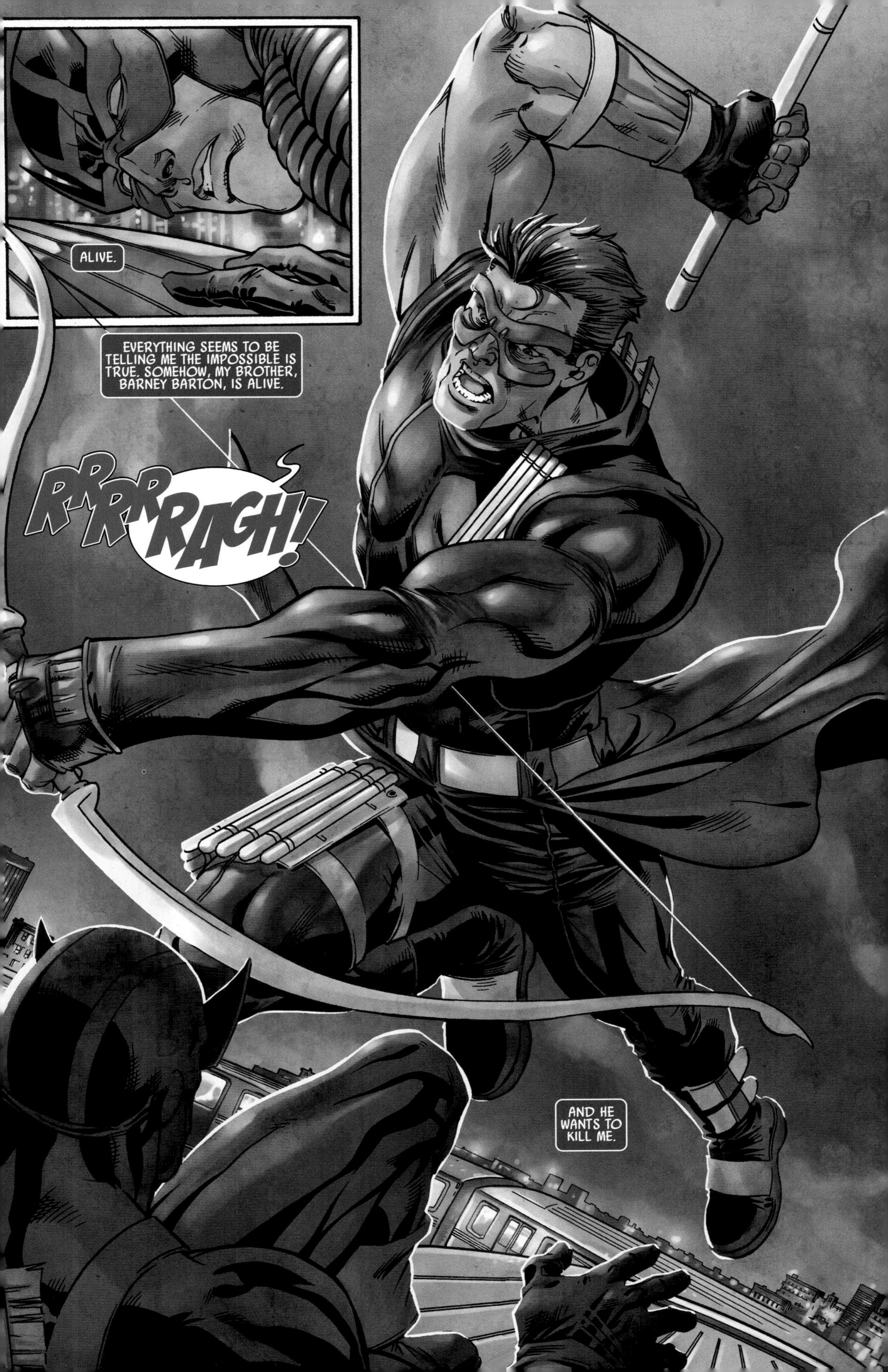
ALIVE.
EVERYTHING SEEMS TO BE TELLING ME THE IMPOSSIBLE IS TRUE. SOMEHOW, MY BROTHER, BARNEY BARTON, IS ALIVE.
RRRRRAGH!
AND HE WANTS TO KILL ME.

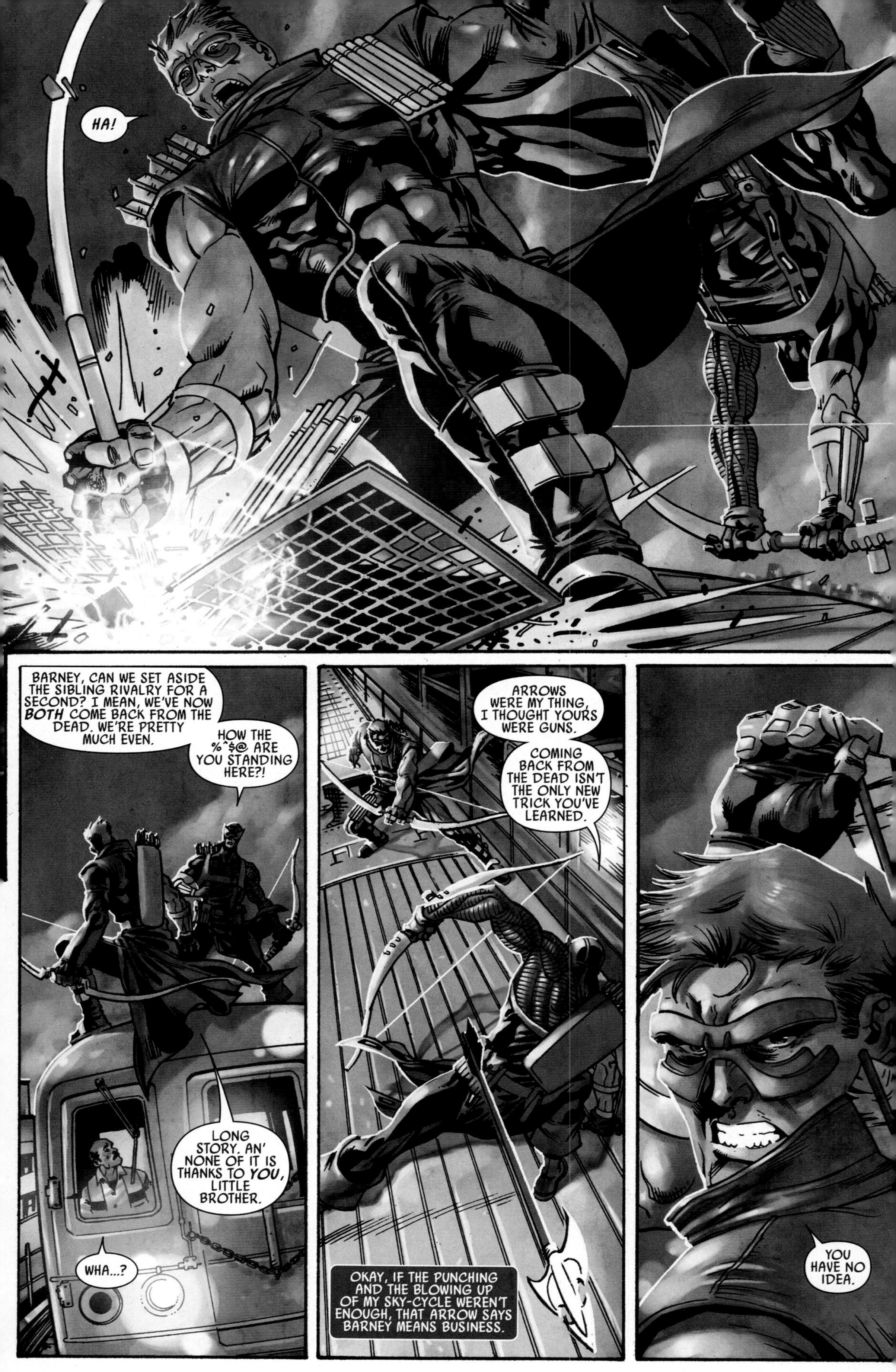
HA!
BARNEY, CAN WE SET ASIDE THE SIBLING RIVALRY FOR A SECOND? I MEAN, WE'VE NOW BOTH COME BACK FROM THE DEAD. WE'RE PRETTY MUCH EVEN.
HOW THE %^$@ ARE YOU STANDING HERE?!
LONG STORY. AN' NONE OF IT IS THANKS TO YOU, LITTLE BROTHER.
WHA...?
ARROWS WERE MY THING, I THOUGHT YOURS WERE GUNS.
COMING BACK FROM THE DEAD ISN'T THE ONLY NEW TRICK YOU'VE LEARNED.
OKAY, IF THE PUNCHING AND THE BLOWING UP OF MY SKY-CYCLE WEREN'T ENOUGH, THAT ARROW SAYS BARNEY MEANS BUSINESS.
YOU HAVE NO IDEA.

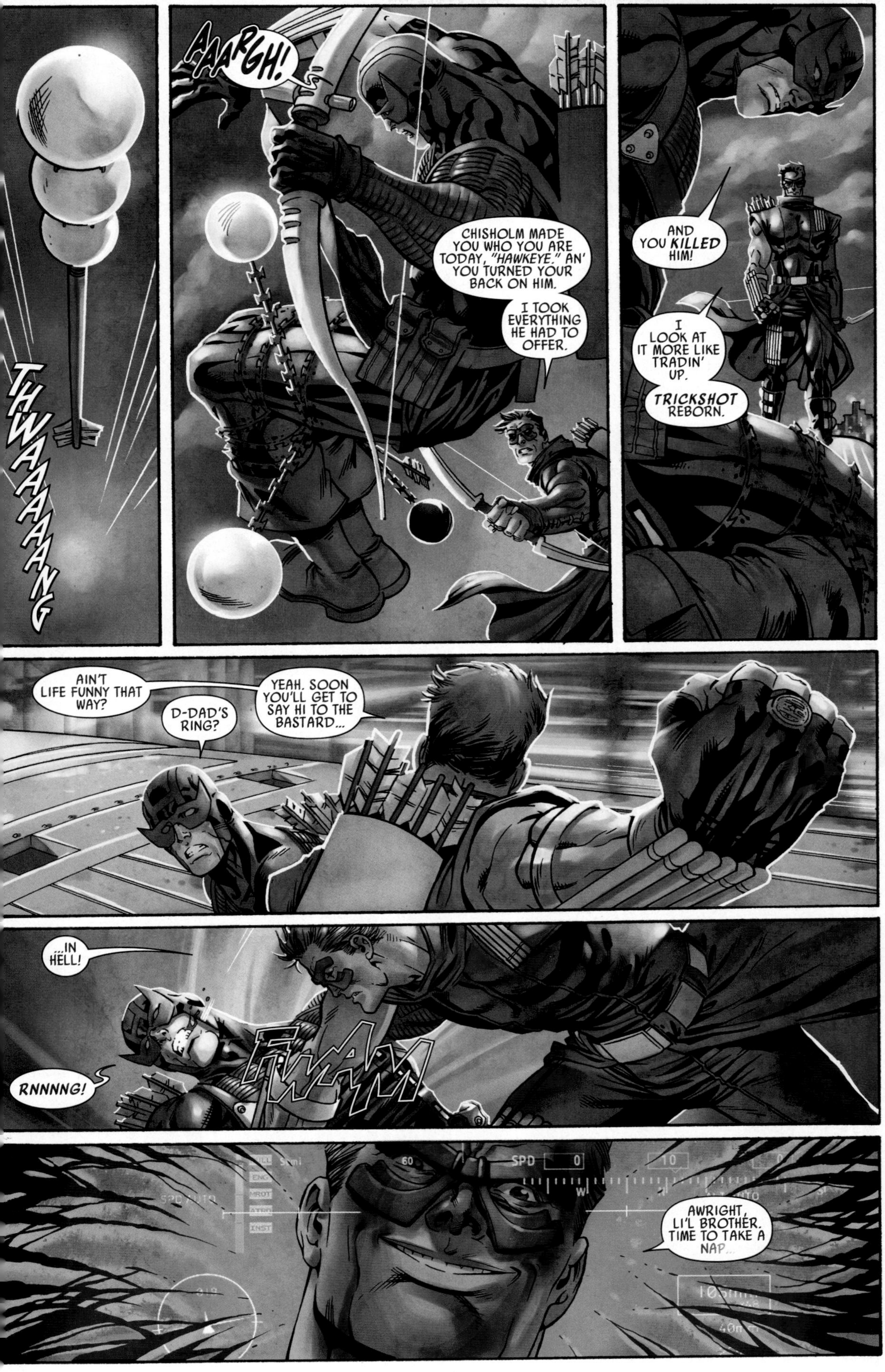
THWAAAAAANG
AAAARGH!
CHISHOLM MADE YOU WHO YOU ARE TODAY, "HAWKEYE." AN' YOU TURNED YOUR BACK ON HIM.
I TOOK EVERYTHING HE HAD TO OFFER.
AND YOU KILLED HIM!
I LOOK AT IT MORE LIKE TRADIN' UP.
TRICKSHOT REBORN.
AIN'T LIFE FUNNY THAT WAY?
D-DAD'S RING?
YEAH. SOON YOU'LL GET TO SAY HI TO THE BASTARD...
...IN HELL!
FWAM
RNNNNG!
AWRIGHT, LI'L BROTHER. TIME TO TAKE A NAP...

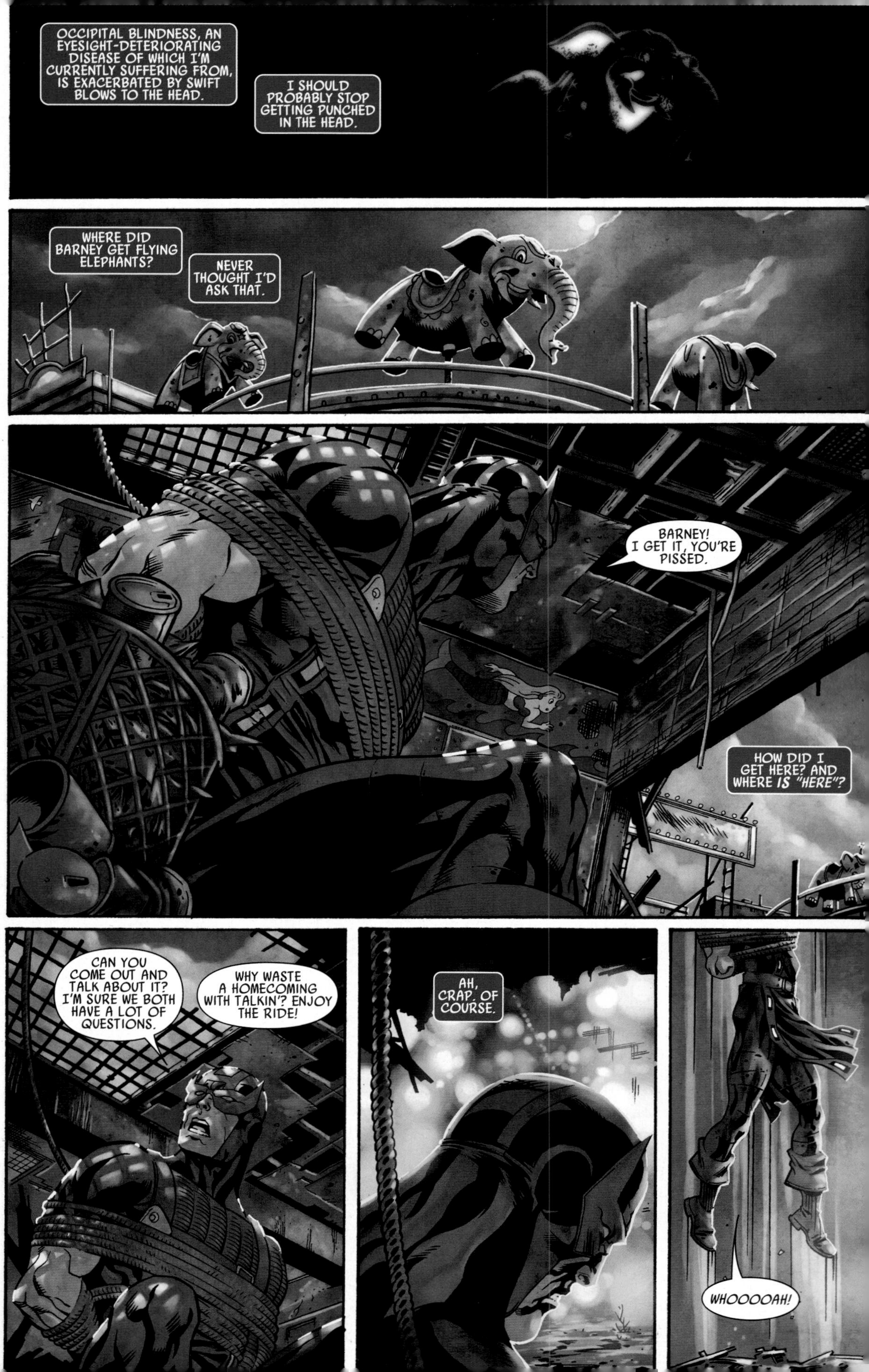

OCCIPITAL BLINDNESS, AN EYESIGHT-DETERIORATING DISEASE OF WHICH I'M CURRENTLY SUFFERING FROM, IS EXACERBATED BY SWIFT BLOWS TO THE HEAD.
I SHOULD PROBABLY STOP GETTING PUNCHED IN THE HEAD.
WHERE DID BARNEY GET FLYING ELEPHANTS?
NEVER THOUGHT I'D ASK THAT.
BARNEY! I GET IT, YOU'RE PISSED.
HOW DID I GET HERE? AND WHERE *IS "HERE"*?
CAN YOU COME OUT AND TALK ABOUT IT? I'M SURE WE BOTH HAVE A LOT OF QUESTIONS.
WHY WASTE A HOMECOMING WITH TALKIN'? ENJOY THE RIDE!
AH, CRAP. OF COURSE.
WHOOOOAH!

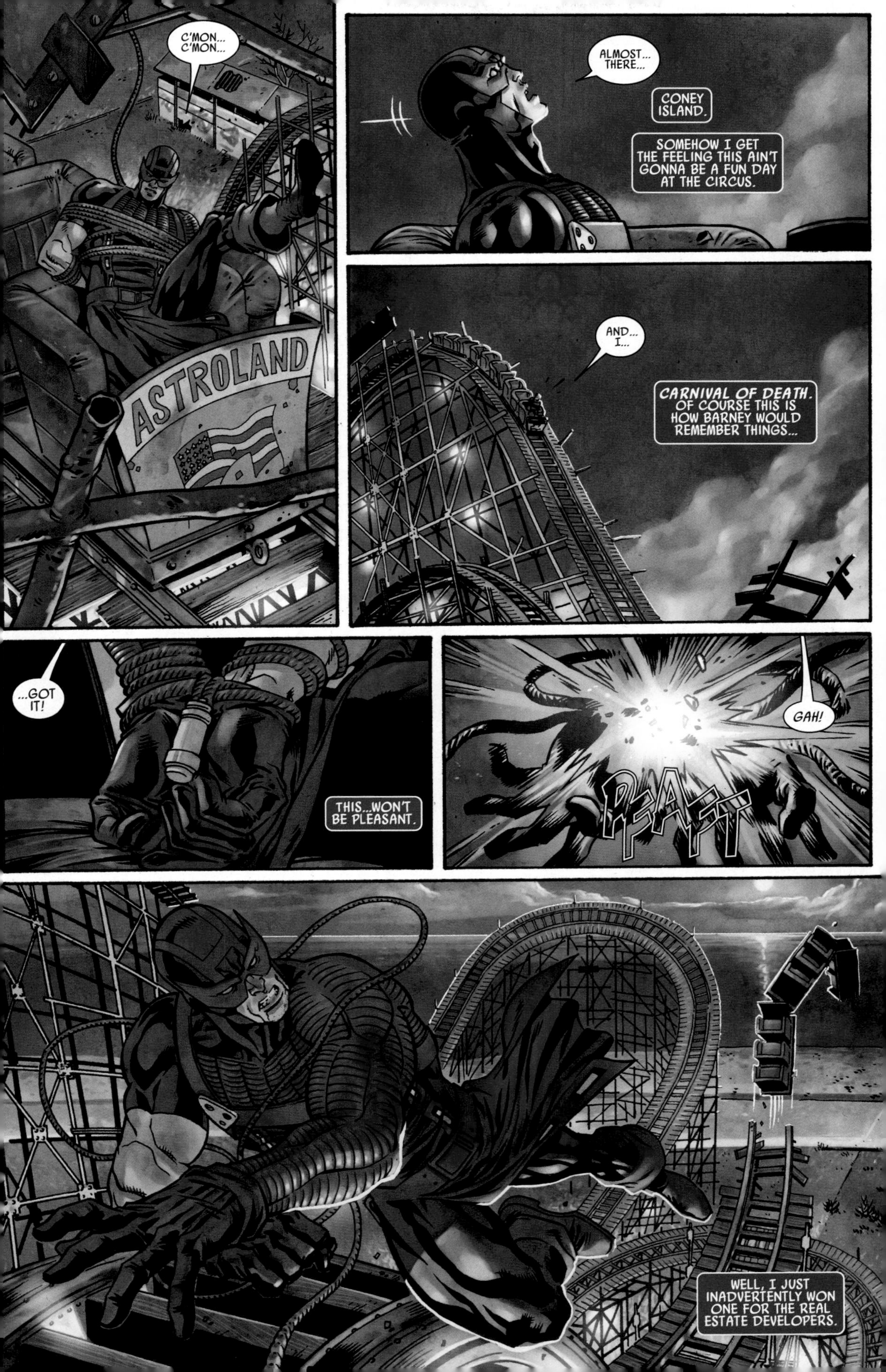
C'MON... C'MON...
ALMOST... THERE...
CONEY ISLAND.
SOMEHOW I GET THE FEELING THIS AIN'T GONNA BE A FUN DAY AT THE CIRCUS.
ASTROLAND
AND... I...
CARNIVAL OF DEATH. OF COURSE THIS IS HOW BARNEY WOULD REMEMBER THINGS...
...GOT IT!
THIS...WON'T BE PLEASANT.
GAH!
PFAFT
WELL, I JUST INADVERTENTLY WON ONE FOR THE REAL ESTATE DEVELOPERS.

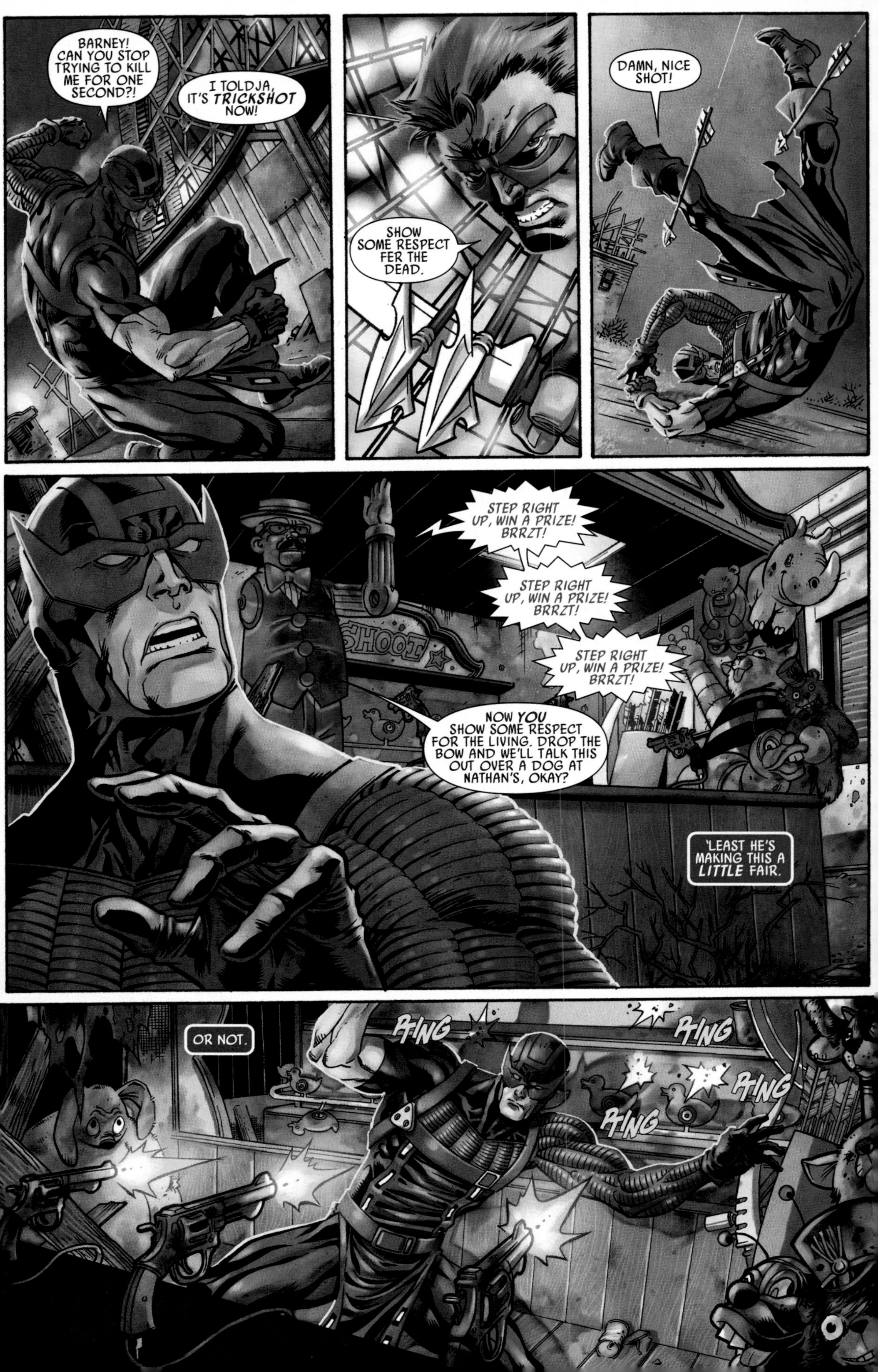
BARNEY! CAN YOU STOP TRYING TO KILL ME FOR ONE SECOND?!
I TOLDJA, IT'S TRICKSHOT NOW!
SHOW SOME RESPECT FER THE DEAD.
DAMN, NICE SHOT!
STEP RIGHT UP, WIN A PRIZE! BRRZT!
STEP RIGHT UP, WIN A PRIZE! BRRZT!
STEP RIGHT UP, WIN A PRIZE! BRRZT!
SHOOT
NOW YOU SHOW SOME RESPECT FOR THE LIVING. DROP THE BOW AND WE'LL TALK THIS OUT OVER A DOG AT NATHAN'S, OKAY?
'LEAST HE'S MAKING THIS A LITTLE FAIR.
OR NOT.
PTING
PTING
PTING
PTING

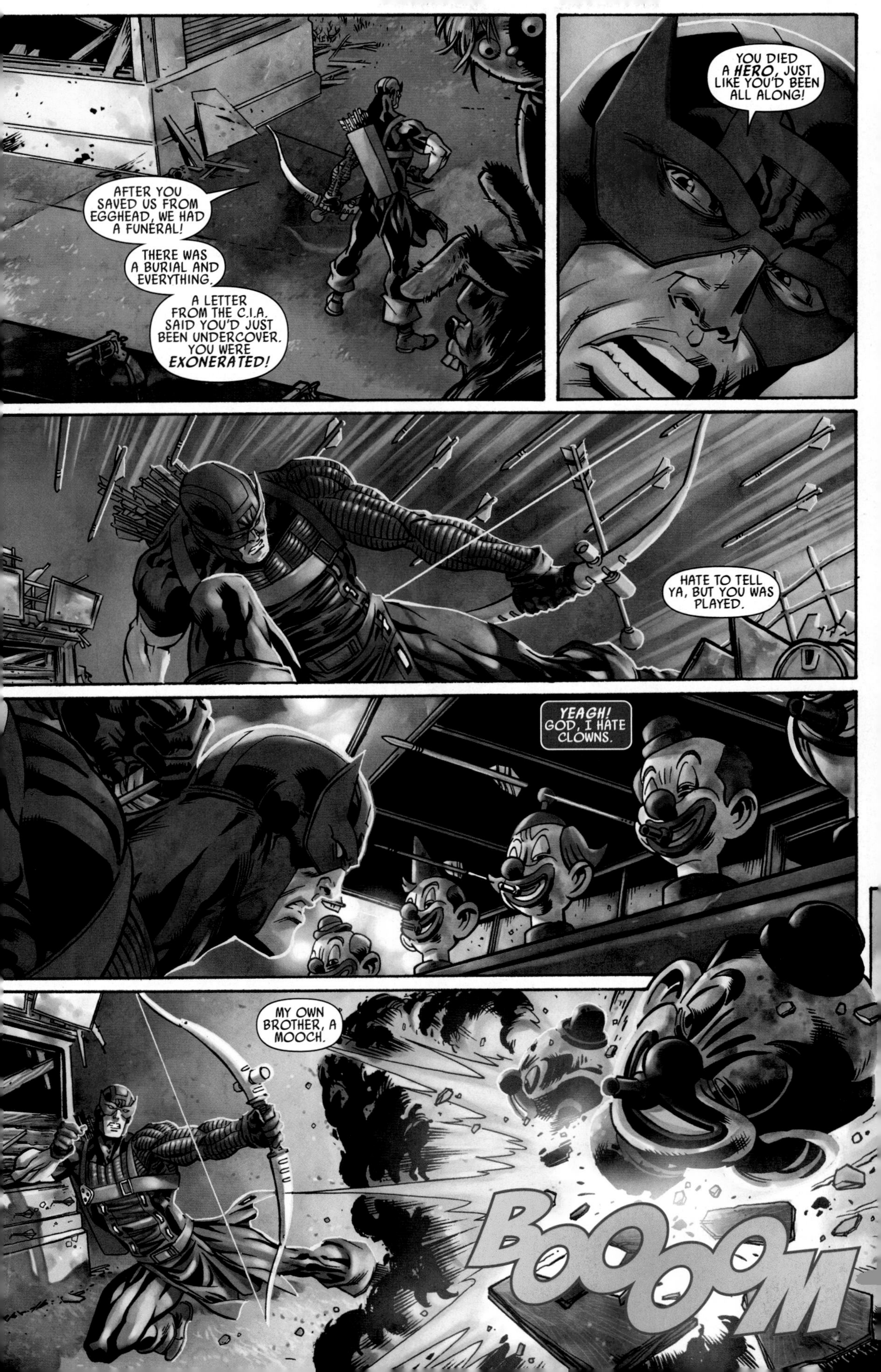
AFTER YOU SAVED US FROM EGGHEAD, WE HAD A FUNERAL!
THERE WAS A BURIAL AND EVERYTHING.
A LETTER FROM THE C.I.A. SAID YOU'D JUST BEEN UNDERCOVER. YOU WERE EXONERATED!
YOU DIED A HERO, JUST LIKE YOU'D BEEN ALL ALONG!
HATE TO TELL YA, BUT YOU WAS PLAYED.
YEAGH! GOD, I HATE CLOWNS.
MY OWN BROTHER, A MOOCH.
BOOOOM

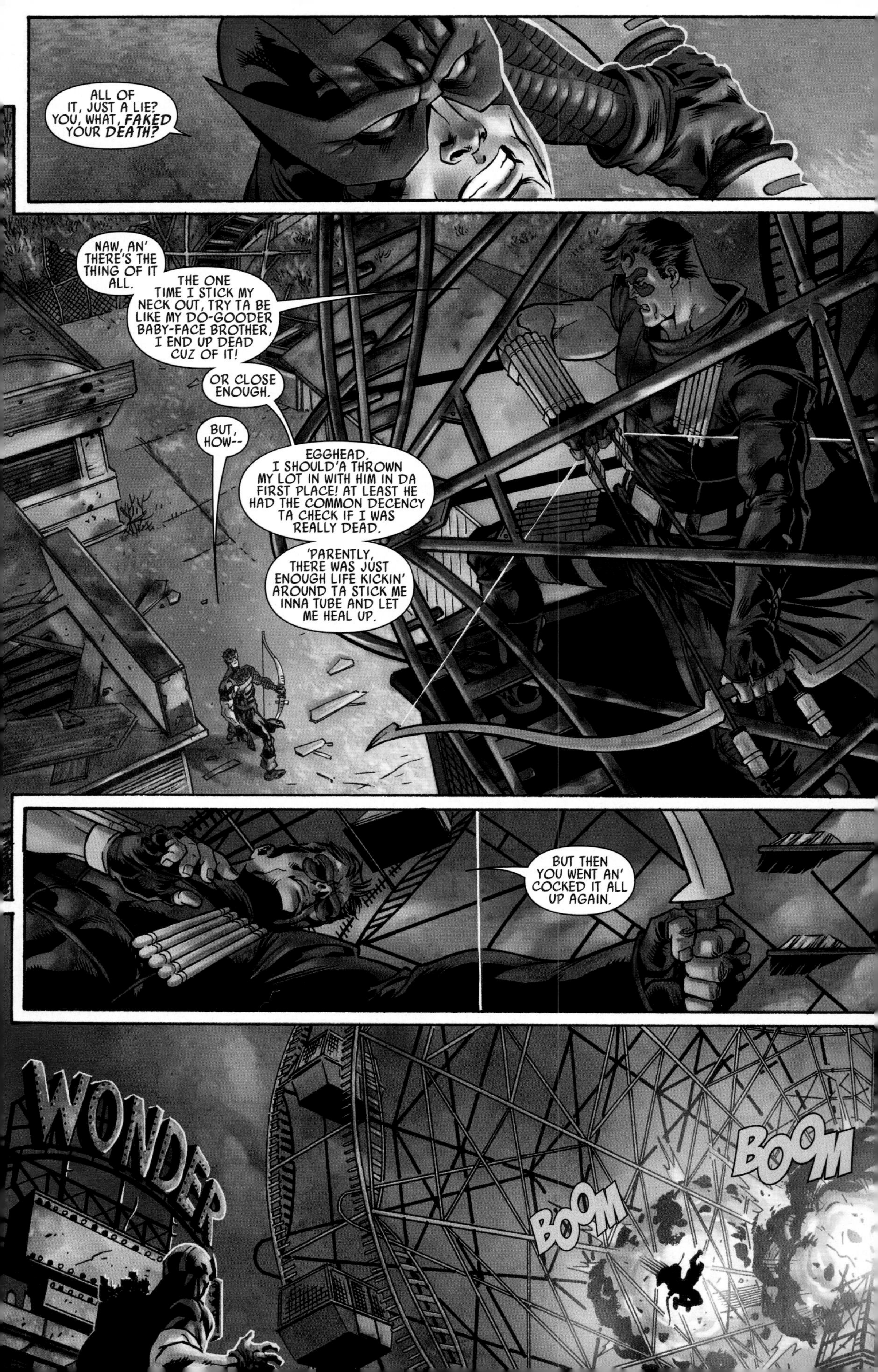
ALL OF IT, JUST A LIE? YOU, WHAT, FAKED YOUR DEATH?
NAW, AN' THERE'S THE THING OF IT ALL.
THE ONE TIME I STICK MY NECK OUT, TRY TA BE LIKE MY DO-GOODER BABY-FACE BROTHER, I END UP DEAD CUZ OF IT!
OR CLOSE ENOUGH.
BUT, HOW--
EGGHEAD. I SHOULD'A THROWN MY LOT IN WITH HIM IN DA FIRST PLACE! AT LEAST HE HAD THE COMMON DECENCY TA CHECK IF I WAS REALLY DEAD.
'PARENTLY, THERE WAS JUST ENOUGH LIFE KICKIN' AROUND TA STICK ME INNA TUBE AND LET ME HEAL UP.
BUT THEN YOU WENT AN' COCKED IT ALL UP AGAIN.
WONDER
BOOM
BOOM

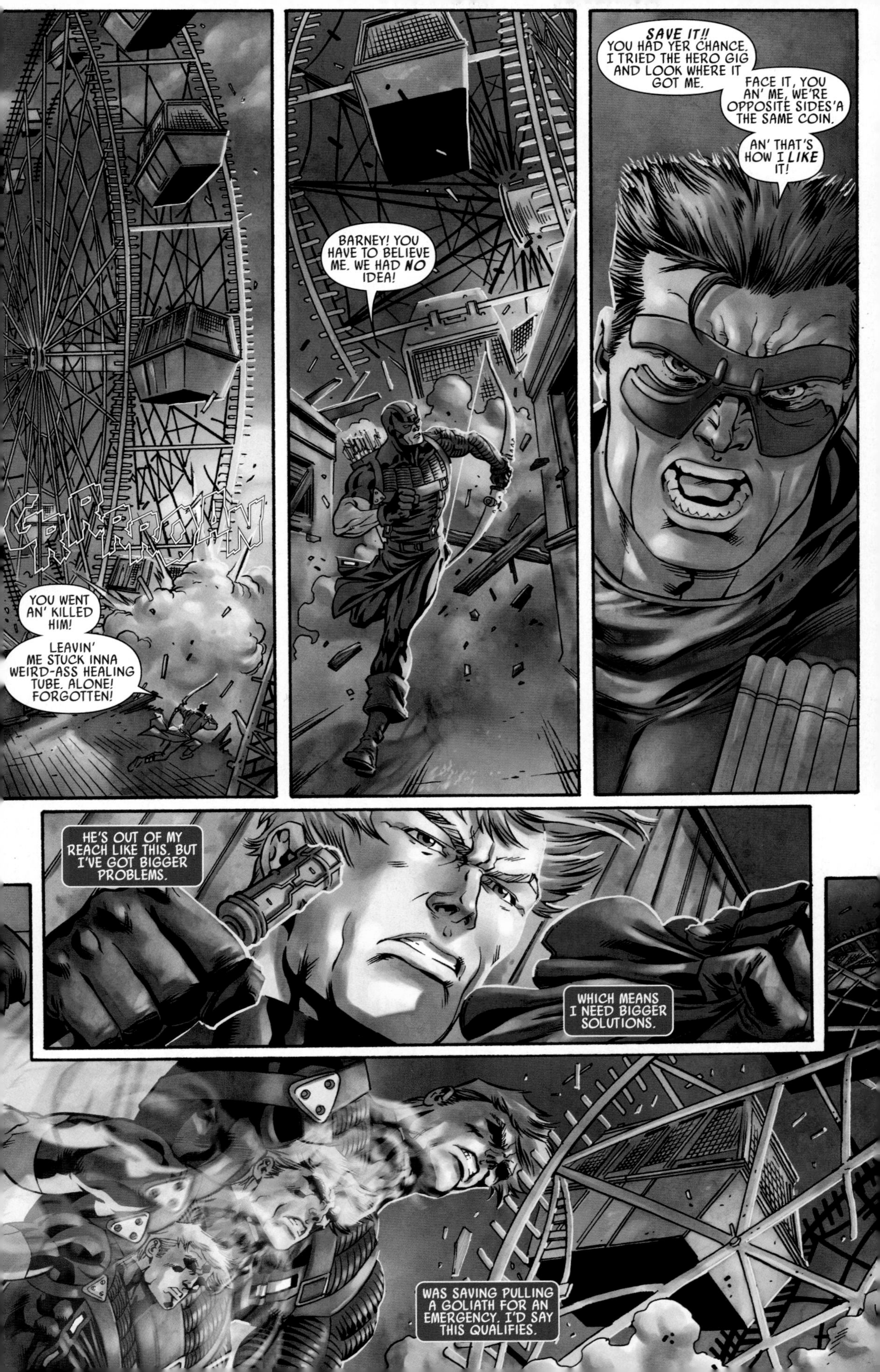
GRRROOM
YOU WENT AN' KILLED HIM!
LEAVIN' ME STUCK INNA WEIRD-ASS HEALING TUBE. ALONE! FORGOTTEN!
BARNEY! YOU HAVE TO BELIEVE ME. WE HAD NO IDEA!
SAVE IT!! YOU HAD YER CHANCE. I TRIED THE HERO GIG AND LOOK WHERE IT GOT ME.
FACE IT, YOU AN' ME, WE'RE OPPOSITE SIDES'A THE SAME COIN.
AN' THAT'S HOW I LIKE IT!
HE'S OUT OF MY REACH LIKE THIS. BUT I'VE GOT BIGGER PROBLEMS.
WHICH MEANS I NEED BIGGER SOLUTIONS.
WAS SAVING PULLING A GOLIATH FOR AN EMERGENCY. I'D SAY THIS QUALIFIES.

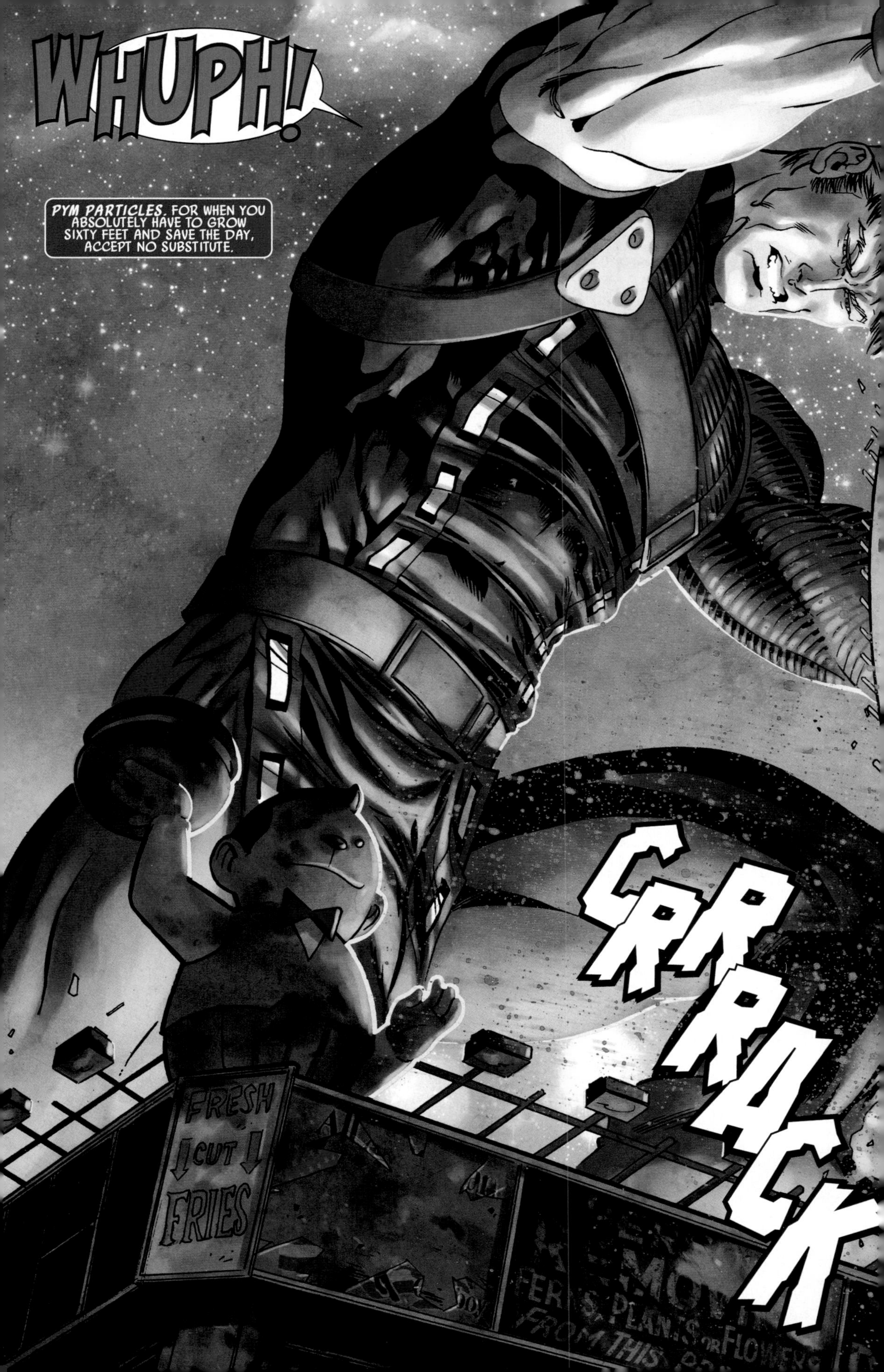
WHUPH!
PYM PARTICLES. FOR WHEN YOU ABSOLUTELY HAVE TO GROW SIXTY FEET AND SAVE THE DAY, ACCEPT NO SUBSTITUTE.
CRRRACK
FRESH CUT FRIES

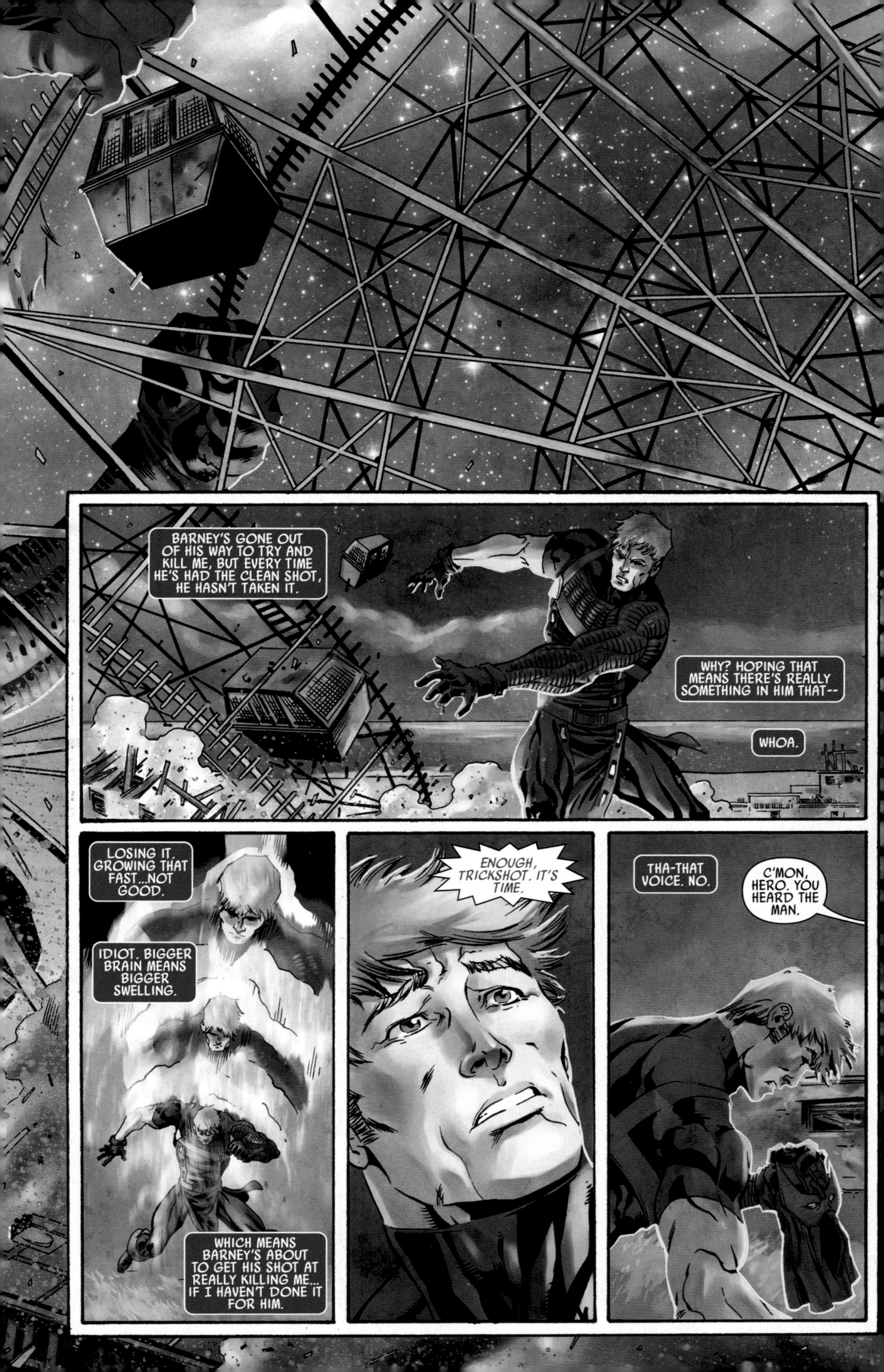
BARNEY'S GONE OUT OF HIS WAY TO TRY AND KILL ME, BUT EVERY TIME HE'S HAD THE CLEAN SHOT, HE HASN'T TAKEN IT.
WHY? HOPING THAT MEANS THERE'S REALLY SOMETHING IN HIM THAT--
WHOA.
LOSING IT. GROWING THAT FAST...NOT GOOD.
IDIOT. BIGGER BRAIN MEANS BIGGER SWELLING.
WHICH MEANS BARNEY'S ABOUT TO GET HIS SHOT AT REALLY KILLING ME... IF I HAVEN'T DONE IT FOR HIM.
ENOUGH, TRICKSHOT. IT'S TIME.
THA-THAT VOICE. NO.
C'MON, HERO. YOU HEARD THE MAN.

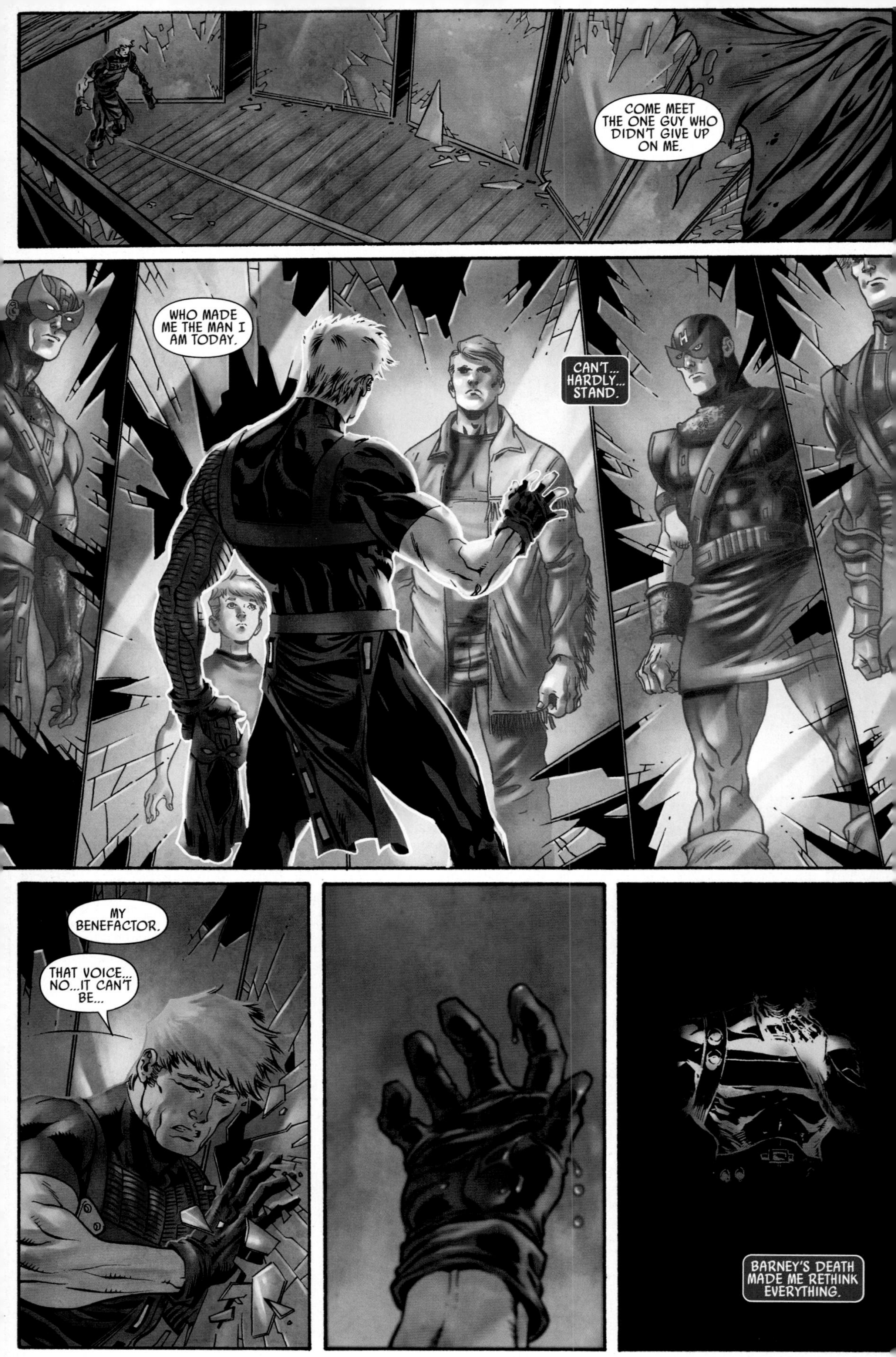
COME MEET THE ONE GUY WHO DIDN'T GIVE UP ON ME.
WHO MADE ME THE MAN I AM TODAY.
CAN'T... HARDLY... STAND.
MY BENEFACTOR.
THAT VOICE... NO...IT CAN'T BE...
BARNEY'S DEATH MADE ME RETHINK EVERYTHING.

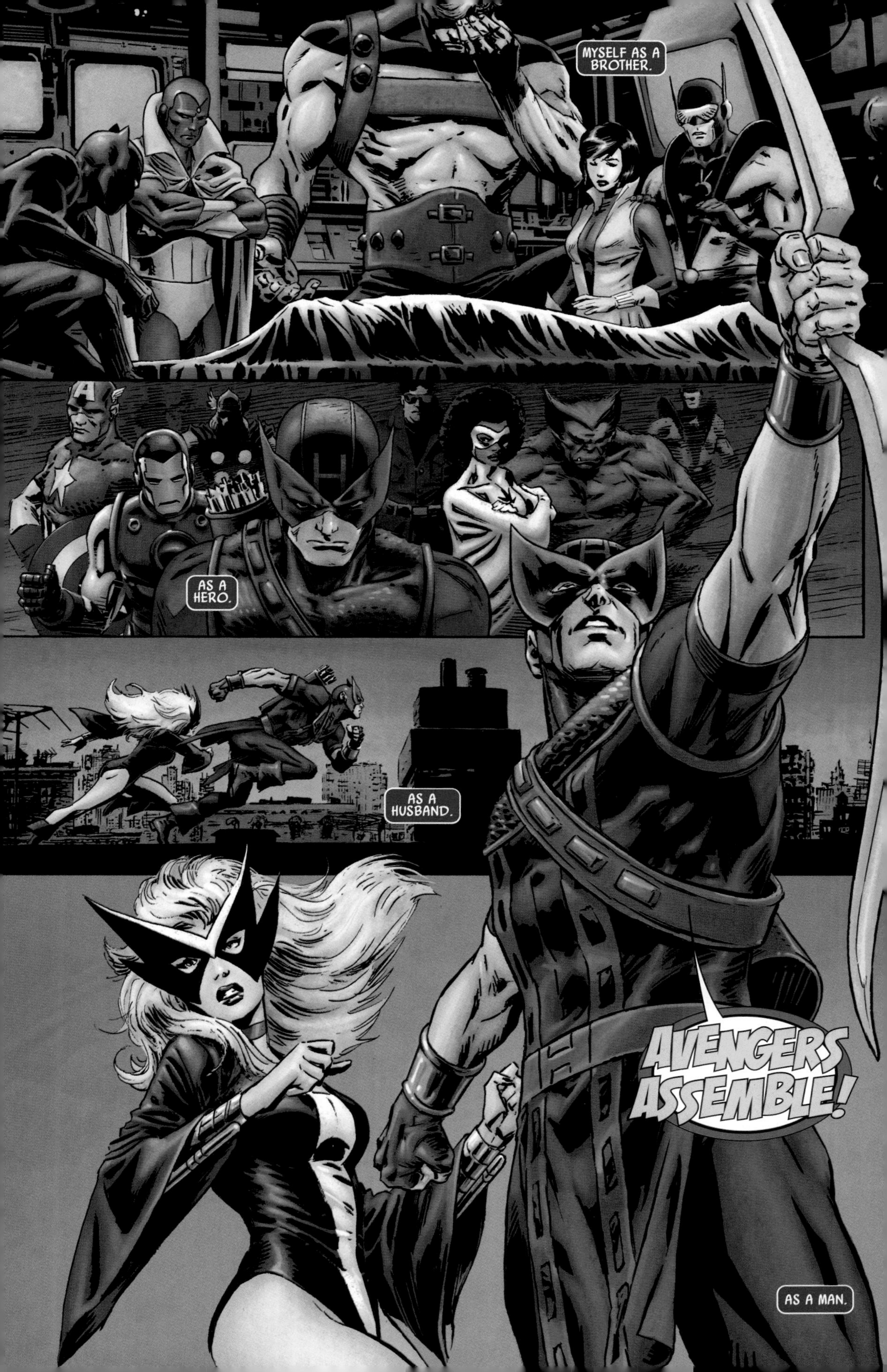
MYSELF AS A BROTHER.
AS A HERO.
AS A HUSBAND.
AVENGERS ASSEMBLE!
AS A MAN.

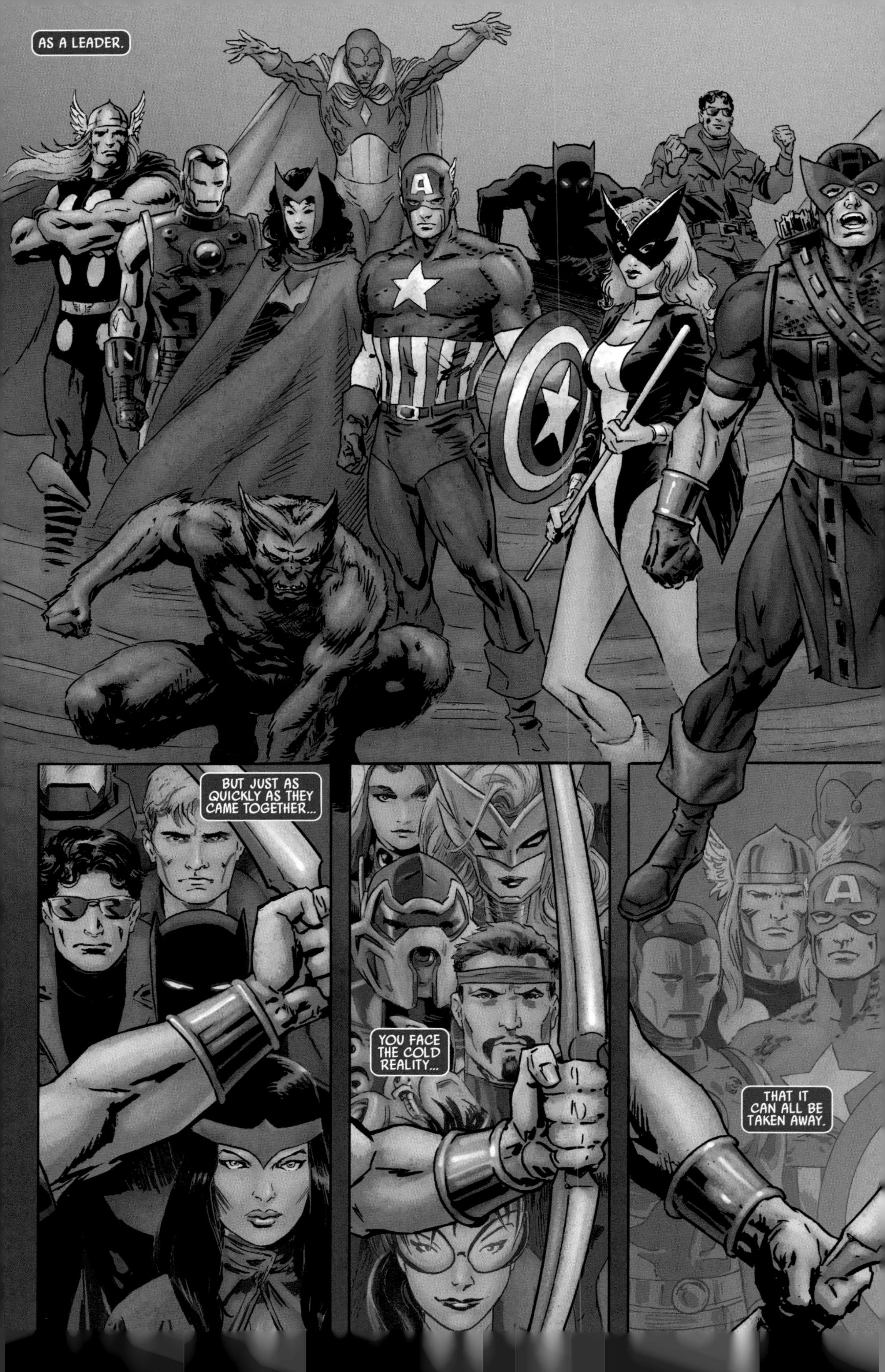
AS A LEADER.
BUT JUST AS QUICKLY AS THEY CAME TOGETHER...
YOU FACE THE COLD REALITY...
THAT IT CAN ALL BE TAKEN AWAY.

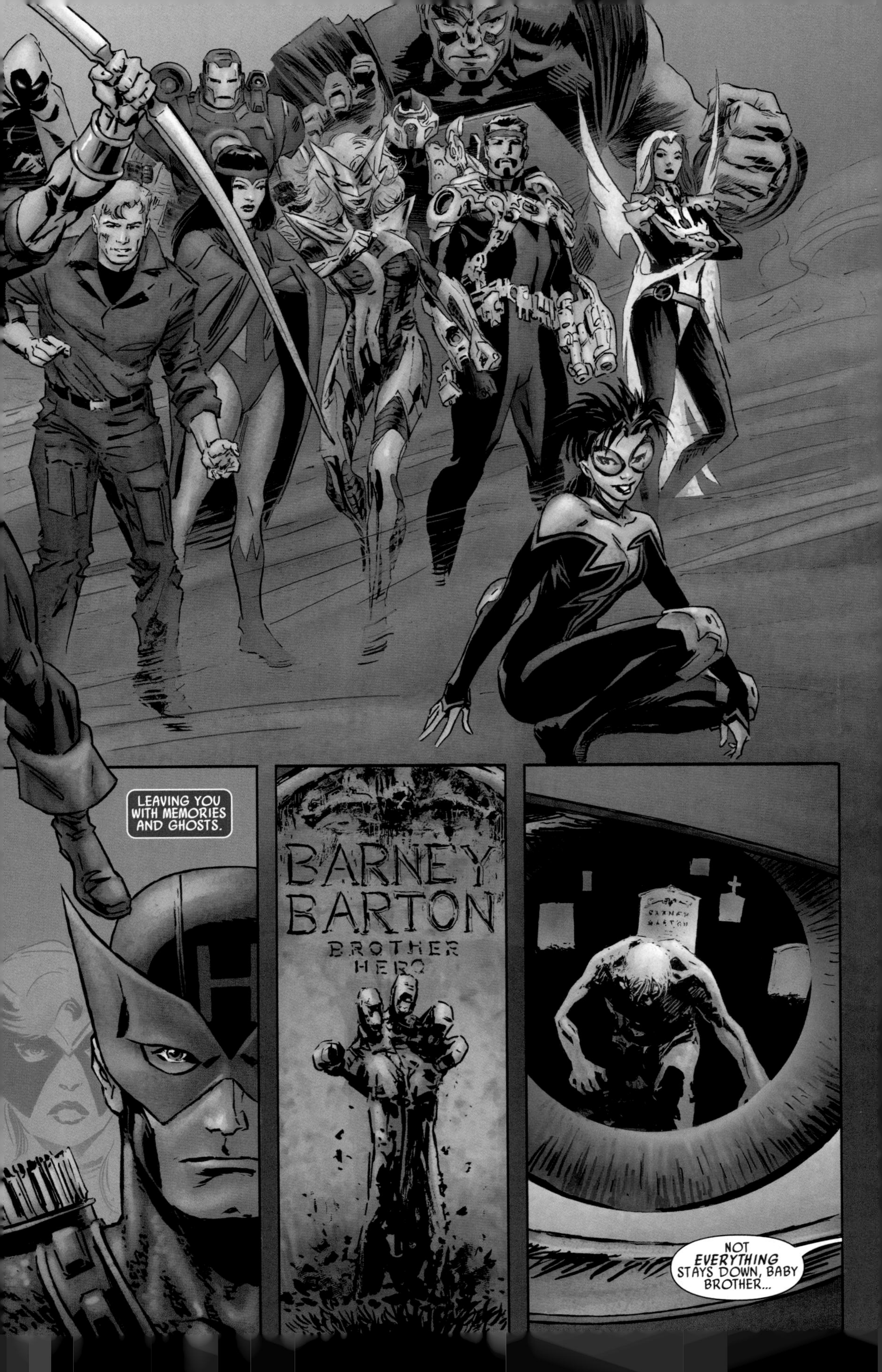
LEAVING YOU WITH MEMORIES AND GHOSTS.
BARNEY BARTON
BROTHER
HERO
NOT *EVERYTHING* STAYS DOWN, BABY BROTHER...

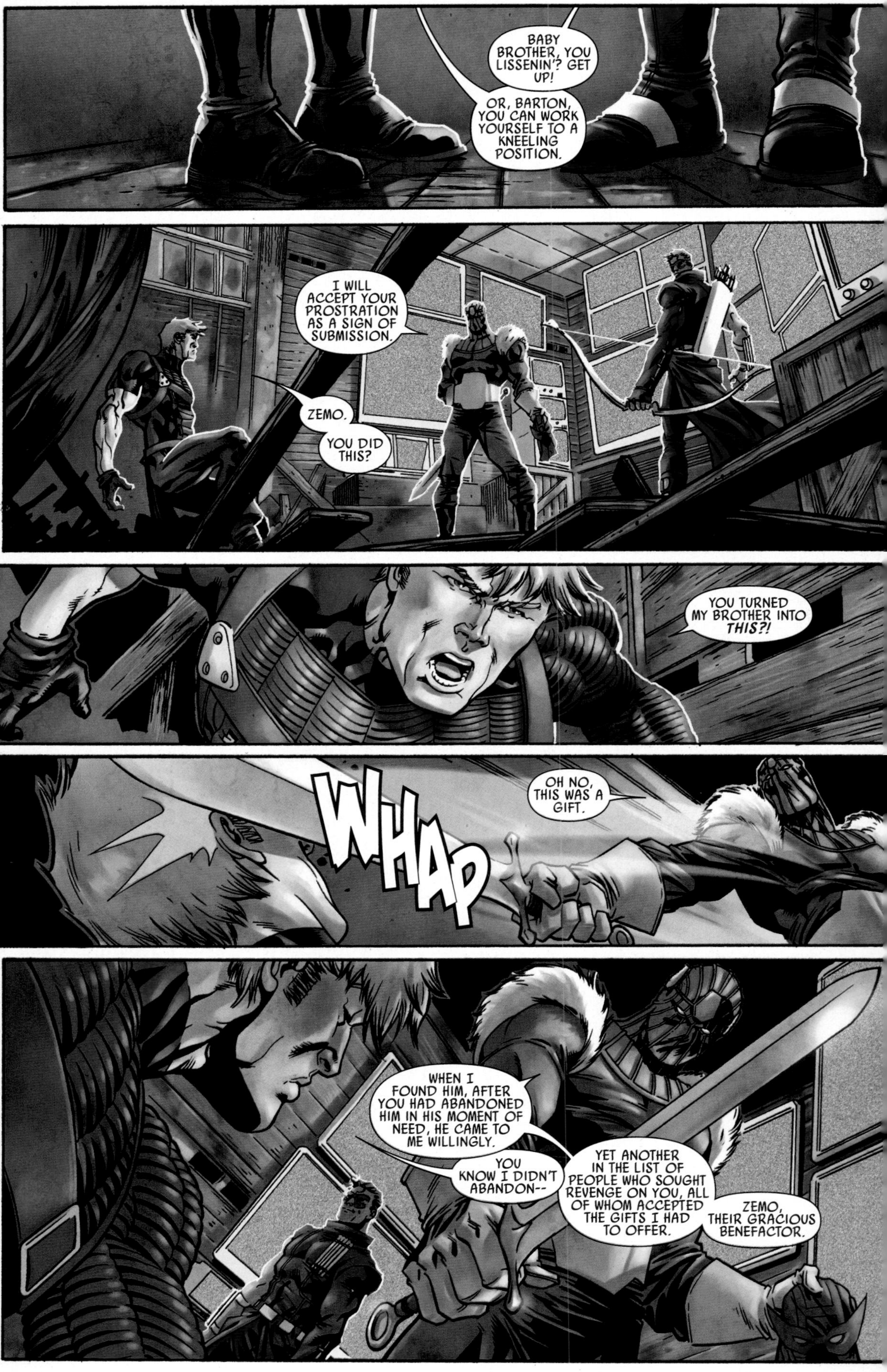

BABY BROTHER, YOU LISSENIN'? GET UP!
OR, BARTON, YOU CAN WORK YOURSELF TO A KNEELING POSITION.
I WILL ACCEPT YOUR PROSTRATION AS A SIGN OF SUBMISSION.
ZEMO.
YOU DID THIS?
YOU TURNED MY BROTHER INTO *THIS?!*
WHAP
OH NO, THIS WAS A GIFT.
WHEN I FOUND HIM, AFTER YOU HAD ABANDONED HIM IN HIS MOMENT OF NEED, HE CAME TO ME WILLINGLY.
YOU KNOW I DIDN'T ABANDON--
YET ANOTHER IN THE LIST OF PEOPLE WHO SOUGHT REVENGE ON YOU, ALL OF WHOM ACCEPTED THE GIFTS I HAD TO OFFER.
ZEMO, THEIR GRACIOUS BENEFACTOR.

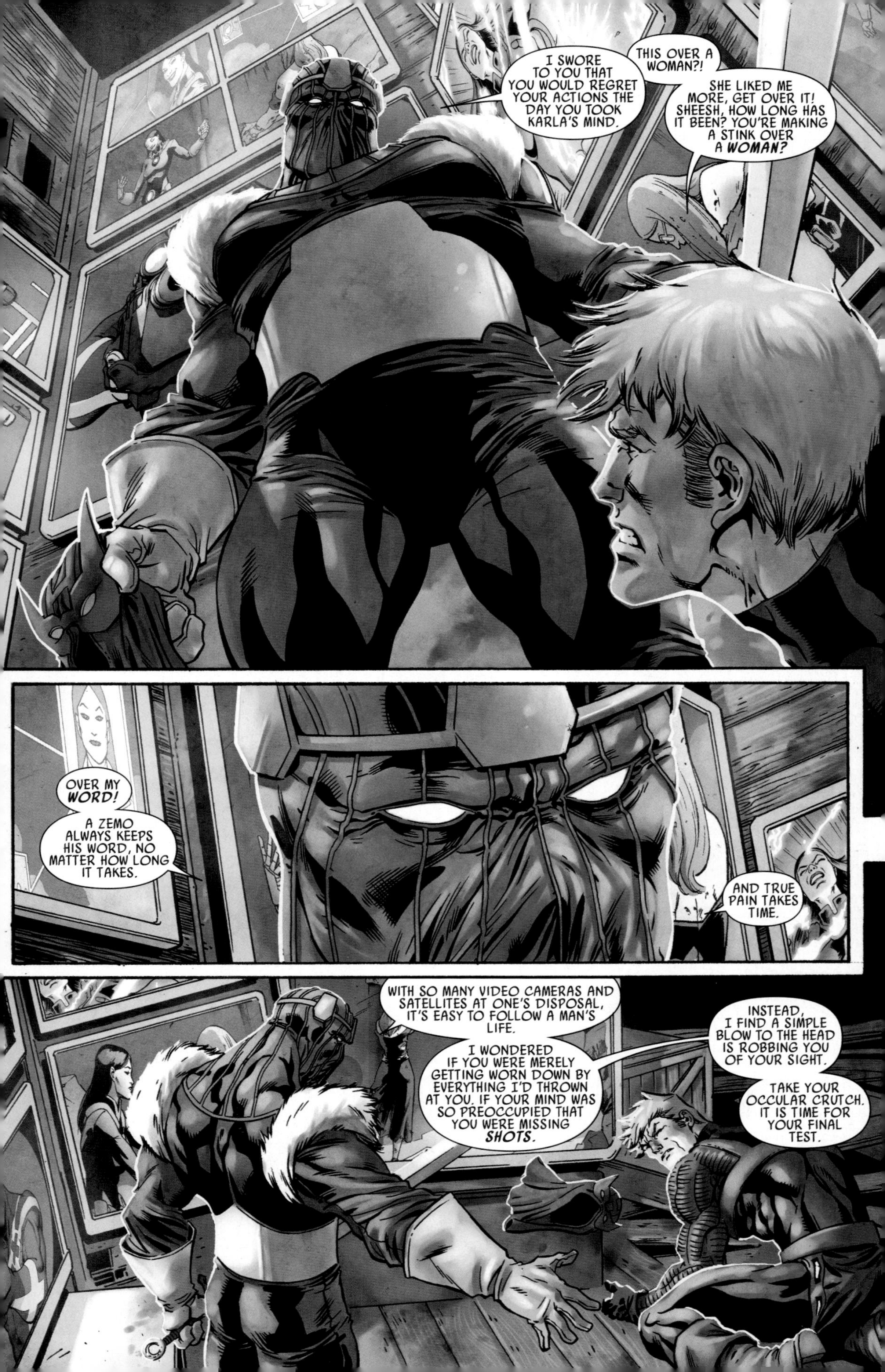
I SWORE TO YOU THAT YOU WOULD REGRET YOUR ACTIONS THE DAY YOU TOOK KARLA'S MIND.
THIS OVER A WOMAN?!
SHE LIKED ME MORE, GET OVER IT! SHEESH, HOW LONG HAS IT BEEN? YOU'RE MAKING A STINK OVER A WOMAN?
OVER MY WORD!
A ZEMO ALWAYS KEEPS HIS WORD, NO MATTER HOW LONG IT TAKES.
AND TRUE PAIN TAKES TIME.
WITH SO MANY VIDEO CAMERAS AND SATELLITES AT ONE'S DISPOSAL, IT'S EASY TO FOLLOW A MAN'S LIFE.
I WONDERED IF YOU WERE MERELY GETTING WORN DOWN BY EVERYTHING I'D THROWN AT YOU. IF YOUR MIND WAS SO PREOCCUPIED THAT YOU WERE MISSING SHOTS.
INSTEAD, I FIND A SIMPLE BLOW TO THE HEAD IS ROBBING YOU OF YOUR SIGHT.
TAKE YOUR OCCULAR CRUTCH. IT IS TIME FOR YOUR FINAL TEST.

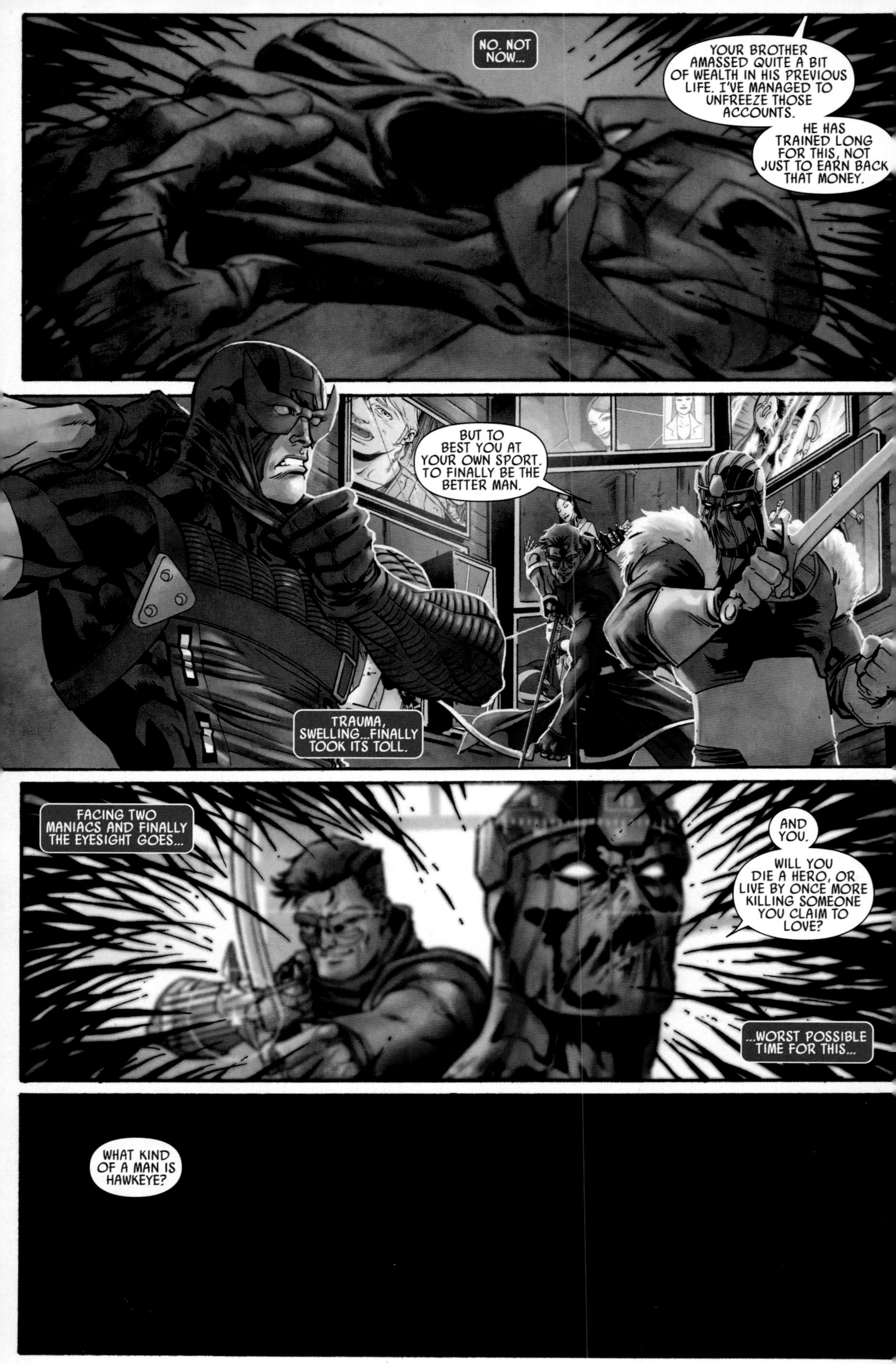
NO. NOT NOW...
YOUR BROTHER AMASSED QUITE A BIT OF WEALTH IN HIS PREVIOUS LIFE. I'VE MANAGED TO UNFREEZE THOSE ACCOUNTS.
HE HAS TRAINED LONG FOR THIS, NOT JUST TO EARN BACK THAT MONEY.
BUT TO BEST YOU AT YOUR OWN SPORT. TO FINALLY BE THE BETTER MAN.
TRAUMA, SWELLING...FINALLY TOOK ITS TOLL.
FACING TWO MANIACS AND FINALLY THE EYESIGHT GOES...
AND YOU.
WILL YOU DIE A HERO, OR LIVE BY ONCE MORE KILLING SOMEONE YOU CLAIM TO LOVE?
...WORST POSSIBLE TIME FOR THIS...
WHAT KIND OF A MAN IS HAWKEYE?

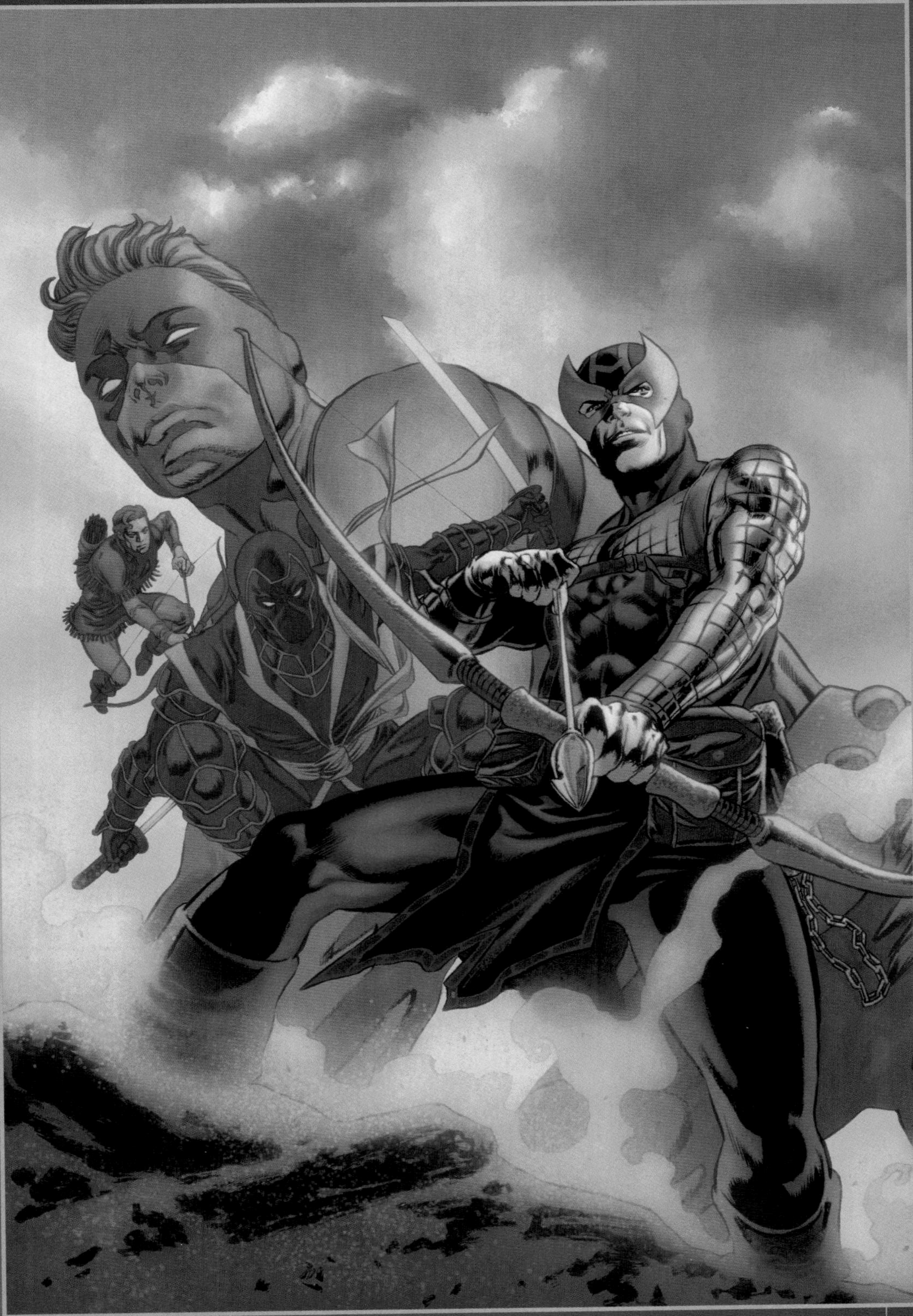

#4

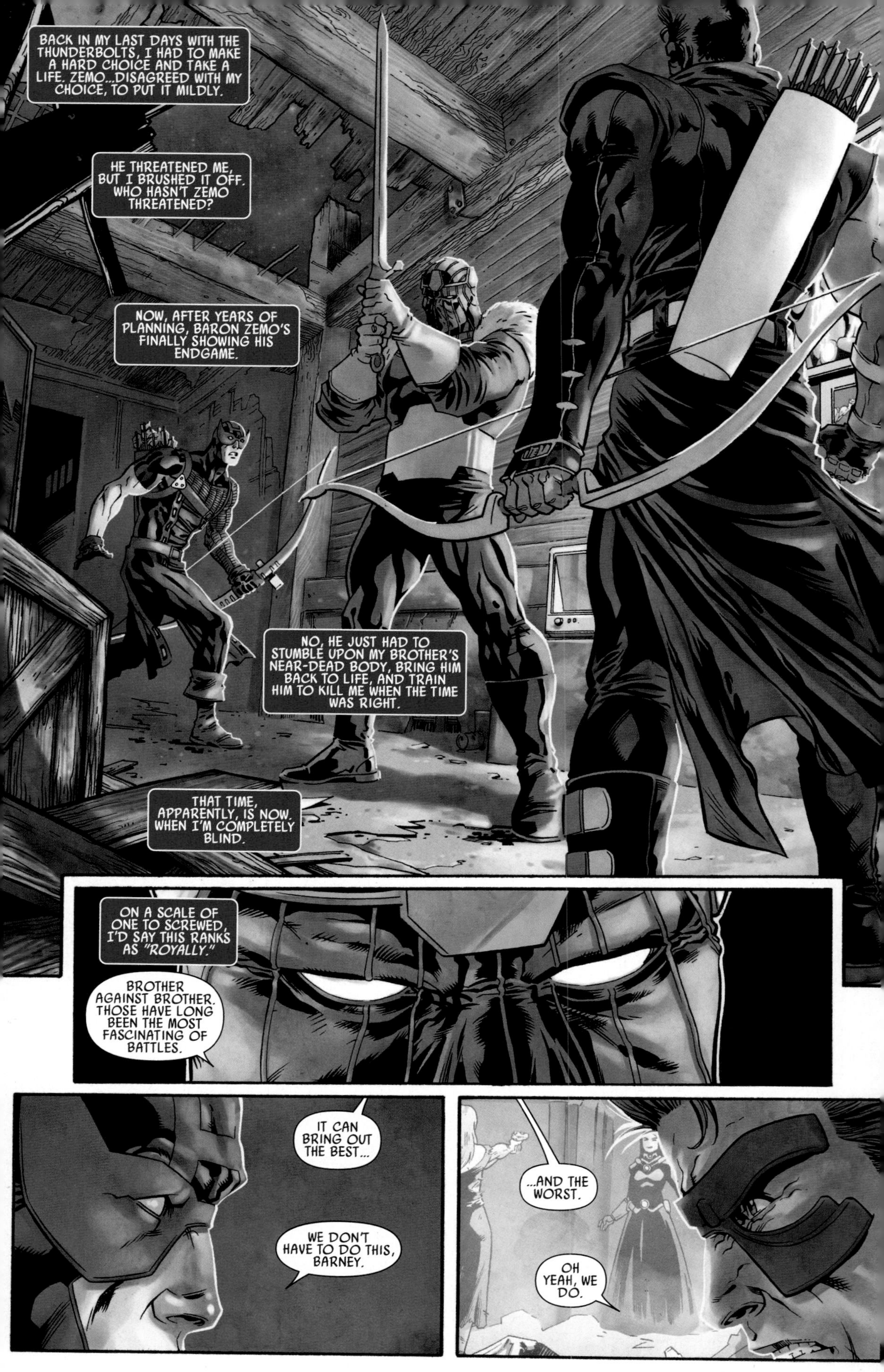
BACK IN MY LAST DAYS WITH THE THUNDERBOLTS, I HAD TO MAKE A HARD CHOICE AND TAKE A LIFE. ZEMO...DISAGREED WITH MY CHOICE, TO PUT IT MILDLY.
HE THREATENED ME, BUT I BRUSHED IT OFF. WHO HASN'T ZEMO THREATENED?
NOW, AFTER YEARS OF PLANNING, BARON ZEMO'S FINALLY SHOWING HIS ENDGAME.
NO, HE JUST HAD TO STUMBLE UPON MY BROTHER'S NEAR-DEAD BODY, BRING HIM BACK TO LIFE, AND TRAIN HIM TO KILL ME WHEN THE TIME WAS RIGHT.
THAT TIME, APPARENTLY, IS NOW. WHEN I'M COMPLETELY BLIND.
ON A SCALE OF ONE TO SCREWED, I'D SAY THIS RANKS AS "ROYALLY."
BROTHER AGAINST BROTHER. THOSE HAVE LONG BEEN THE MOST FASCINATING OF BATTLES.
IT CAN BRING OUT THE BEST...
WE DON'T HAVE TO DO THIS, BARNEY.
...AND THE WORST.
OH YEAH, WE DO.

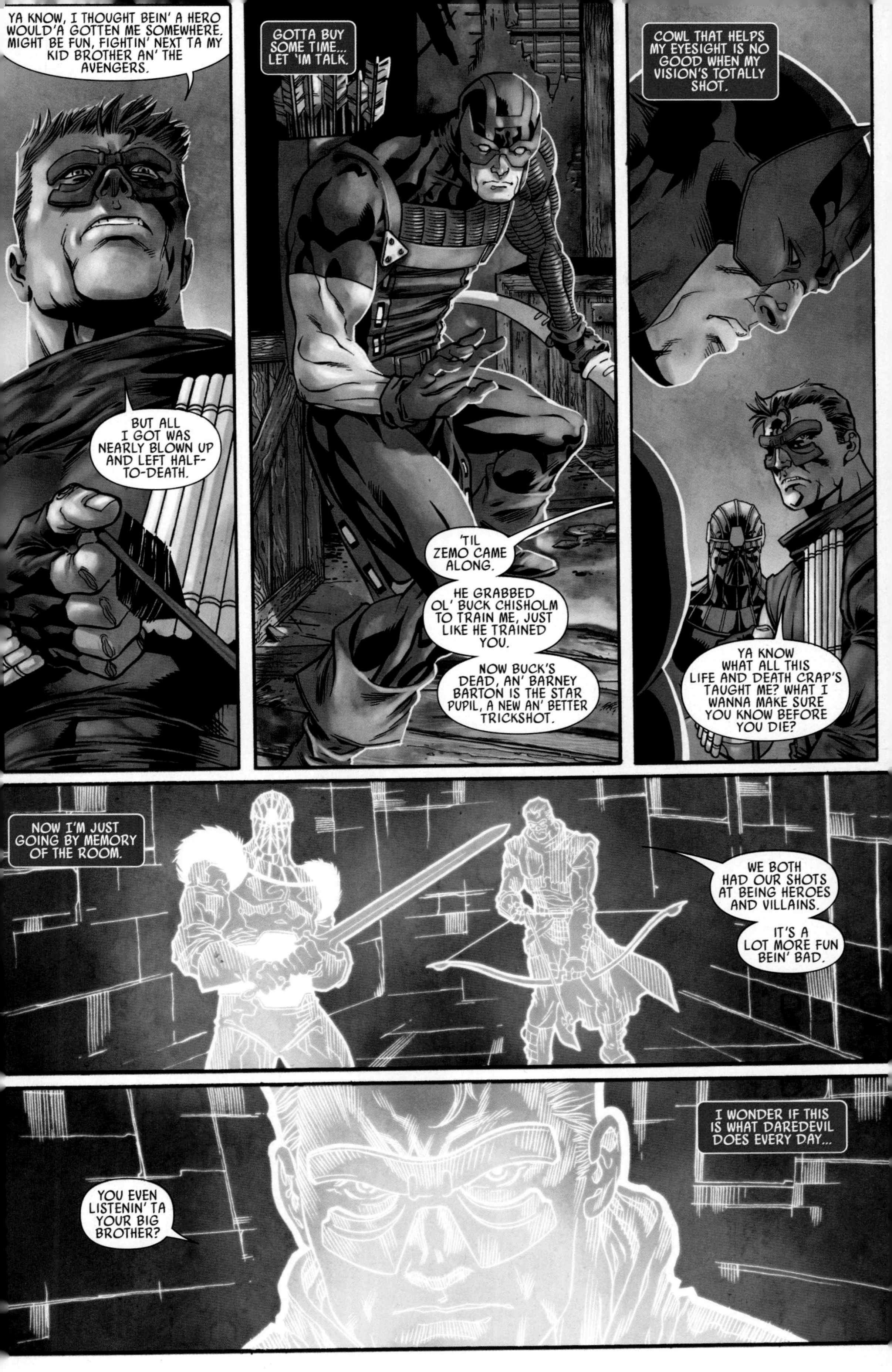
YA KNOW, I THOUGHT BEIN' A HERO WOULD'A GOTTEN ME SOMEWHERE. MIGHT BE FUN, FIGHTIN' NEXT TA MY KID BROTHER AN' THE AVENGERS.
BUT ALL I GOT WAS NEARLY BLOWN UP AND LEFT HALF-TO-DEATH.
GOTTA BUY SOME TIME... LET 'IM TALK.
'TIL ZEMO CAME ALONG.
HE GRABBED OL' BUCK CHISHOLM TO TRAIN ME, JUST LIKE HE TRAINED YOU.
NOW BUCK'S DEAD, AN' BARNEY BARTON IS THE STAR PUPIL, A NEW AN' BETTER TRICKSHOT.
COWL THAT HELPS MY EYESIGHT IS NO GOOD WHEN MY VISION'S TOTALLY SHOT.
YA KNOW WHAT ALL THIS LIFE AND DEATH CRAP'S TAUGHT ME? WHAT I WANNA MAKE SURE YOU KNOW BEFORE YOU DIE?
NOW I'M JUST GOING BY MEMORY OF THE ROOM.
WE BOTH HAD OUR SHOTS AT BEING HEROES AND VILLAINS.
IT'S A LOT MORE FUN BEIN' BAD.
I WONDER IF THIS IS WHAT DAREDEVIL DOES EVERY DAY...
YOU EVEN LISTENIN' TA YOUR BIG BROTHER?

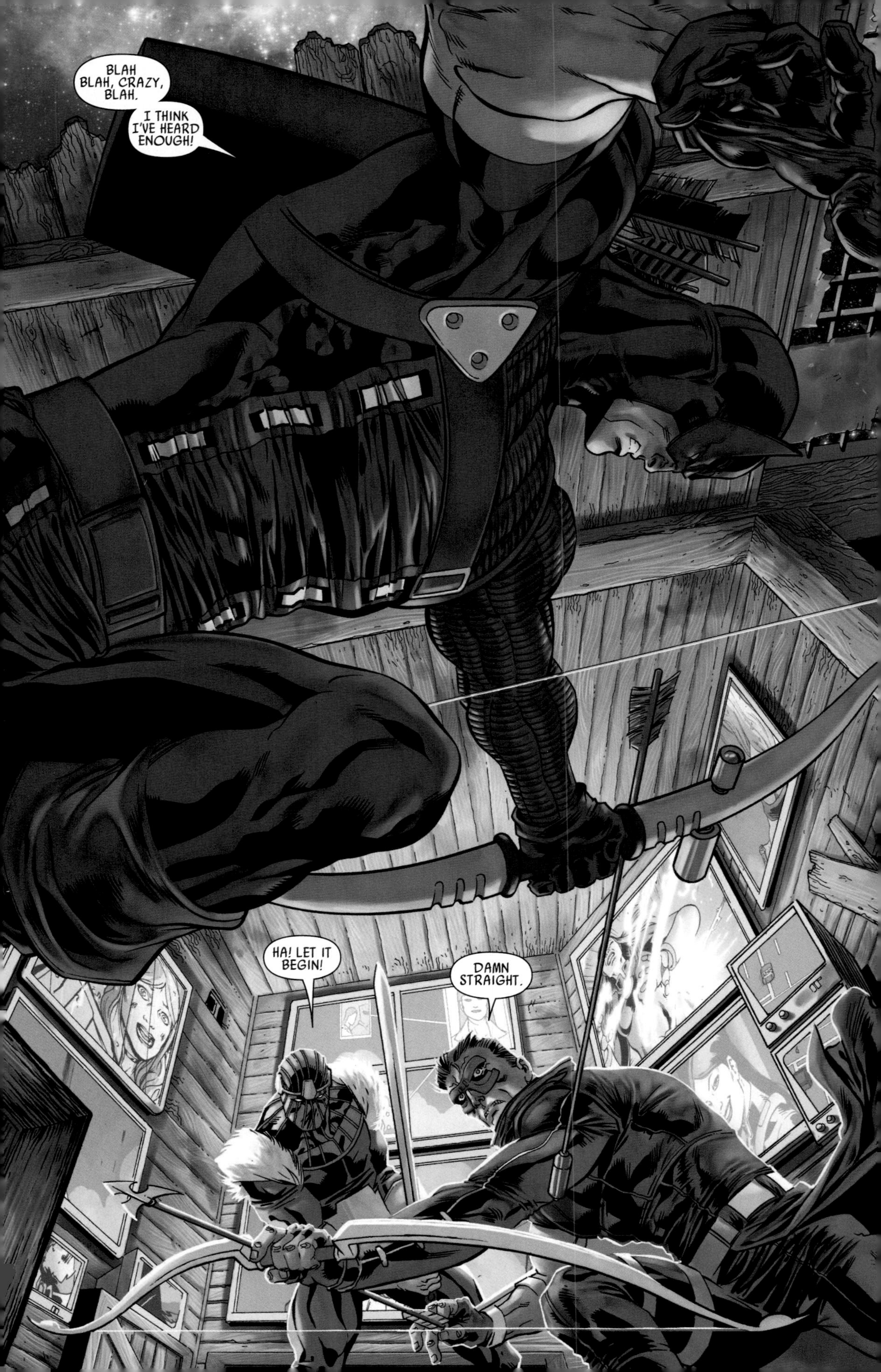
BLAH BLAH, CRAZY, BLAH.
I THINK I'VE HEARD ENOUGH!
HA! LET IT BEGIN!
DAMN STRAIGHT.

BARNEY'S NEVER BEEN THE BRIGHTEST BULB, BUT HE'S ACTUALLY RIGHT.

SOMETIMES YOU JUST HAVE TO FIGHT DIRTY.

THAT'S WHERE TRICK ARROWS COME IN HANDY.

POP

POP

POP

SKREEEEE

FWOOOOOSH

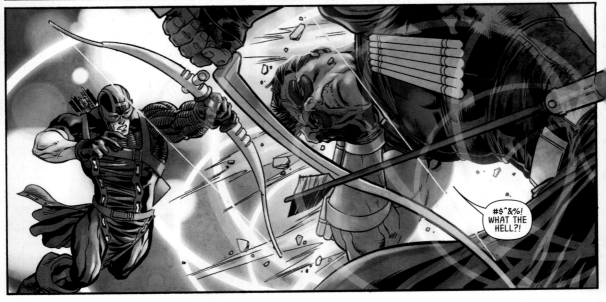

#$^&%! WHAT THE HELL?!

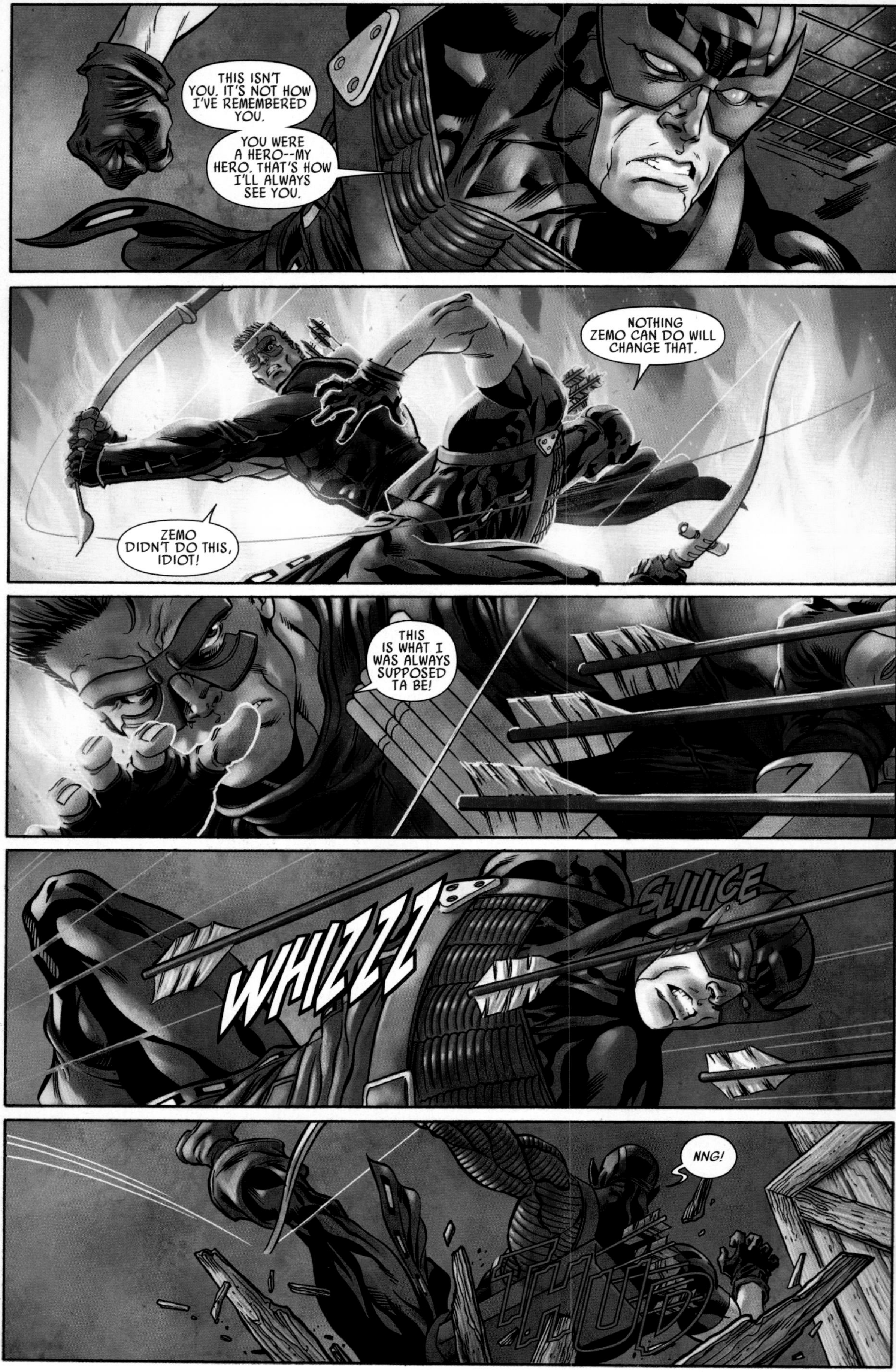
THIS ISN'T YOU. IT'S NOT HOW I'VE REMEMBERED YOU.
YOU WERE A HERO--MY HERO. THAT'S HOW I'LL ALWAYS SEE YOU.
NOTHING ZEMO CAN DO WILL CHANGE THAT.
ZEMO DIDN'T DO THIS, IDIOT!
THIS IS WHAT I WAS ALWAYS SUPPOSED TA BE!
WHIZZZ
SLIIICE
NNG!
THUD

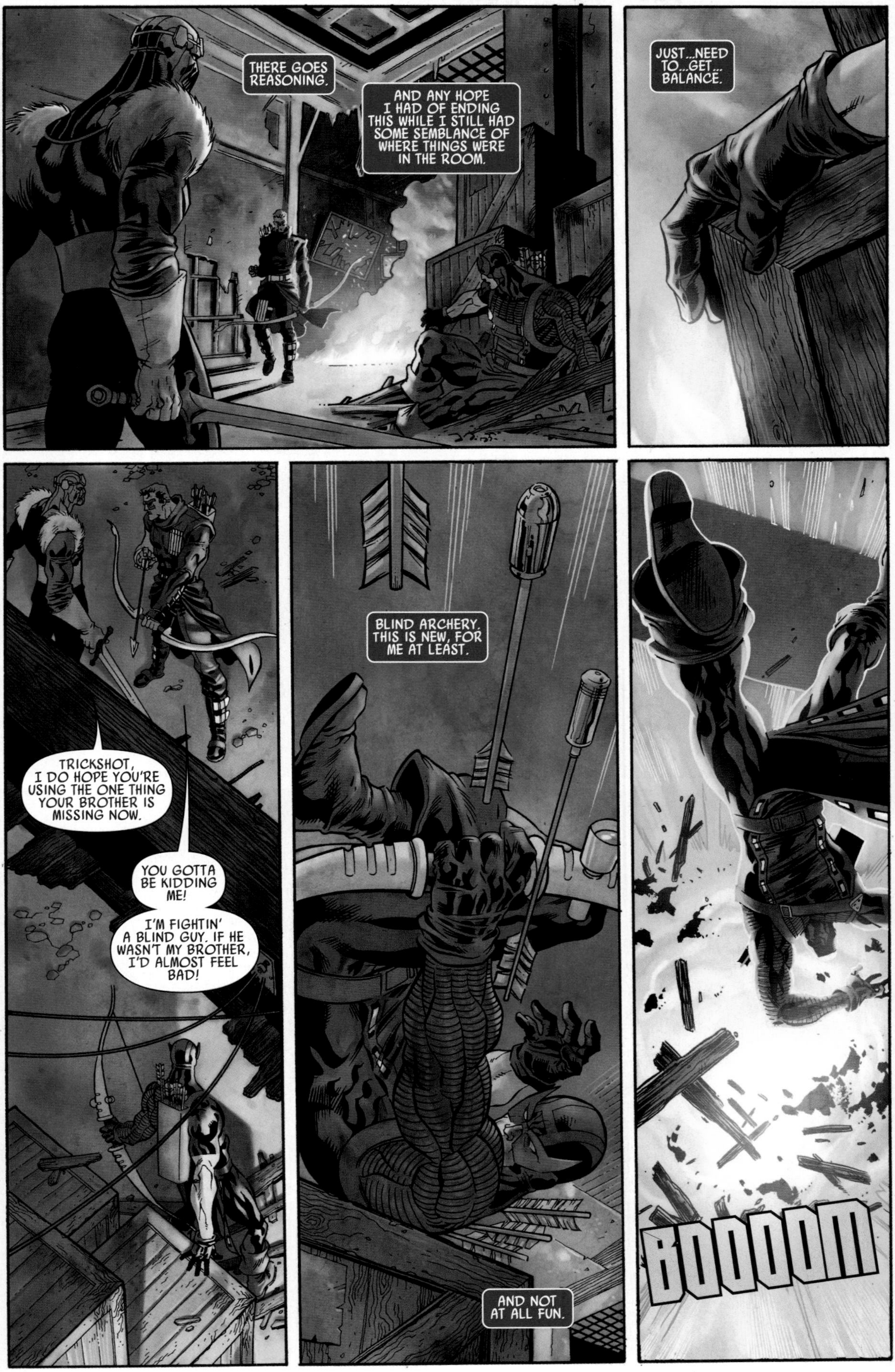
THERE GOES REASONING.
AND ANY HOPE I HAD OF ENDING THIS WHILE I STILL HAD SOME SEMBLANCE OF WHERE THINGS WERE IN THE ROOM.
JUST...NEED TO...GET... BALANCE.
TRICKSHOT, I DO HOPE YOU'RE USING THE ONE THING YOUR BROTHER IS MISSING NOW.
YOU GOTTA BE KIDDING ME!
I'M FIGHTIN' A BLIND GUY. IF HE WASN'T MY BROTHER, I'D ALMOST FEEL BAD!
BLIND ARCHERY. THIS IS NEW, FOR ME AT LEAST.
AND NOT AT ALL FUN.
BOOOOM

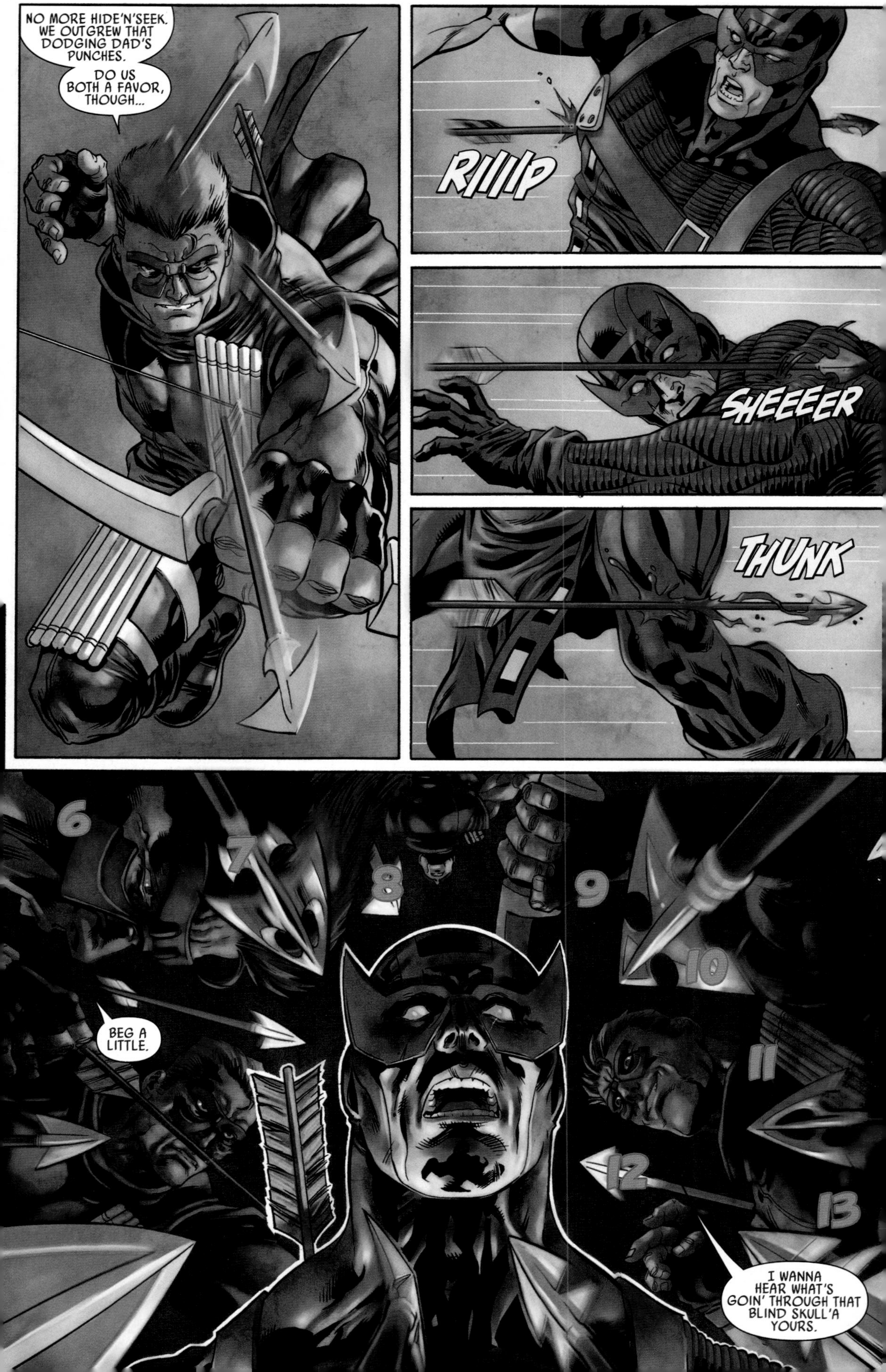
NO MORE HIDE'N'SEEK. WE OUTGREW THAT DODGING DAD'S PUNCHES.
DO US BOTH A FAVOR, THOUGH...
RIIIIP
SHEEEER
THUNK
6
7
8
9
10
BEG A LITTLE.
11
12
13
I WANNA HEAR WHAT'S GOIN' THROUGH THAT BLIND SKULL'A YOURS.

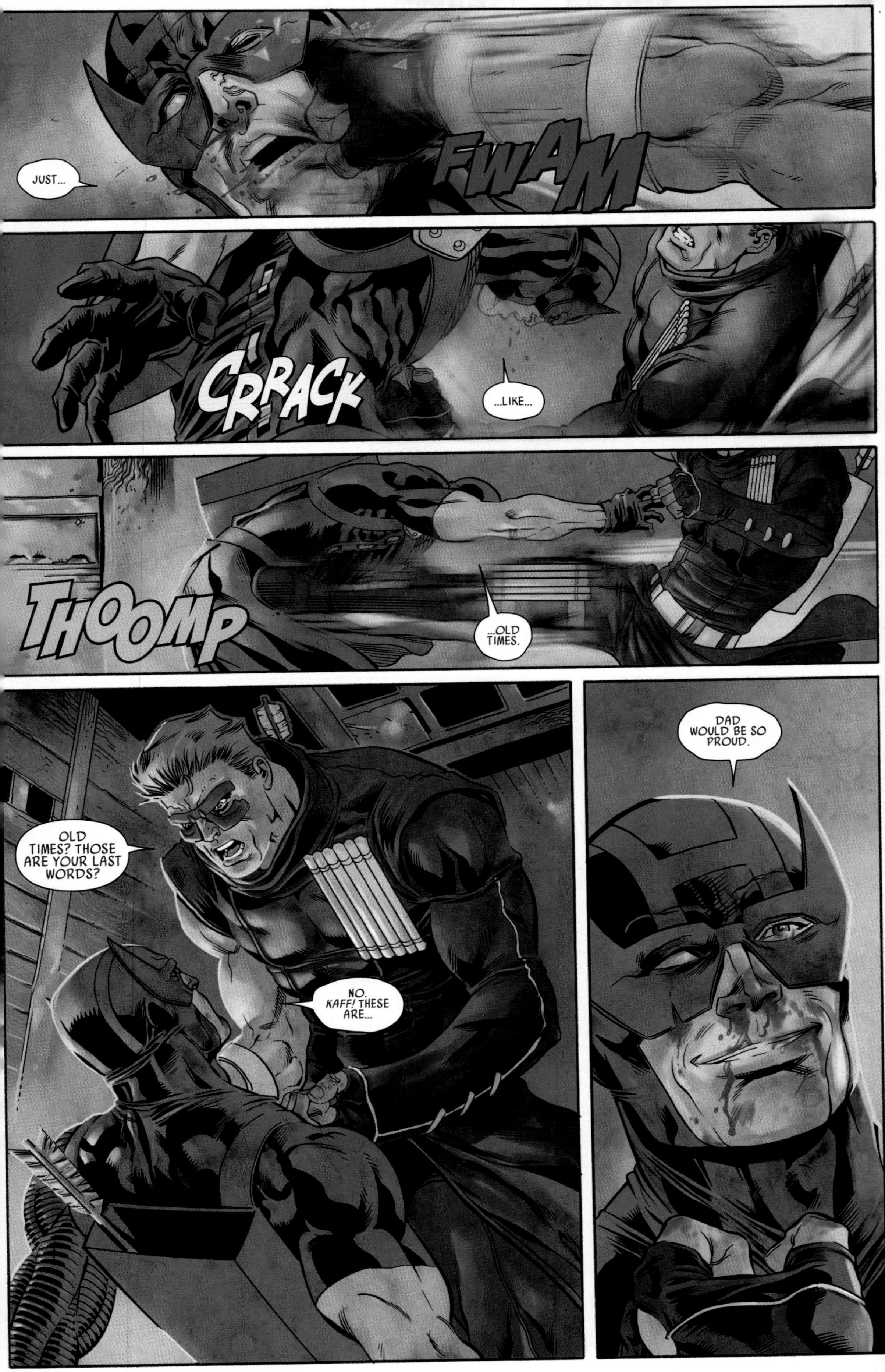
JUST...
FWAM
CRRACK
...LIKE...
THOOMP
...OLD TIMES.
OLD TIMES? THOSE ARE YOUR LAST WORDS?
NO. KAFF! THESE ARE...
DAD WOULD BE SO PROUD.

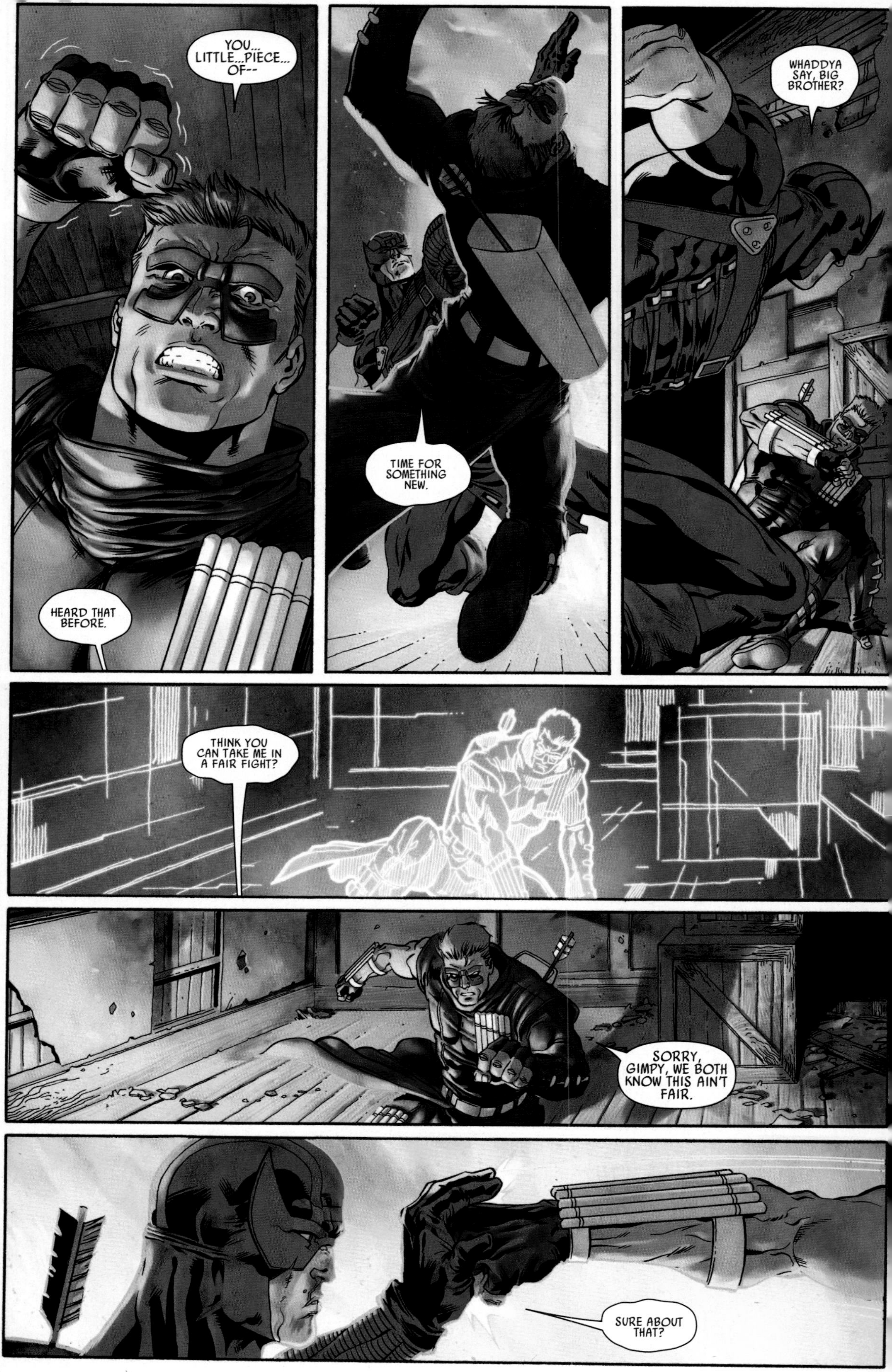
YOU... LITTLE...PIECE... OF--
HEARD THAT BEFORE.
TIME FOR SOMETHING NEW.
WHADDYA SAY, BIG BROTHER?
THINK YOU CAN TAKE ME IN A FAIR FIGHT?
SORRY, GIMPY, WE BOTH KNOW THIS AIN'T FAIR.
SURE ABOUT THAT?

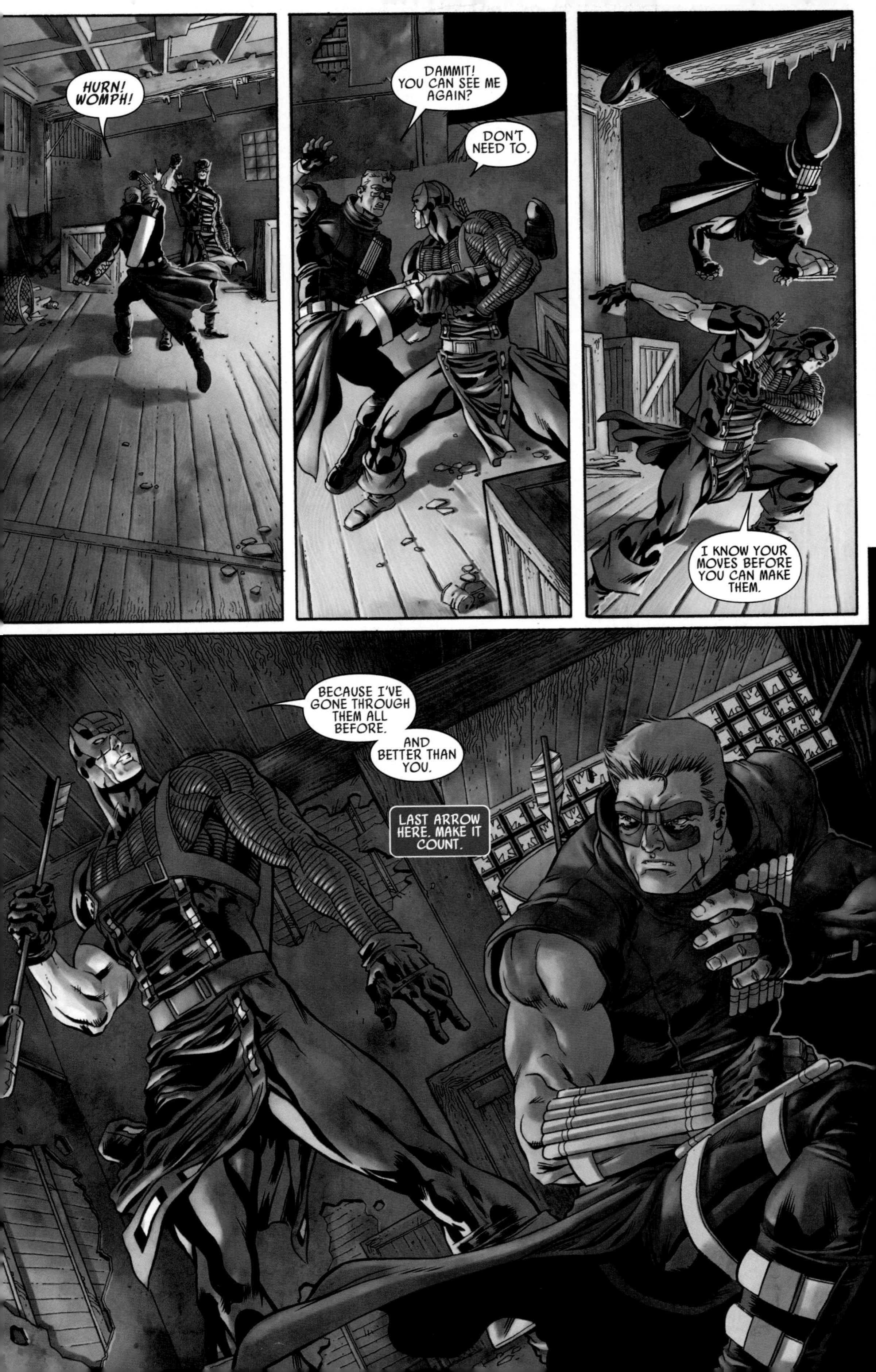
HURN! WOMPH!
DAMMIT! YOU CAN SEE ME AGAIN?
DON'T NEED TO.
I KNOW YOUR MOVES BEFORE YOU CAN MAKE THEM.
BECAUSE I'VE GONE THROUGH THEM ALL BEFORE.
AND BETTER THAN YOU.
LAST ARROW HERE. MAKE IT COUNT.

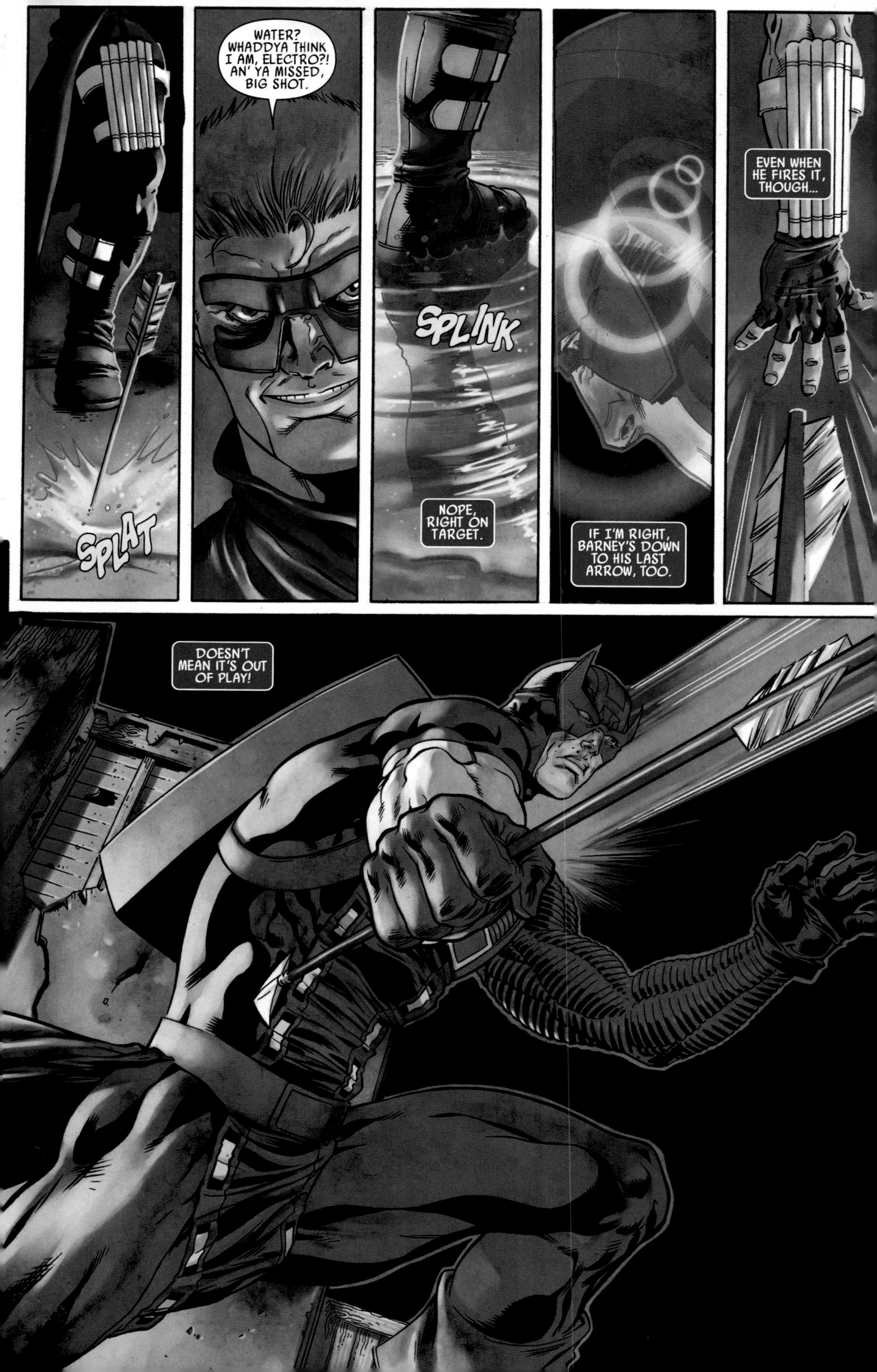
SPLAT
WATER? WHADDYA THINK I AM, ELECTRO?! AN' YA MISSED, BIG SHOT.
SPLINK
NOPE, RIGHT ON TARGET.
IF I'M RIGHT, BARNEY'S DOWN TO HIS LAST ARROW, TOO.
EVEN WHEN HE FIRES IT, THOUGH...
DOESN'T MEAN IT'S OUT OF PLAY!

WHAT THE %^$& ?!

FIRST LESSON-- MAKE EVERY SHOT COUNT.

SECOND LESSON-- ANYTHING CAN BE A WEAPON IN THE RIGHT HANDS!

THWAAANG

I'D LOVE FOR YOU TO BE AS GOOD AS ME ONE DAY. BROTHER, FIGHTING SIDE BY SIDE.

YEARGH!

THUNK

BUT FIRST... YOU KINDA HAFTA BE GOOD!

DAD BEAT UP ON INNOCENTS BECAUSE HE LIKED IT. TRUST ME, BARNEY, I HATE THIS.

WHAM

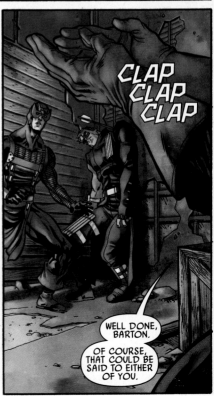

CLAP CLAP CLAP

WELL DONE, BARTON.

OF COURSE, THAT COULD BE SAID TO EITHER OF YOU.

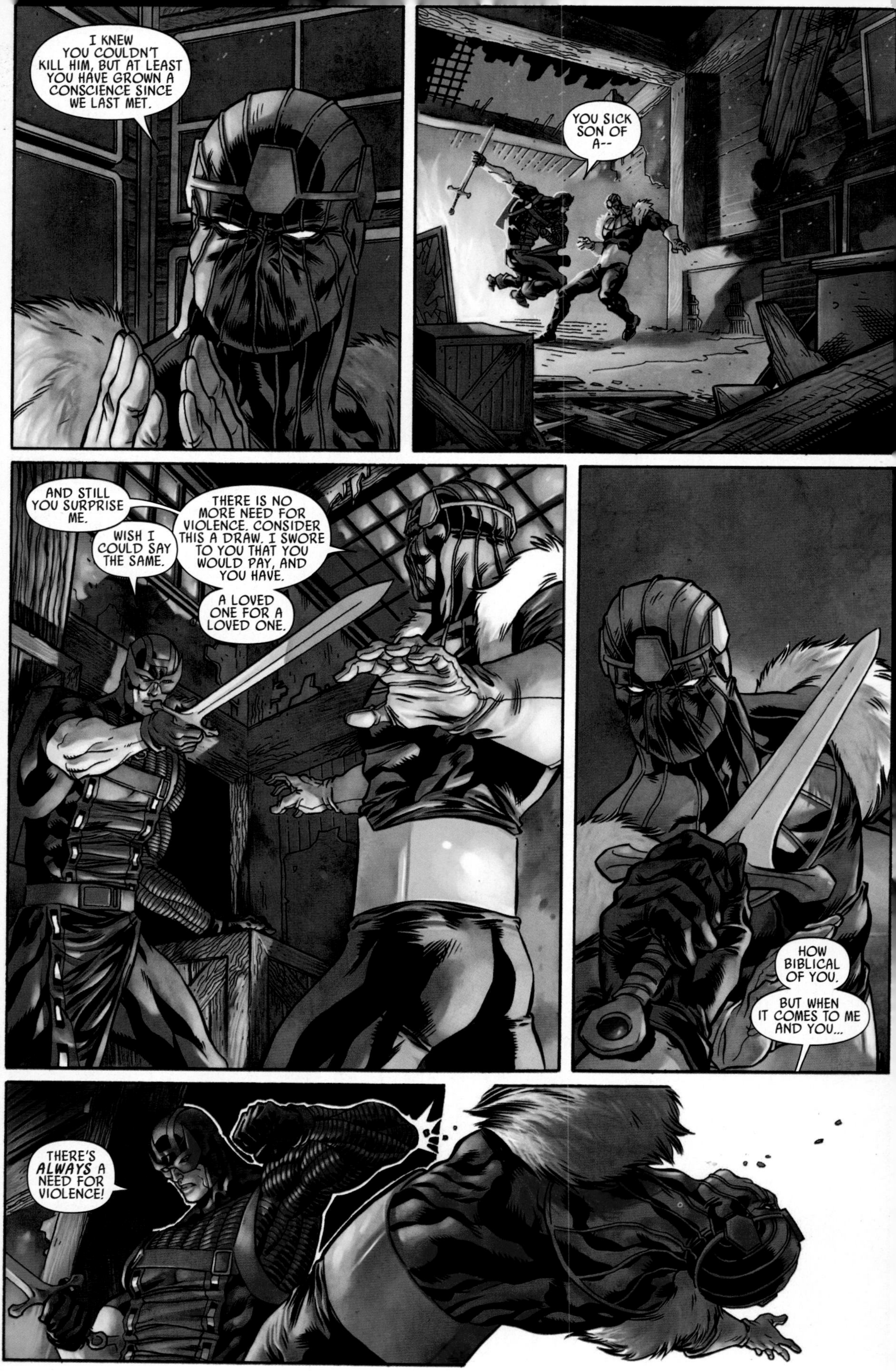
I KNEW YOU COULDN'T KILL HIM, BUT AT LEAST YOU HAVE GROWN A CONSCIENCE SINCE WE LAST MET.
YOU SICK SON OF A--
AND STILL YOU SURPRISE ME.
THERE IS NO MORE NEED FOR VIOLENCE. CONSIDER THIS A DRAW. I SWORE TO YOU THAT YOU WOULD PAY, AND YOU HAVE.
WISH I COULD SAY THE SAME.
A LOVED ONE FOR A LOVED ONE.
HOW BIBLICAL OF YOU.
BUT WHEN IT COMES TO ME AND YOU...
THERE'S *ALWAYS* A NEED FOR VIOLENCE!

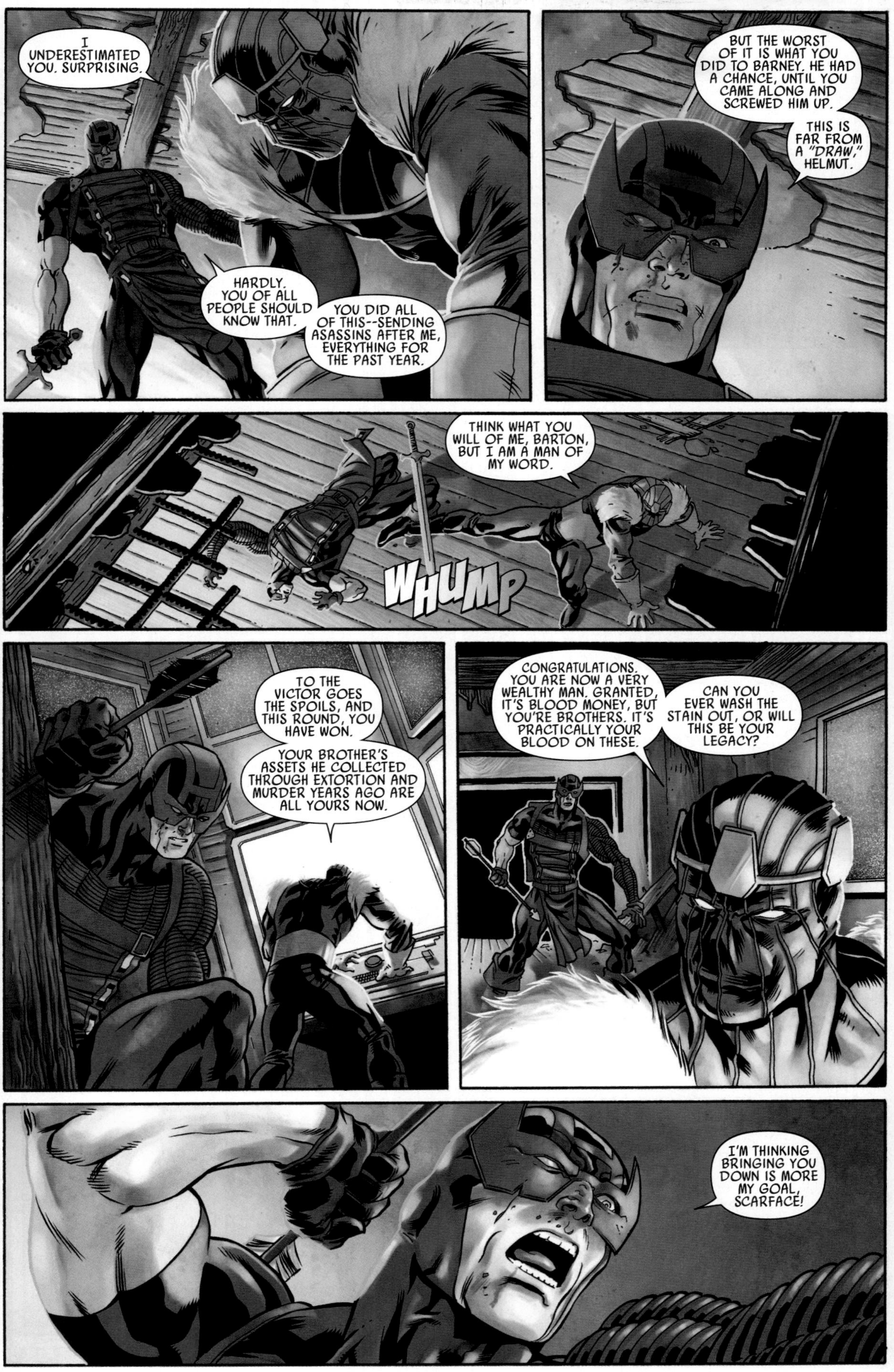
I UNDERESTIMATED YOU. SURPRISING.
HARDLY. YOU OF ALL PEOPLE SHOULD KNOW THAT.
YOU DID ALL OF THIS--SENDING ASASSINS AFTER ME, EVERYTHING FOR THE PAST YEAR.
BUT THE WORST OF IT IS WHAT YOU DID TO BARNEY. HE HAD A CHANCE, UNTIL YOU CAME ALONG AND SCREWED HIM UP.
THIS IS FAR FROM A "DRAW," HELMUT.
THINK WHAT YOU WILL OF ME, BARTON, BUT I AM A MAN OF MY WORD.
WHUMP
TO THE VICTOR GOES THE SPOILS, AND THIS ROUND, YOU HAVE WON.
YOUR BROTHER'S ASSETS HE COLLECTED THROUGH EXTORTION AND MURDER YEARS AGO ARE ALL YOURS NOW.
CONGRATULATIONS. YOU ARE NOW A VERY WEALTHY MAN. GRANTED, IT'S BLOOD MONEY, BUT YOU'RE BROTHERS. IT'S PRACTICALLY YOUR BLOOD ON THESE.
CAN YOU EVER WASH THE STAIN OUT, OR WILL THIS BE YOUR LEGACY?
I'M THINKING BRINGING YOU DOWN IS MORE MY GOAL, SCARFACE!

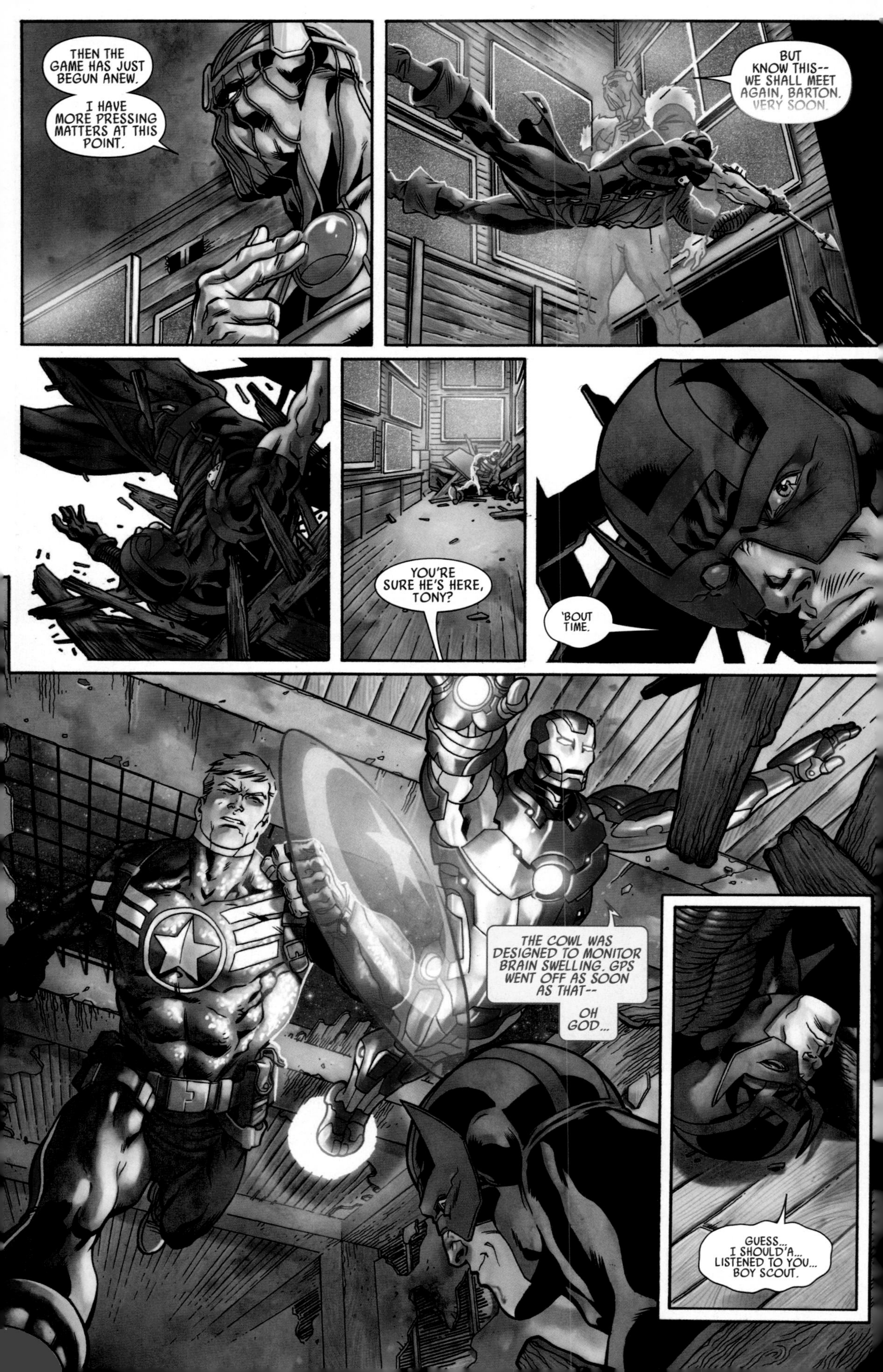
THEN THE GAME HAS JUST BEGUN ANEW.
I HAVE MORE PRESSING MATTERS AT THIS POINT.
BUT KNOW THIS-- WE SHALL MEET AGAIN, BARTON. VERY SOON.
YOU'RE SURE HE'S HERE, TONY?
'BOUT TIME.
THE COWL WAS DESIGNED TO MONITOR BRAIN SWELLING. GPS WENT OFF AS SOON AS THAT--
OH GOD...
GUESS... I SHOULD'A... LISTENED TO YOU... BOY SCOUT.

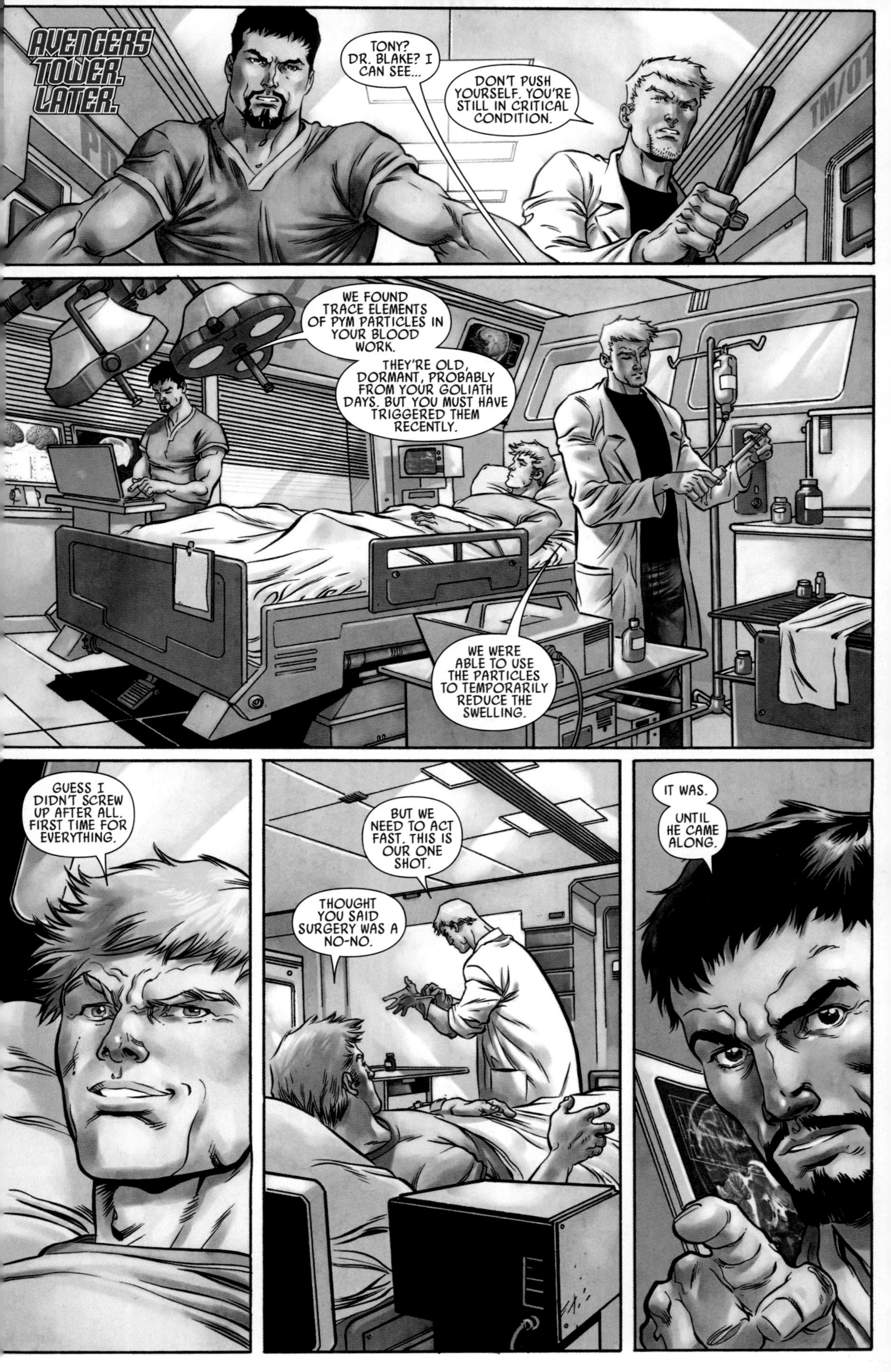
AVENGERS TOWER. LATER.
TONY? DR. BLAKE? I CAN SEE...
DON'T PUSH YOURSELF. YOU'RE STILL IN CRITICAL CONDITION.
WE FOUND TRACE ELEMENTS OF PYM PARTICLES IN YOUR BLOOD WORK.
THEY'RE OLD, DORMANT, PROBABLY FROM YOUR GOLIATH DAYS. BUT YOU MUST HAVE TRIGGERED THEM RECENTLY.
WE WERE ABLE TO USE THE PARTICLES TO TEMPORARILY REDUCE THE SWELLING.
GUESS I DIDN'T SCREW UP AFTER ALL. FIRST TIME FOR EVERYTHING.
BUT WE NEED TO ACT FAST. THIS IS OUR ONE SHOT.
THOUGHT YOU SAID SURGERY WAS A NO-NO.
IT WAS.
UNTIL HE CAME ALONG.

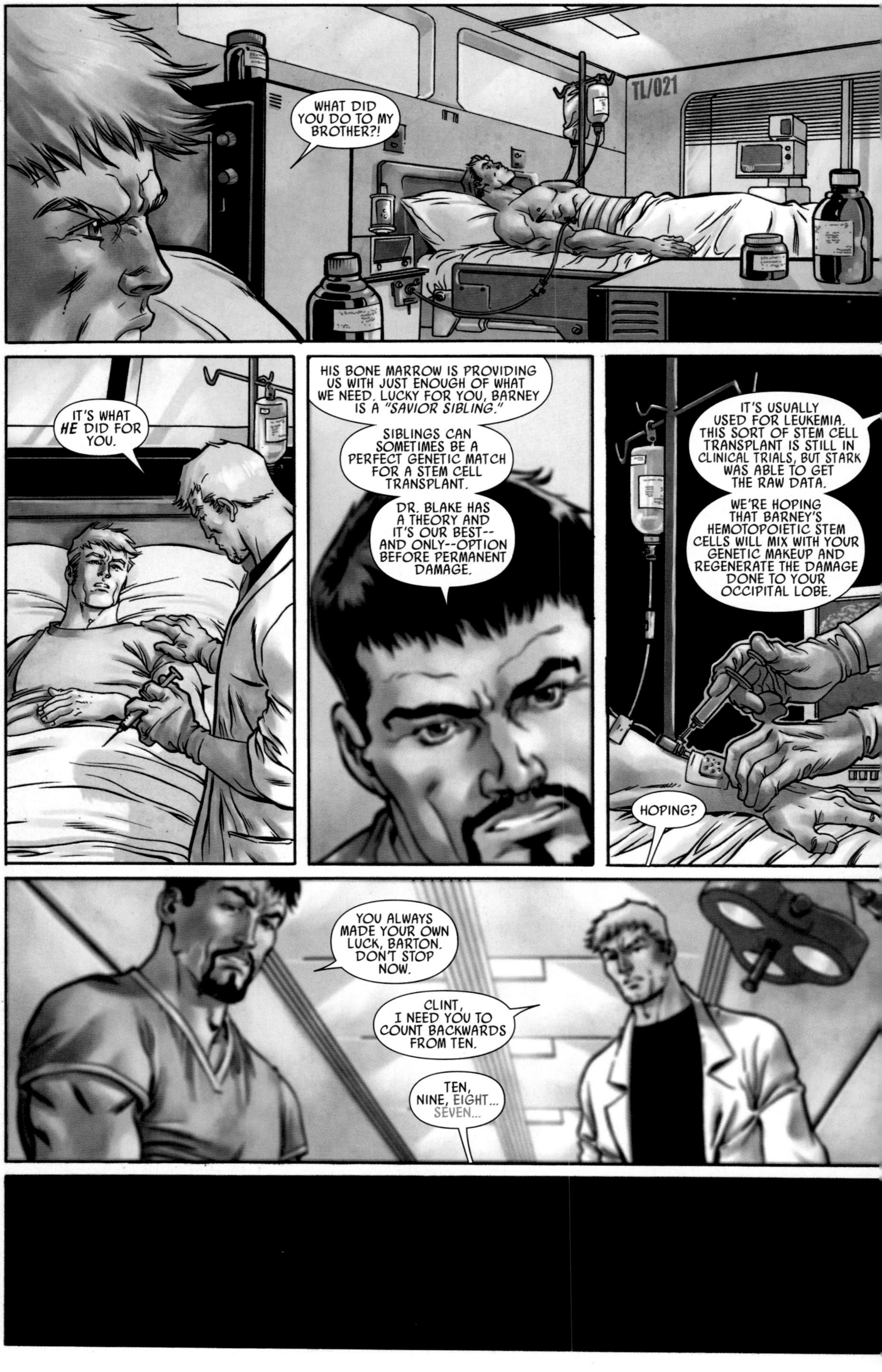
WHAT DID YOU DO TO MY BROTHER?!
IT'S WHAT HE DID FOR YOU.
HIS BONE MARROW IS PROVIDING US WITH JUST ENOUGH OF WHAT WE NEED. LUCKY FOR YOU, BARNEY IS A "SAVIOR SIBLING."
SIBLINGS CAN SOMETIMES BE A PERFECT GENETIC MATCH FOR A STEM CELL TRANSPLANT.
DR. BLAKE HAS A THEORY AND IT'S OUR BEST--AND ONLY--OPTION BEFORE PERMANENT DAMAGE.
IT'S USUALLY USED FOR LEUKEMIA. THIS SORT OF STEM CELL TRANSPLANT IS STILL IN CLINICAL TRIALS, BUT STARK WAS ABLE TO GET THE RAW DATA.
WE'RE HOPING THAT BARNEY'S HEMOTOPOIETIC STEM CELLS WILL MIX WITH YOUR GENETIC MAKEUP AND REGENERATE THE DAMAGE DONE TO YOUR OCCIPITAL LOBE.
HOPING?
YOU ALWAYS MADE YOUR OWN LUCK, BARTON. DON'T STOP NOW.
CLINT, I NEED YOU TO COUNT BACKWARDS FROM TEN.
TEN, NINE, EIGHT... SEVEN...

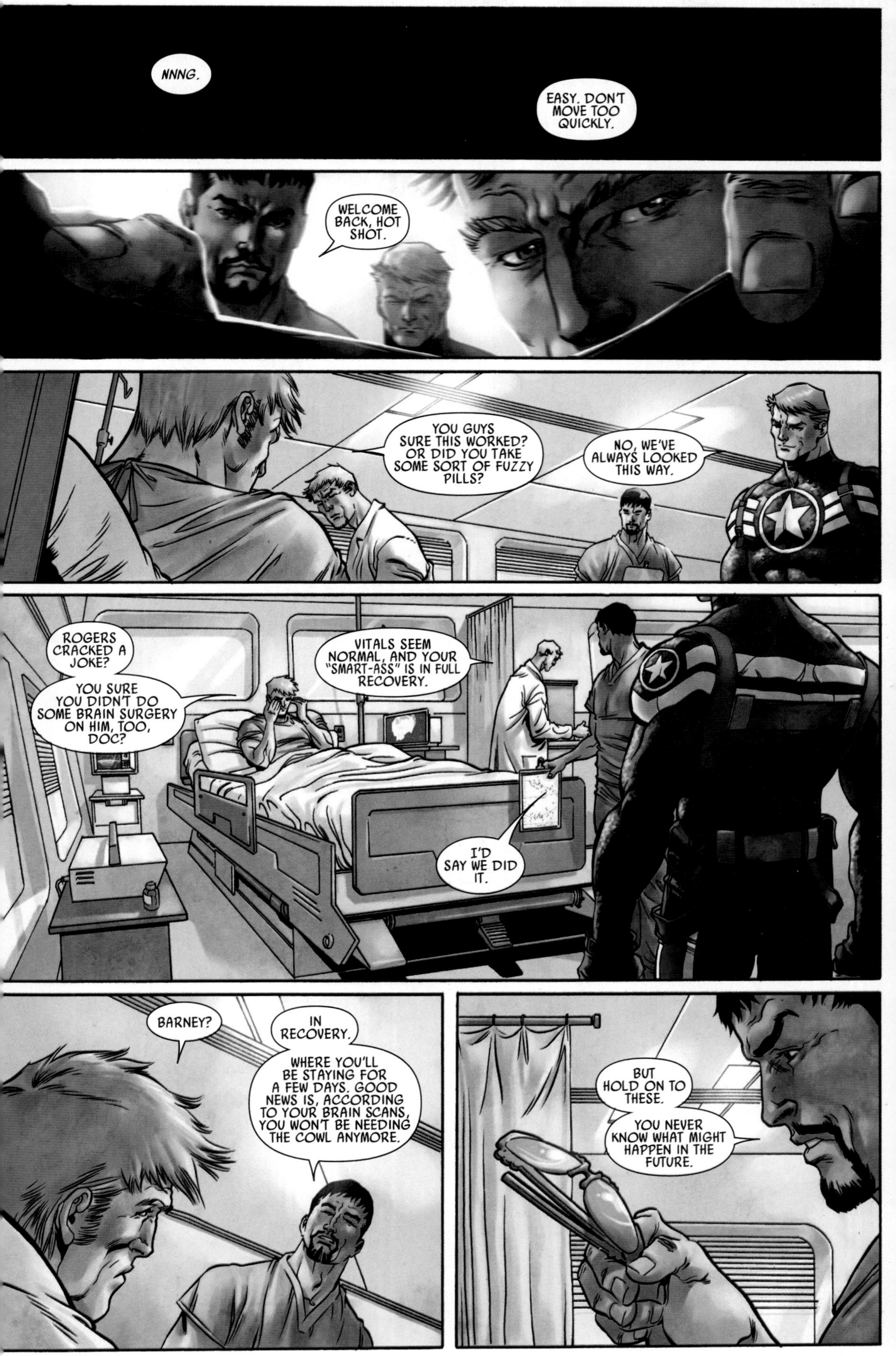
NNNG.
EASY. DON'T MOVE TOO QUICKLY.
WELCOME BACK, HOT SHOT.
YOU GUYS SURE THIS WORKED? OR DID YOU TAKE SOME SORT OF FUZZY PILLS?
NO, WE'VE ALWAYS LOOKED THIS WAY.
ROGERS CRACKED A JOKE?
YOU SURE YOU DIDN'T DO SOME BRAIN SURGERY ON HIM, TOO, DOC?
VITALS SEEM NORMAL, AND YOUR "SMART-ASS" IS IN FULL RECOVERY.
I'D SAY WE DID IT.
BARNEY?
IN RECOVERY.
WHERE YOU'LL BE STAYING FOR A FEW DAYS. GOOD NEWS IS, ACCORDING TO YOUR BRAIN SCANS, YOU WON'T BE NEEDING THE COWL ANYMORE.
BUT HOLD ON TO THESE.
YOU NEVER KNOW WHAT MIGHT HAPPEN IN THE FUTURE.

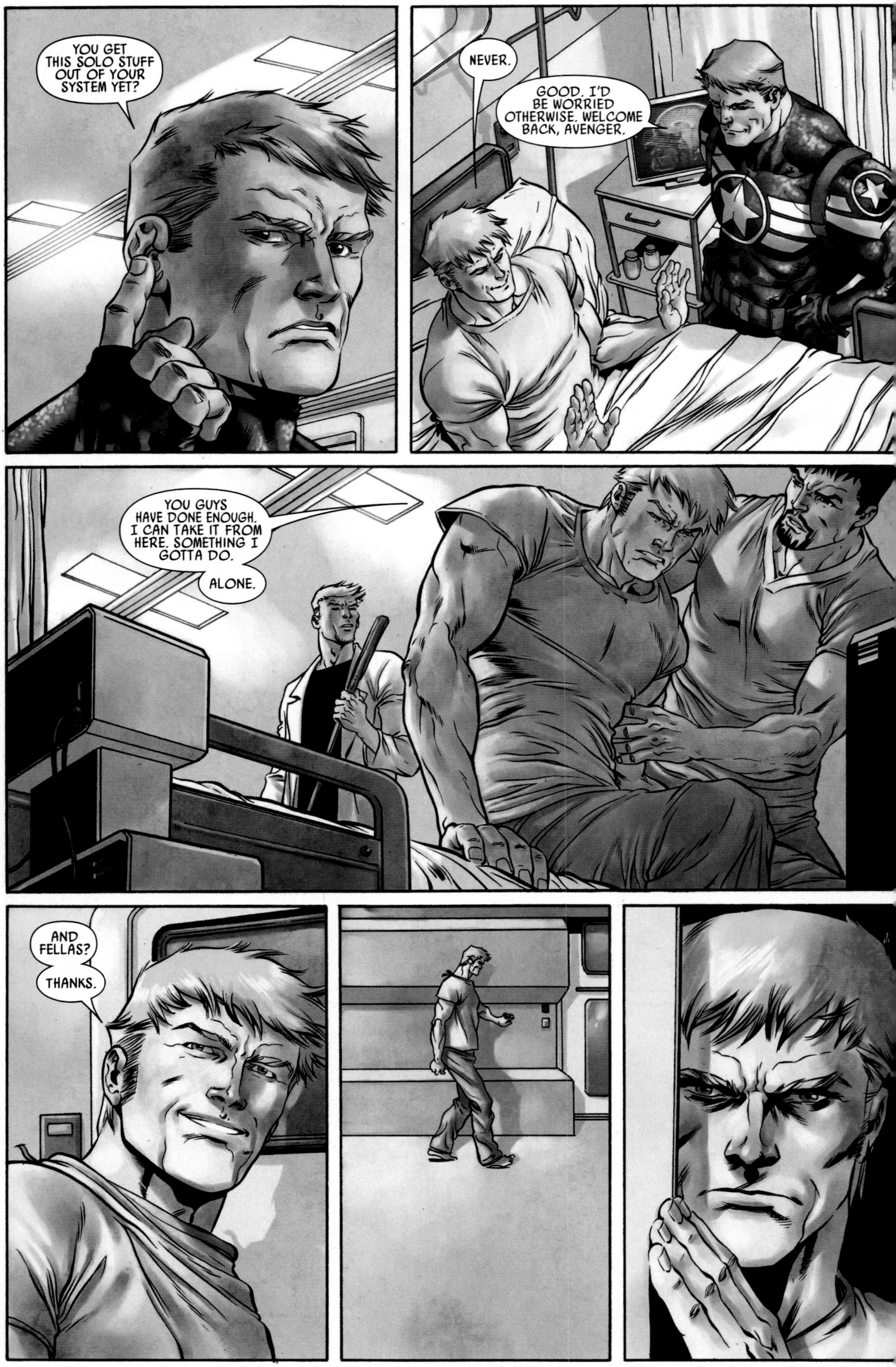
YOU GET THIS SOLO STUFF OUT OF YOUR SYSTEM YET?
NEVER.
GOOD. I'D BE WORRIED OTHERWISE. WELCOME BACK, AVENGER.
YOU GUYS HAVE DONE ENOUGH. I CAN TAKE IT FROM HERE. SOMETHING I GOTTA DO.
ALONE.
AND FELLAS?
THANKS.

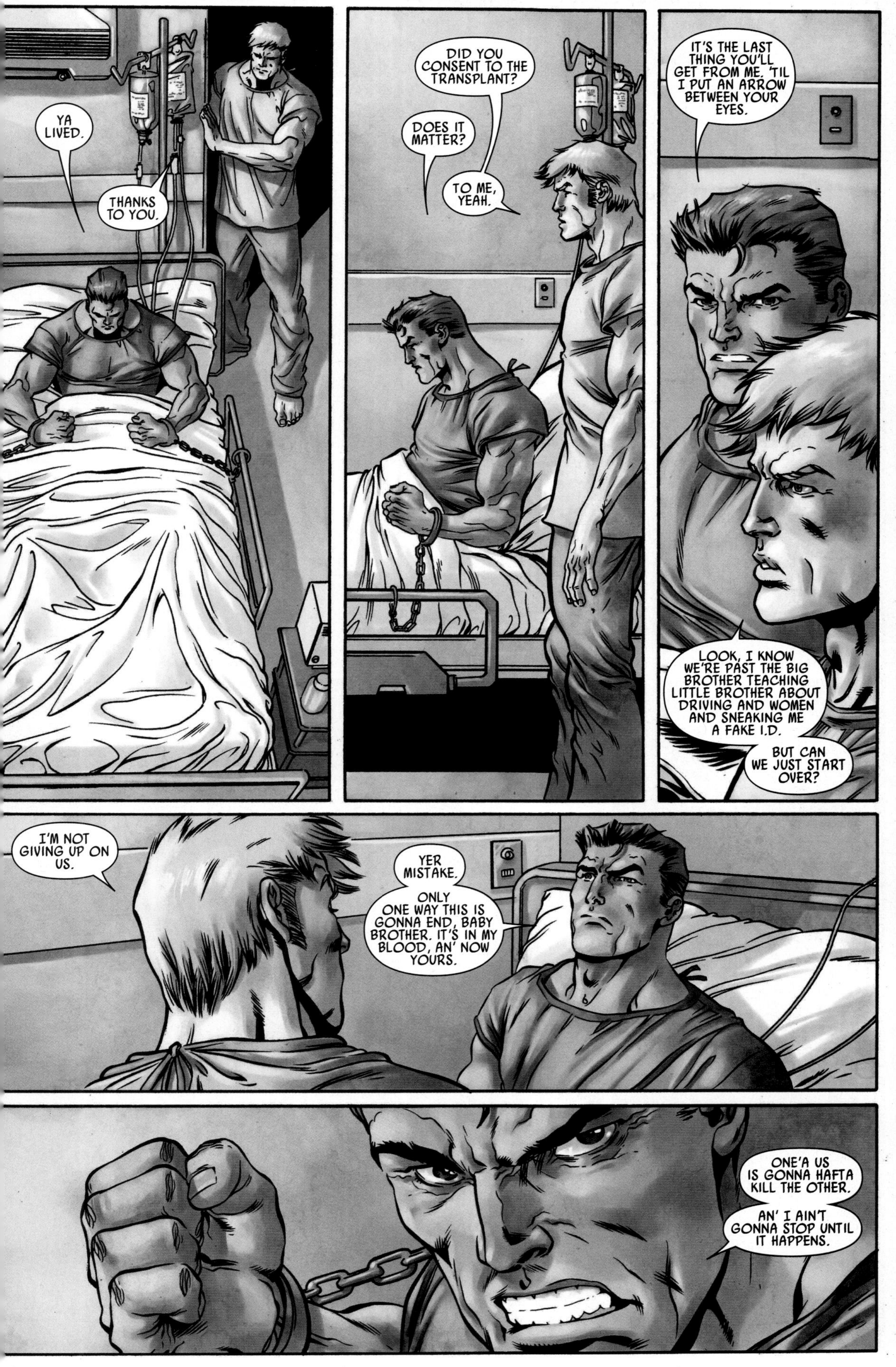
YA LIVED.
THANKS TO YOU.
DID YOU CONSENT TO THE TRANSPLANT?
DOES IT MATTER?
TO ME, YEAH.
IT'S THE LAST THING YOU'LL GET FROM ME. 'TIL I PUT AN ARROW BETWEEN YOUR EYES.
LOOK, I KNOW WE'RE PAST THE BIG BROTHER TEACHING LITTLE BROTHER ABOUT DRIVING AND WOMEN AND SNEAKING ME A FAKE I.D.
BUT CAN WE JUST START OVER?
I'M NOT GIVING UP ON US.
YER MISTAKE.
ONLY ONE WAY THIS IS GONNA END, BABY BROTHER. IT'S IN MY BLOOD, AN' NOW YOURS.
ONE'A US IS GONNA HAFTA KILL THE OTHER.
AN' I AIN'T GONNA STOP UNTIL IT HAPPENS.

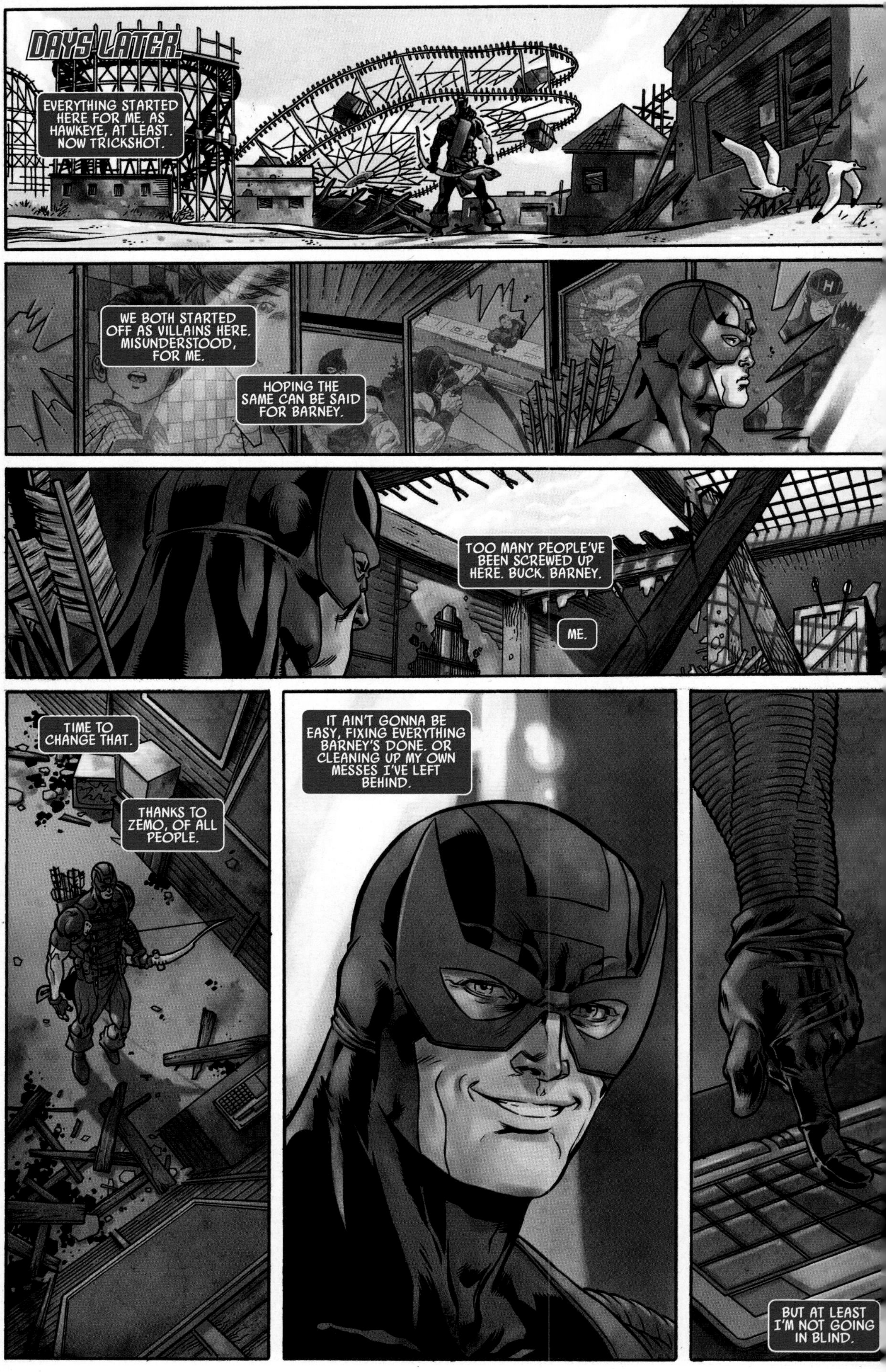
DAYS LATER.
EVERYTHING STARTED HERE FOR ME. AS HAWKEYE, AT LEAST. NOW TRICKSHOT.
WE BOTH STARTED OFF AS VILLAINS HERE. MISUNDERSTOOD, FOR ME.
HOPING THE SAME CAN BE SAID FOR BARNEY.
TOO MANY PEOPLE'VE BEEN SCREWED UP HERE. BUCK. BARNEY.
ME.
TIME TO CHANGE THAT.
THANKS TO ZEMO, OF ALL PEOPLE.
IT AIN'T GONNA BE EASY, FIXING EVERYTHING BARNEY'S DONE. OR CLEANING UP MY OWN MESSES I'VE LEFT BEHIND.
BUT AT LEAST I'M NOT GOING IN BLIND.

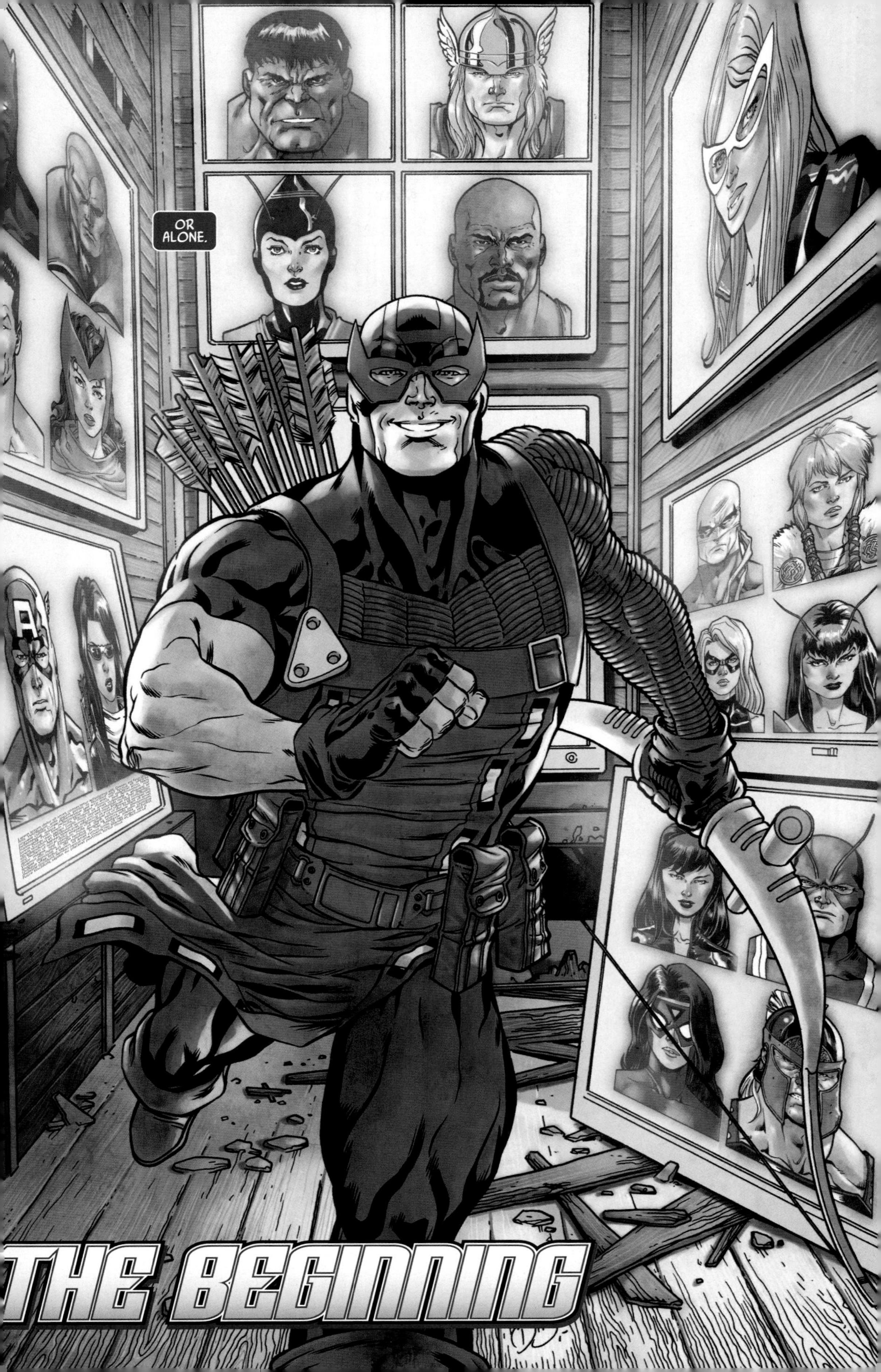
OR ALONE.
THE BEGINNING

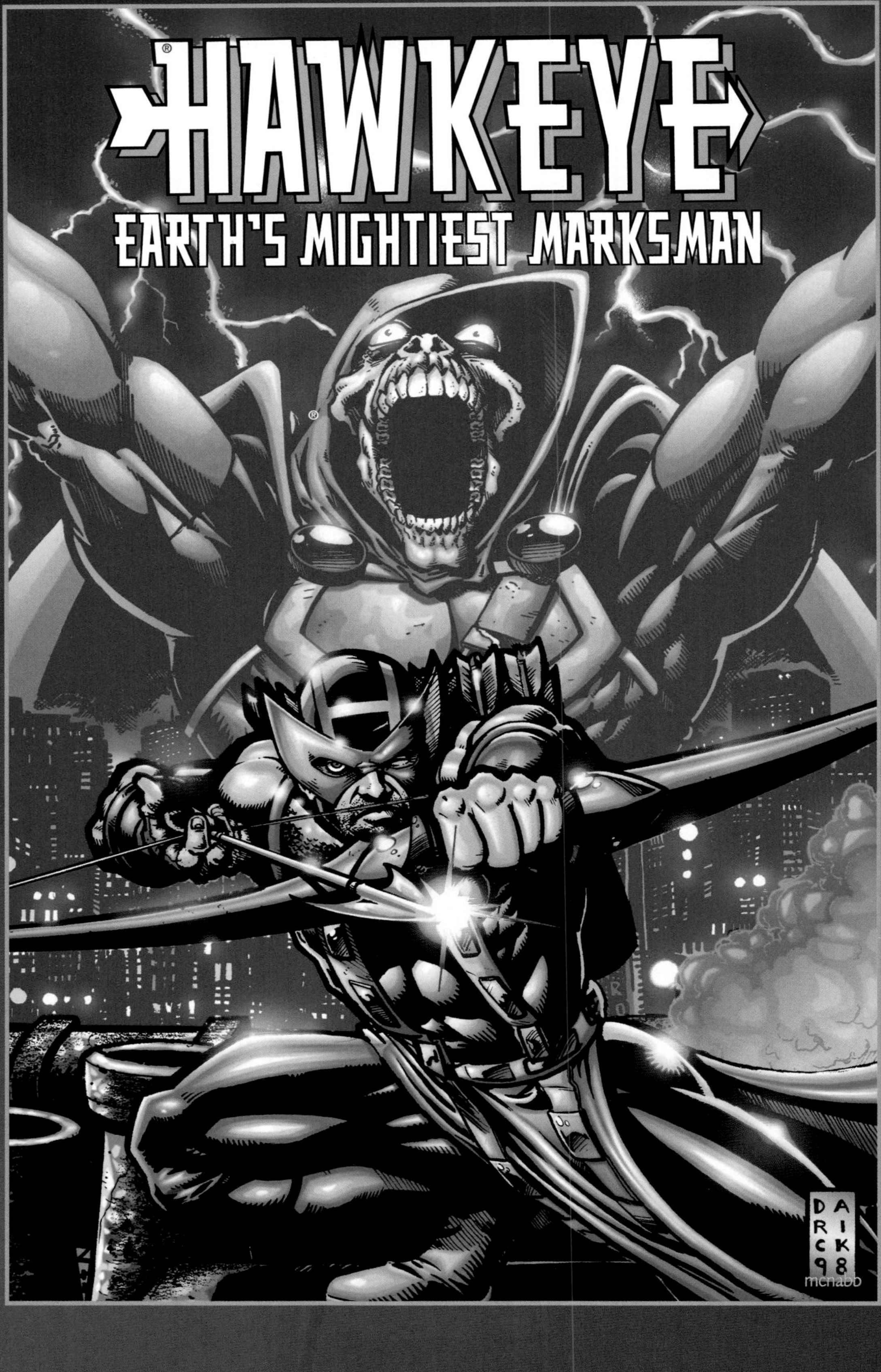

HAWKEYE
EARTH'S MIGHTIEST MARKSMAN
DARICK 98
mcnabb

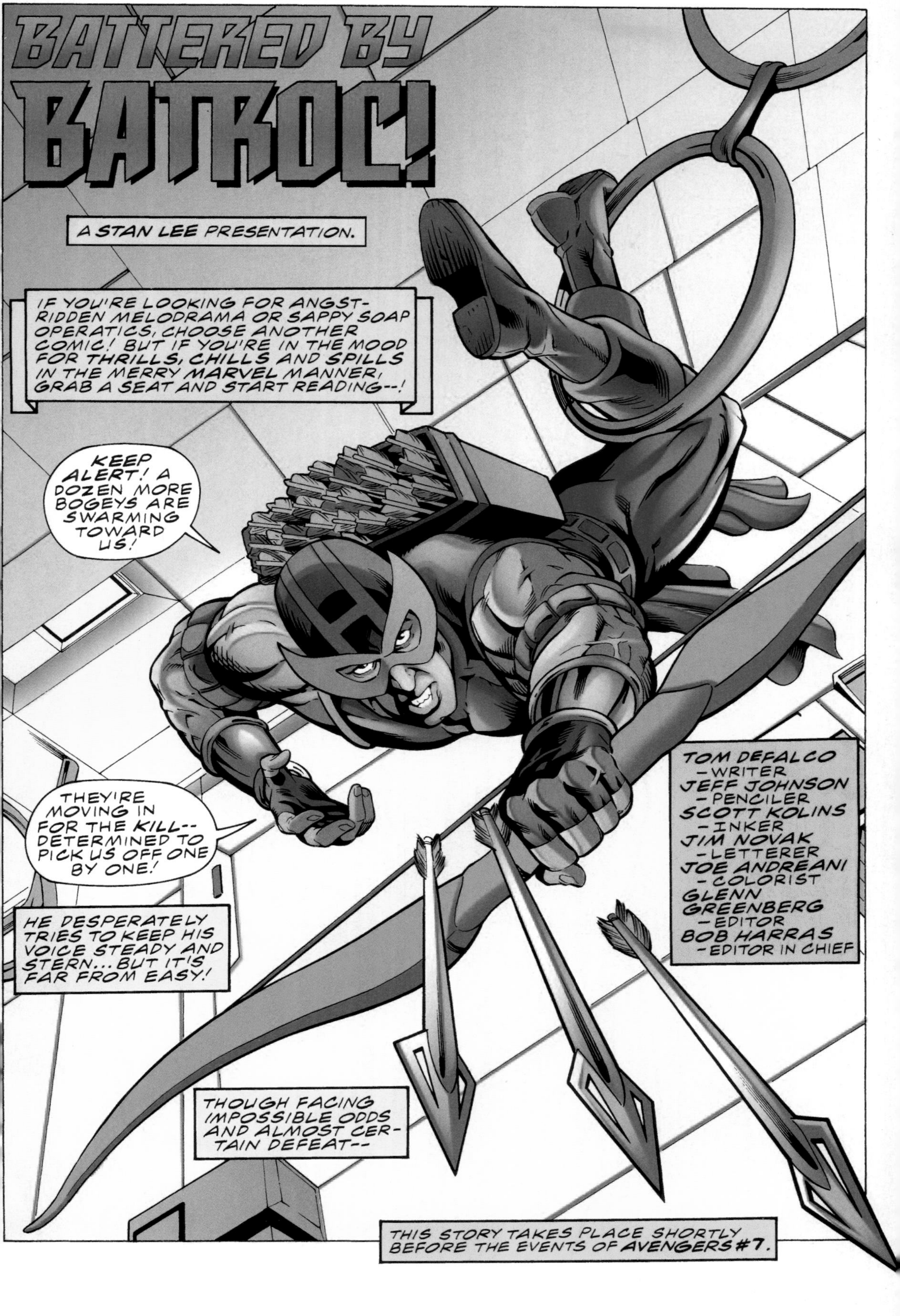

BATTERED BY BATROC!
A STAN LEE PRESENTATION.
IF YOU'RE LOOKING FOR ANGST-RIDDEN MELODRAMA OR SAPPY SOAP OPERATICS, CHOOSE ANOTHER COMIC! BUT IF YOU'RE IN THE MOOD FOR THRILLS, CHILLS AND SPILLS IN THE MERRY MARVEL MANNER, GRAB A SEAT AND START READING--!
KEEP ALERT! A DOZEN MORE BOGEYS ARE SWARMING TOWARD US!
THEY'RE MOVING IN FOR THE KILL-- DETERMINED TO PICK US OFF ONE BY ONE!
HE DESPERATELY TRIES TO KEEP HIS VOICE STEADY AND STERN... BUT IT'S FAR FROM EASY!
TOM DEFALCO -WRITER JEFF JOHNSON -PENCILER SCOTT KOLINS -INKER JIM NOVAK -LETTERER JOE ANDREANI -COLORIST GLENN GREENBERG -EDITOR BOB HARRAS -EDITOR IN CHIEF
THOUGH FACING IMPOSSIBLE ODDS AND ALMOST CERTAIN DEFEAT--
THIS STORY TAKES PLACE SHORTLY BEFORE THE EVENTS OF AVENGERS #7.

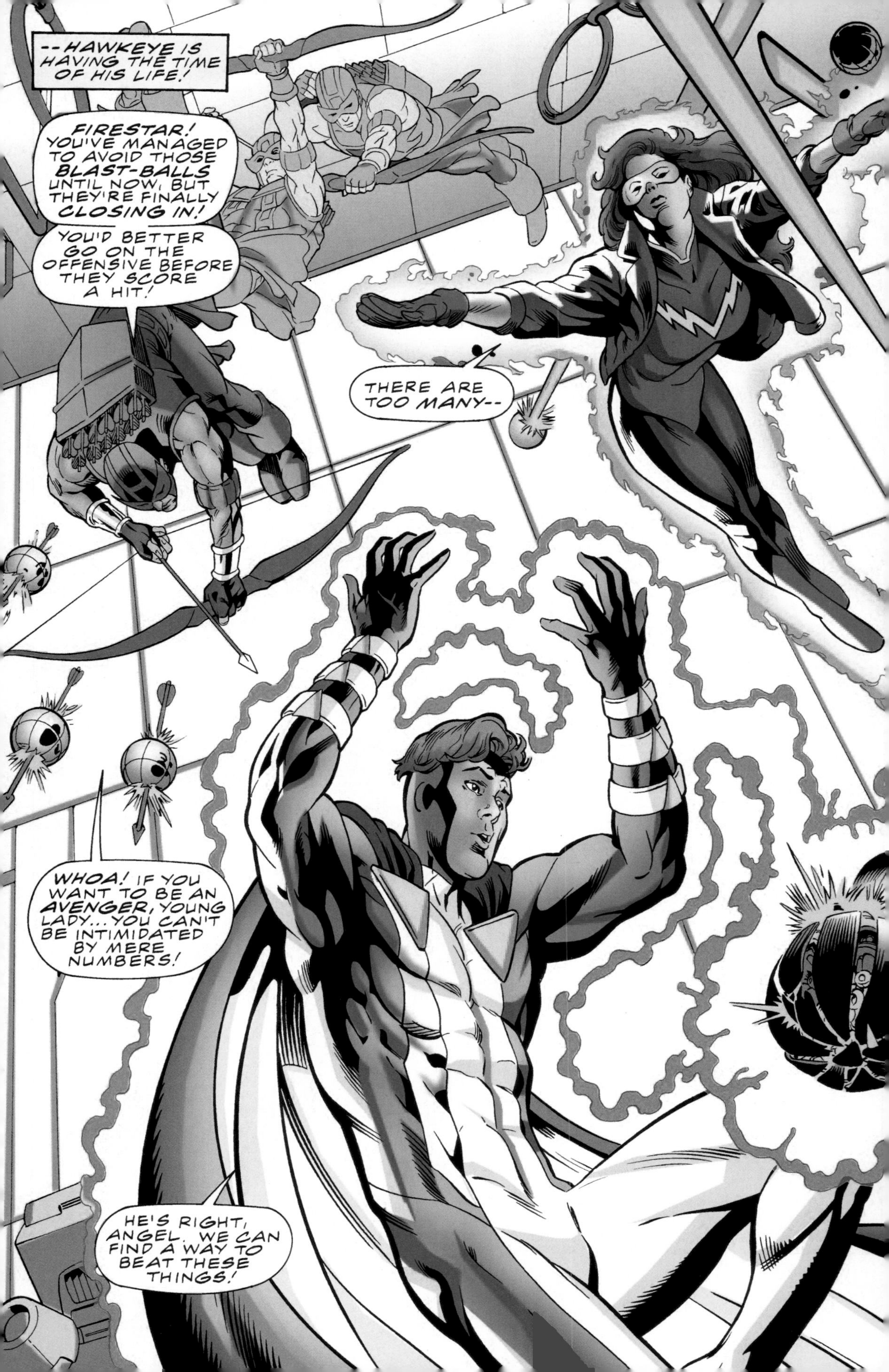
--HAWKEYE IS HAVING THE TIME OF HIS LIFE!
FIRESTAR! YOU'VE MANAGED TO AVOID THOSE BLAST-BALLS UNTIL NOW, BUT THEY'RE FINALLY CLOSING IN!
YOU'D BETTER GO ON THE OFFENSIVE BEFORE THEY SCORE A HIT!
THERE ARE TOO MANY--
WHOA! IF YOU WANT TO BE AN AVENGER, YOUNG LADY... YOU CAN'T BE INTIMIDATED BY MERE NUMBERS!
HE'S RIGHT, ANGEL. WE CAN FIND A WAY TO BEAT THESE THINGS!

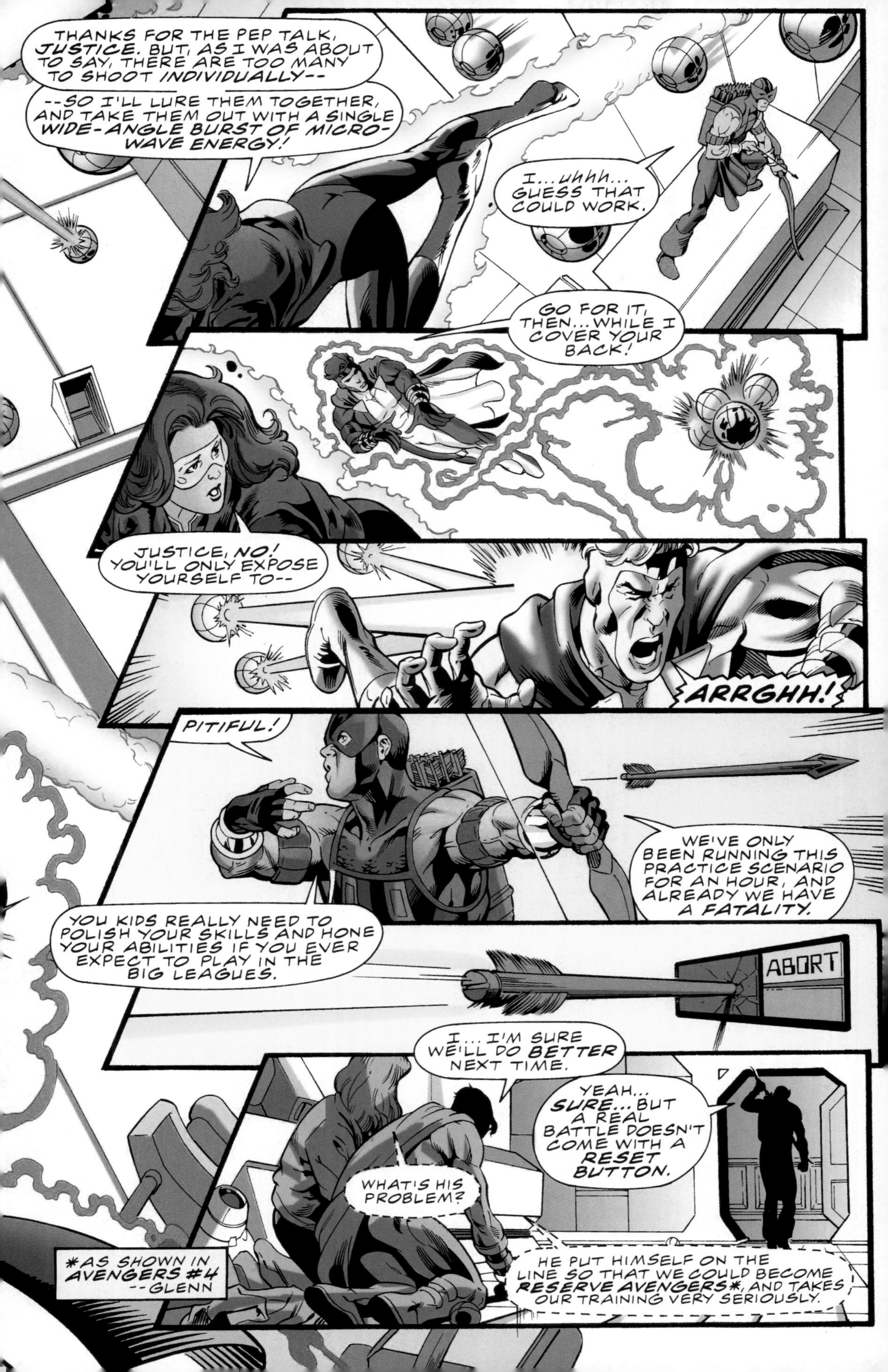
THANKS FOR THE PEP TALK, JUSTICE. BUT, AS I WAS ABOUT TO SAY, THERE ARE TOO MANY TO SHOOT INDIVIDUALLY--
--SO I'LL LURE THEM TOGETHER, AND TAKE THEM OUT WITH A SINGLE WIDE-ANGLE BURST OF MICRO-WAVE ENERGY!
I...uhhh... GUESS THAT COULD WORK.
GO FOR IT, THEN...WHILE I COVER YOUR BACK!
JUSTICE, NO! YOU'LL ONLY EXPOSE YOURSELF TO--
ARRGHH!
PITIFUL!
WE'VE ONLY BEEN RUNNING THIS PRACTICE SCENARIO FOR AN HOUR, AND ALREADY WE HAVE A FATALITY.
YOU KIDS REALLY NEED TO POLISH YOUR SKILLS AND HONE YOUR ABILITIES IF YOU EVER EXPECT TO PLAY IN THE BIG LEAGUES.
ABORT
I... I'M SURE WE'LL DO BETTER NEXT TIME.
YEAH... SURE... BUT A REAL BATTLE DOESN'T COME WITH A RESET BUTTON.
WHAT'S HIS PROBLEM?
HE PUT HIMSELF ON THE LINE SO THAT WE COULD BECOME RESERVE AVENGERS*, AND TAKES OUR TRAINING VERY SERIOUSLY.
*AS SHOWN IN AVENGERS #4 --GLENN

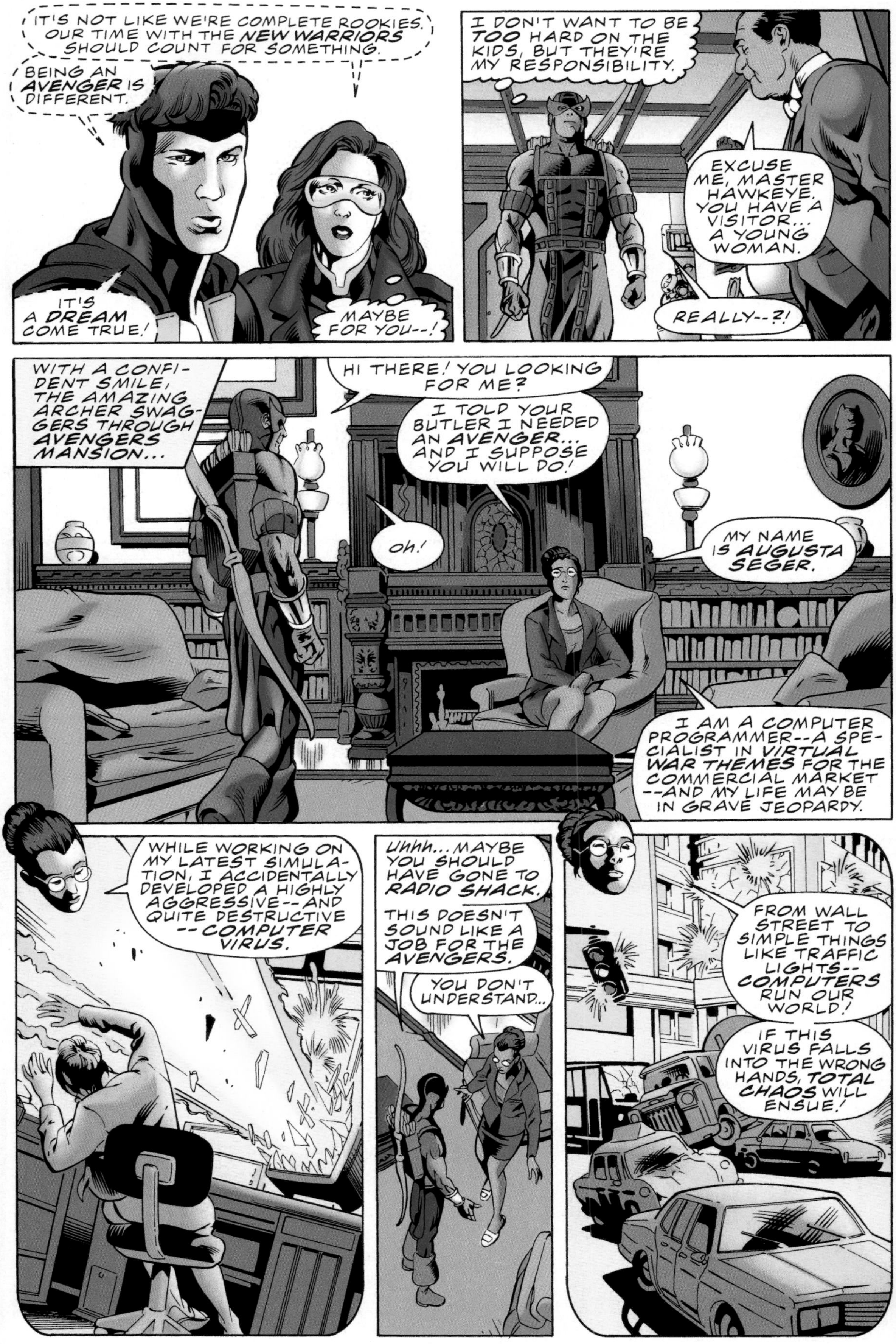
IT'S NOT LIKE WE'RE COMPLETE ROOKIES. OUR TIME WITH THE NEW WARRIORS SHOULD COUNT FOR SOMETHING.
BEING AN AVENGER IS DIFFERENT.
IT'S A DREAM COME TRUE!
MAYBE FOR YOU--!
I DON'T WANT TO BE TOO HARD ON THE KIDS, BUT THEY'RE MY RESPONSIBILITY.
EXCUSE ME, MASTER HAWKEYE. YOU HAVE A VISITOR... A YOUNG WOMAN.
REALLY--?!
WITH A CONFIDENT SMILE, THE AMAZING ARCHER SWAGGERS THROUGH AVENGERS MANSION...
HI THERE! YOU LOOKING FOR ME?
I TOLD YOUR BUTLER I NEEDED AN AVENGER... AND I SUPPOSE YOU WILL DO!
oh!
MY NAME IS AUGUSTA SEGER.
I AM A COMPUTER PROGRAMMER--A SPECIALIST IN VIRTUAL WAR THEMES FOR THE COMMERCIAL MARKET --AND MY LIFE MAY BE IN GRAVE JEOPARDY.
WHILE WORKING ON MY LATEST SIMULATION, I ACCIDENTALLY DEVELOPED A HIGHLY AGGRESSIVE--AND QUITE DESTRUCTIVE --COMPUTER VIRUS.
Unhh... MAYBE YOU SHOULD HAVE GONE TO RADIO SHACK.
THIS DOESN'T SOUND LIKE A JOB FOR THE AVENGERS.
YOU DON'T UNDERSTAND...
FROM WALL STREET TO SIMPLE THINGS LIKE TRAFFIC LIGHTS-- COMPUTERS RUN OUR WORLD!
IF THIS VIRUS FALLS INTO THE WRONG HANDS, TOTAL CHAOS WILL ENSUE!

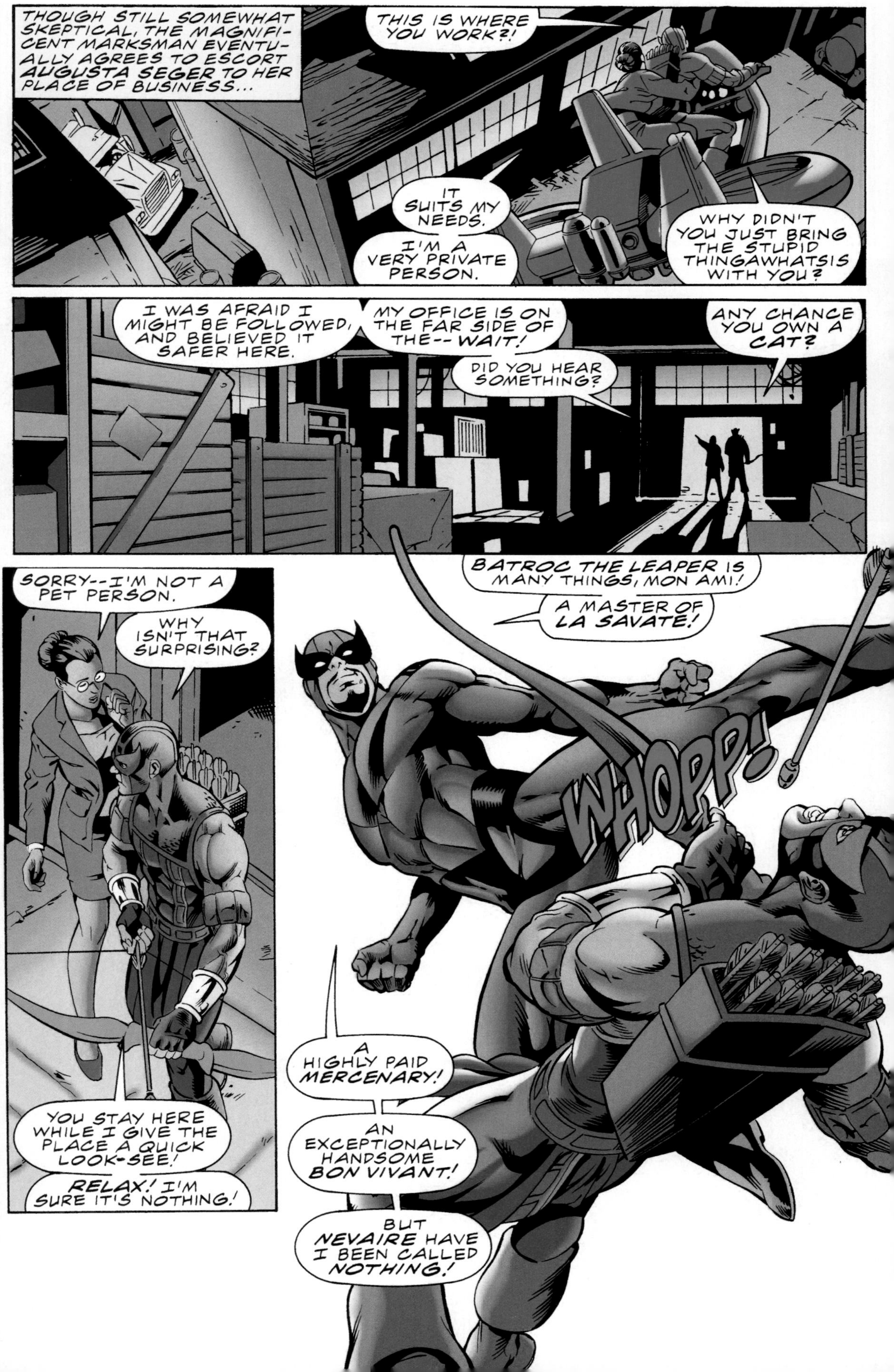
THOUGH STILL SOMEWHAT SKEPTICAL, THE MAGNIFICENT MARKSMAN EVENTUALLY AGREES TO ESCORT AUGUSTA SEGER TO HER PLACE OF BUSINESS...
THIS IS WHERE YOU WORK?!
IT SUITS MY NEEDS.
I'M A VERY PRIVATE PERSON.
WHY DIDN'T YOU JUST BRING THE STUPID THINGAWHATSIS WITH YOU?
I WAS AFRAID I MIGHT BE FOLLOWED, AND BELIEVED IT SAFER HERE.
MY OFFICE IS ON THE FAR SIDE OF THE--WAIT!
DID YOU HEAR SOMETHING?
ANY CHANCE YOU OWN A CAT?
SORRY--I'M NOT A PET PERSON.
WHY ISN'T THAT SURPRISING?
YOU STAY HERE WHILE I GIVE THE PLACE A QUICK LOOK-SEE!
RELAX! I'M SURE IT'S NOTHING!
BATROC THE LEAPER IS MANY THINGS, MON AMI!
A MASTER OF LA SAVATE!
WHOPP!
A HIGHLY PAID MERCENARY!
AN EXCEPTIONALLY HANDSOME BON VIVANT!
BUT NEVAIRE HAVE I BEEN CALLED NOTHING!

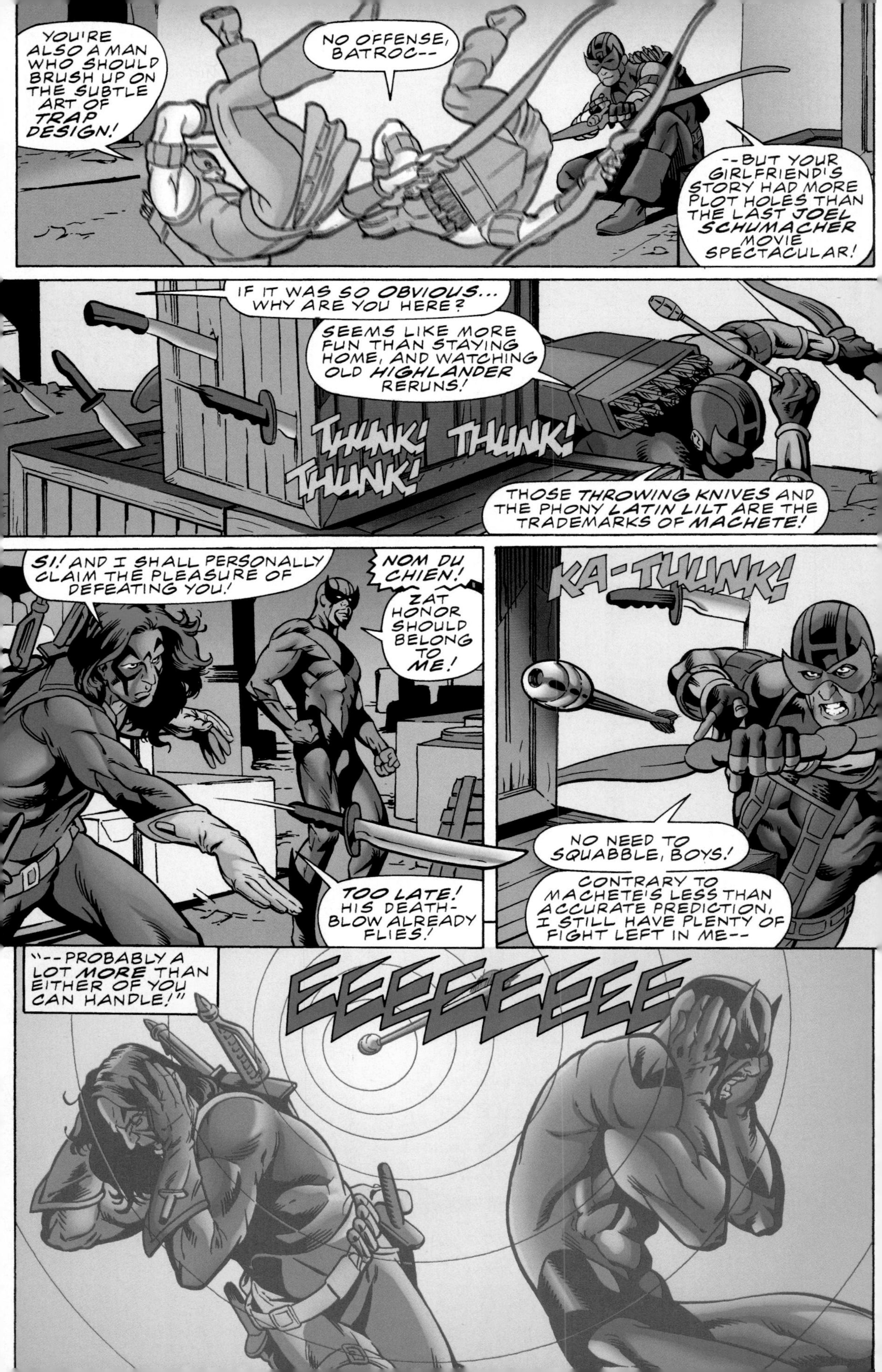
YOU'RE ALSO A MAN WHO SHOULD BRUSH UP ON THE SUBTLE ART OF TRAP DESIGN!
NO OFFENSE, BATROC--
--BUT YOUR GIRLFRIEND'S STORY HAD MORE PLOT HOLES THAN THE LAST JOEL SCHUMACHER MOVIE SPECTACULAR!
IF IT WAS SO OBVIOUS... WHY ARE YOU HERE?
SEEMS LIKE MORE FUN THAN STAYING HOME, AND WATCHING OLD HIGHLANDER RERUNS!
THUNK! THUNK! THUNK!
THOSE THROWING KNIVES AND THE PHONY LATIN LILT ARE THE TRADEMARKS OF MACHETE!
SI! AND I SHALL PERSONALLY CLAIM THE PLEASURE OF DEFEATING YOU!
NOM DU CHIEN!
ZAT HONOR SHOULD BELONG TO ME!
TOO LATE! HIS DEATH-BLOW ALREADY FLIES!
KA-THUNK!
NO NEED TO SQUABBLE, BOYS!
CONTRARY TO MACHETE'S LESS THAN ACCURATE PREDICTION, I STILL HAVE PLENTY OF FIGHT LEFT IN ME--
"--PROBABLY A LOT MORE THAN EITHER OF YOU CAN HANDLE!"
EEEEEEEEE

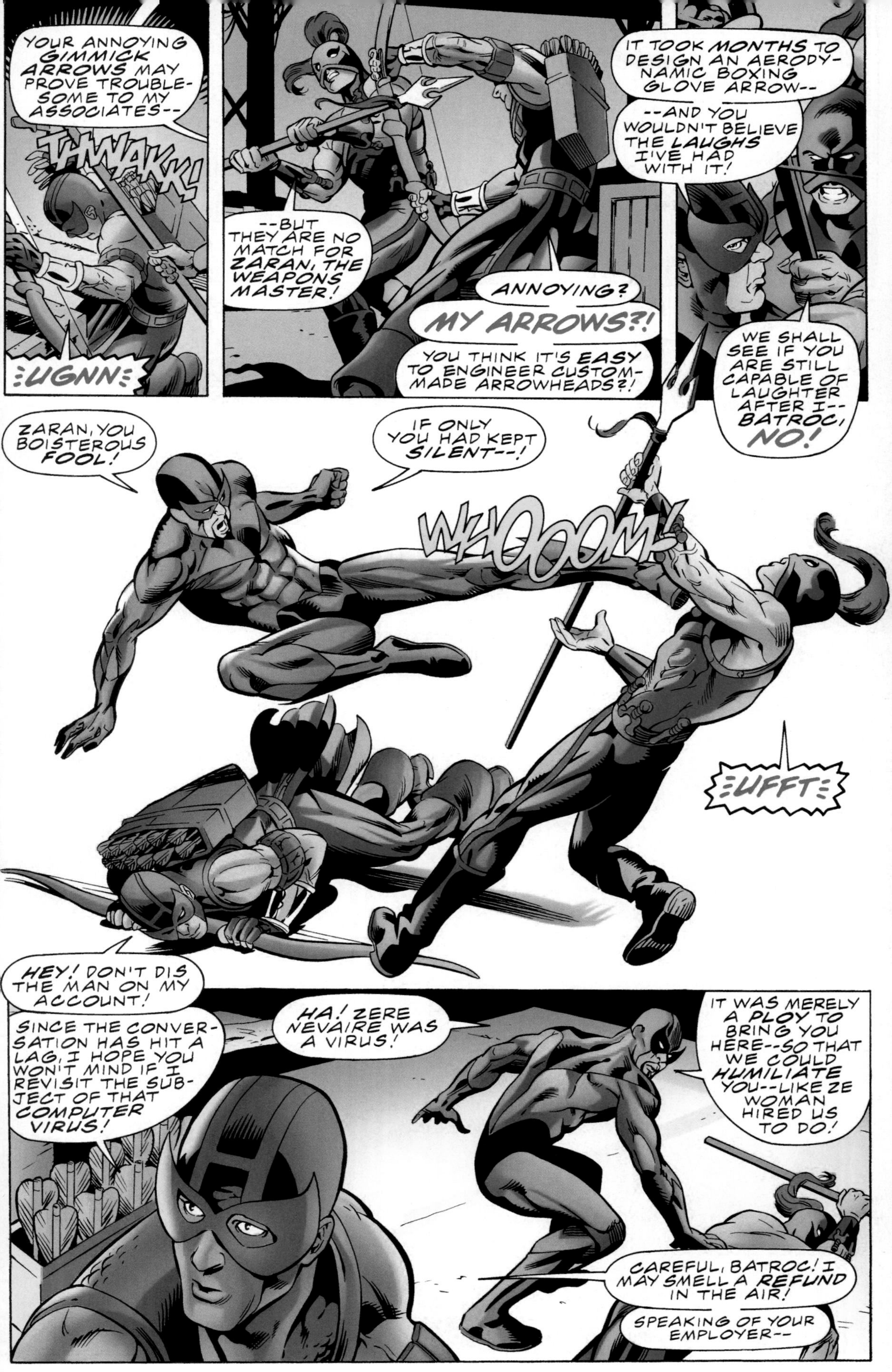
YOUR ANNOYING GIMMICK ARROWS MAY PROVE TROUBLESOME TO MY ASSOCIATES--
THWAKK!
UGNN
--BUT THEY ARE NO MATCH FOR ZARAN, THE WEAPONS MASTER!
ANNOYING? MY ARROWS?!
YOU THINK IT'S EASY TO ENGINEER CUSTOM-MADE ARROWHEADS?!
IT TOOK MONTHS TO DESIGN AN AERODYNAMIC BOXING GLOVE ARROW--
--AND YOU WOULDN'T BELIEVE THE LAUGHS I'VE HAD WITH IT!
WE SHALL SEE IF YOU ARE STILL CAPABLE OF LAUGHTER AFTER I-- BATROC, NO!
ZARAN, YOU BOISTEROUS FOOL!
IF ONLY YOU HAD KEPT SILENT--!
WHOOOM!
UFFT
HEY! DON'T DIS THE MAN ON MY ACCOUNT!
SINCE THE CONVERSATION HAS HIT A LAG, I HOPE YOU WON'T MIND IF I REVISIT THE SUBJECT OF THAT COMPUTER VIRUS!
HA! ZERE NEVAIRE WAS A VIRUS!
IT WAS MERELY A PLOY TO BRING YOU HERE--SO THAT WE COULD HUMILIATE YOU--LIKE ZE WOMAN HIRED US TO DO!
CAREFUL, BATROC! I MAY SMELL A REFUND IN THE AIR!
SPEAKING OF YOUR EMPLOYER--

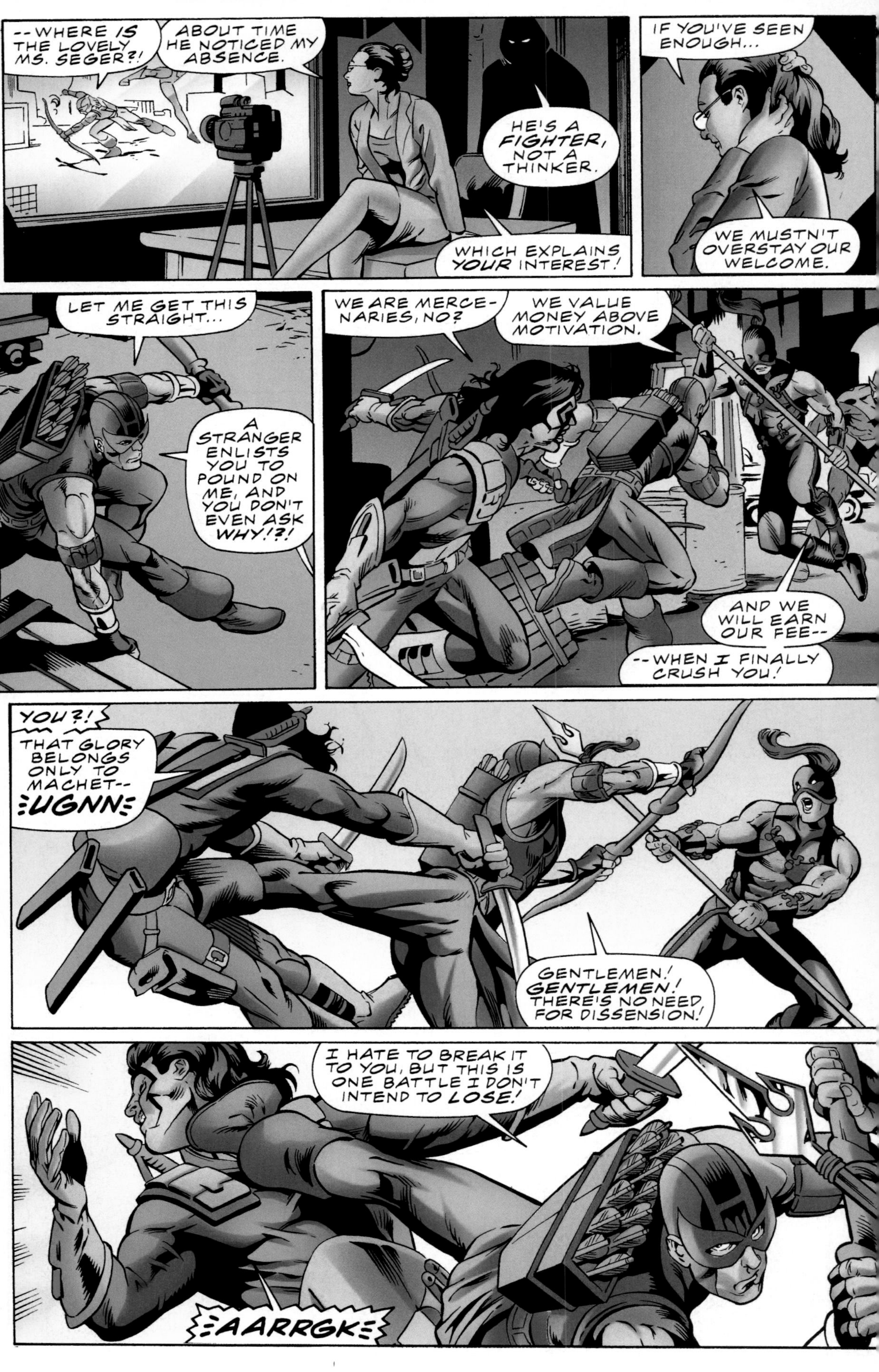
--WHERE *IS* THE LOVELY MS. SEGER?!
ABOUT TIME HE NOTICED MY ABSENCE.
HE'S A *FIGHTER*, NOT A THINKER.
WHICH EXPLAINS *YOUR* INTEREST!
IF YOU'VE SEEN ENOUGH...
WE MUSTN'T OVERSTAY OUR WELCOME.
LET ME GET THIS STRAIGHT...
A STRANGER ENLISTS YOU TO POUND ON ME, AND YOU DON'T EVEN ASK *WHY!?!*
WE ARE MERCENARIES, NO?
WE VALUE MONEY ABOVE MOTIVATION.
AND WE WILL EARN OUR FEE--
--WHEN *I* FINALLY CRUSH YOU!
YOU?!
THAT GLORY BELONGS ONLY TO MACHET--
UGNN
GENTLEMEN! *GENTLEMEN!* THERE'S NO NEED FOR DISSENSION!
I HATE TO BREAK IT TO YOU, BUT THIS IS ONE BATTLE I DON'T INTEND TO *LOSE!*
AARRGK

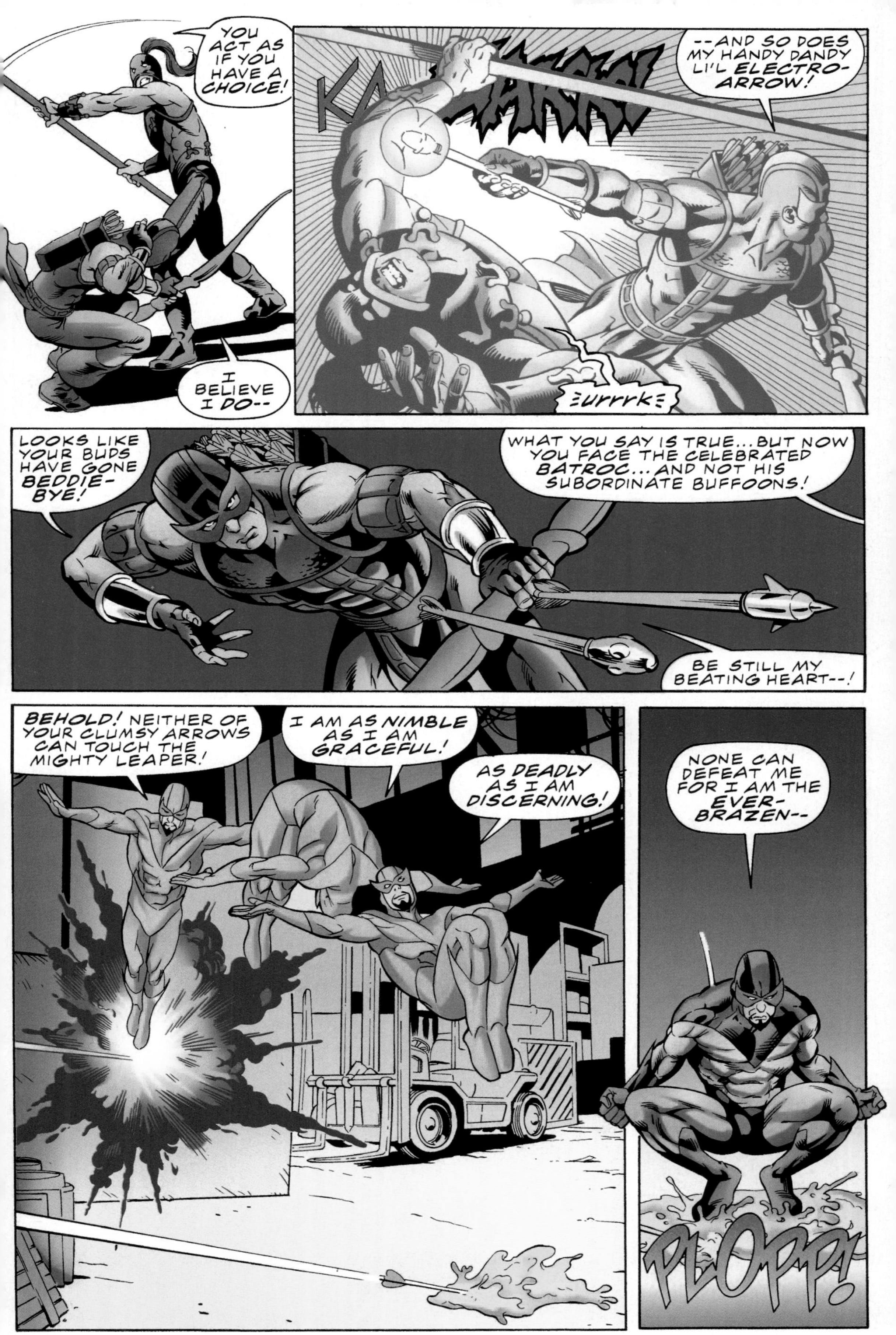
YOU ACT AS IF YOU HAVE A CHOICE!
I BELIEVE I DO--
KA-ZAKK!
--AND SO DOES MY HANDY DANDY LI'L ELECTRO-ARROW!
urrrk
LOOKS LIKE YOUR BUDS HAVE GONE BEDDIE-BYE!
WHAT YOU SAY IS TRUE... BUT NOW YOU FACE THE CELEBRATED BATROC... AND NOT HIS SUBORDINATE BUFFOONS!
BE STILL MY BEATING HEART--!
BEHOLD! NEITHER OF YOUR CLUMSY ARROWS CAN TOUCH THE MIGHTY LEAPER!
I AM AS NIMBLE AS I AM GRACEFUL!
AS DEADLY AS I AM DISCERNING!
NONE CAN DEFEAT ME FOR I AM THE EVER-BRAZEN--
PLOPP!

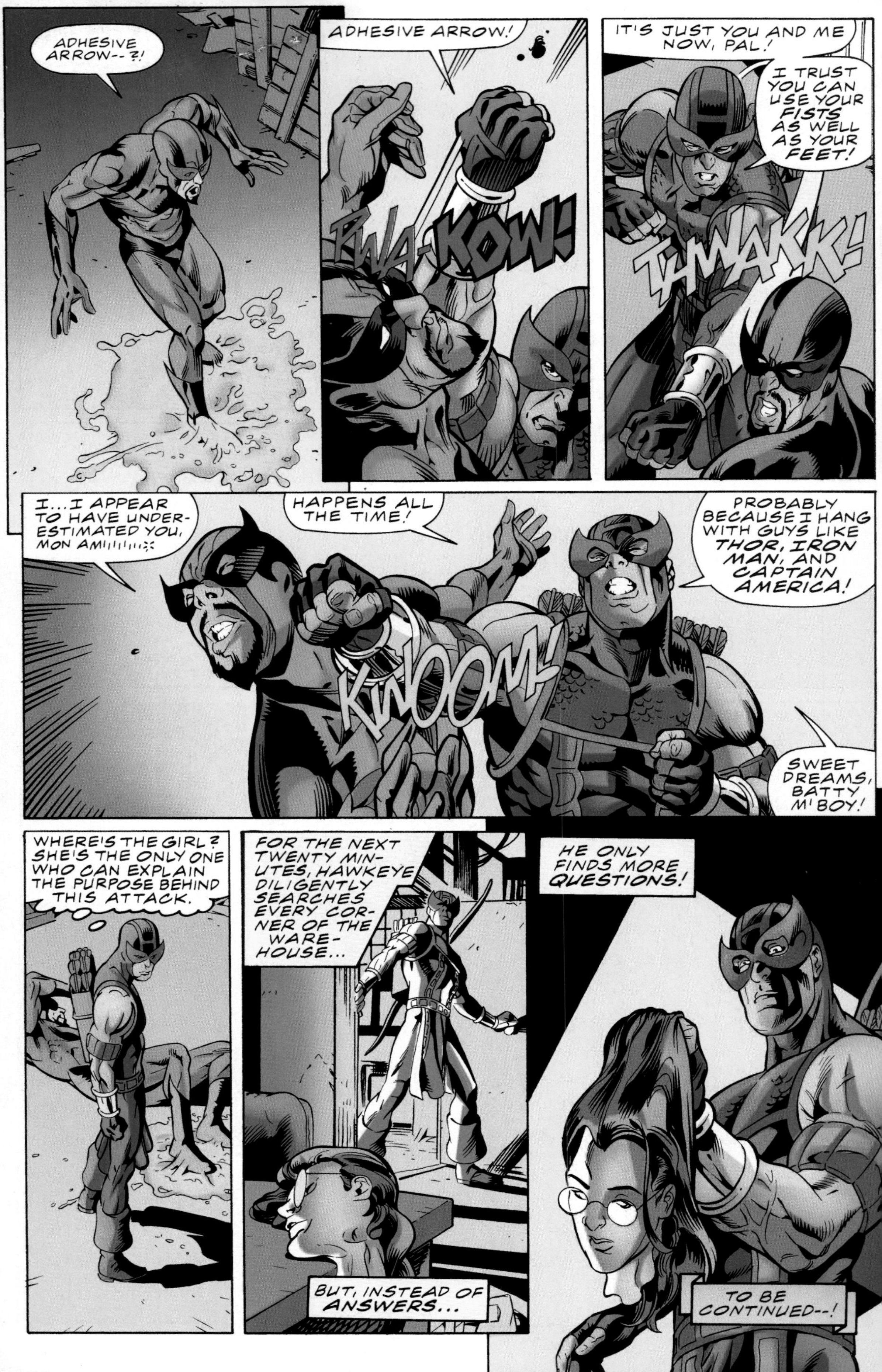
ADHESIVE ARROW-- ?!
ADHESIVE ARROW!
PWA-KOW!
IT'S JUST YOU AND ME NOW, PAL!
I TRUST YOU CAN USE YOUR FISTS AS WELL AS YOUR FEET!
THWAKK!
I...I APPEAR TO HAVE UNDER-ESTIMATED YOU, MON AMI...
HAPPENS ALL THE TIME!
PROBABLY BECAUSE I HANG WITH GUYS LIKE THOR, IRON MAN, AND CAPTAIN AMERICA!
KWOOM!
SWEET DREAMS, BATTY M'BOY!
WHERE'S THE GIRL? SHE'S THE ONLY ONE WHO CAN EXPLAIN THE PURPOSE BEHIND THIS ATTACK.
FOR THE NEXT TWENTY MINUTES, HAWKEYE DILIGENTLY SEARCHES EVERY CORNER OF THE WAREHOUSE...
BUT, INSTEAD OF ANSWERS...
HE ONLY FINDS MORE QUESTIONS!
TO BE CONTINUED--!

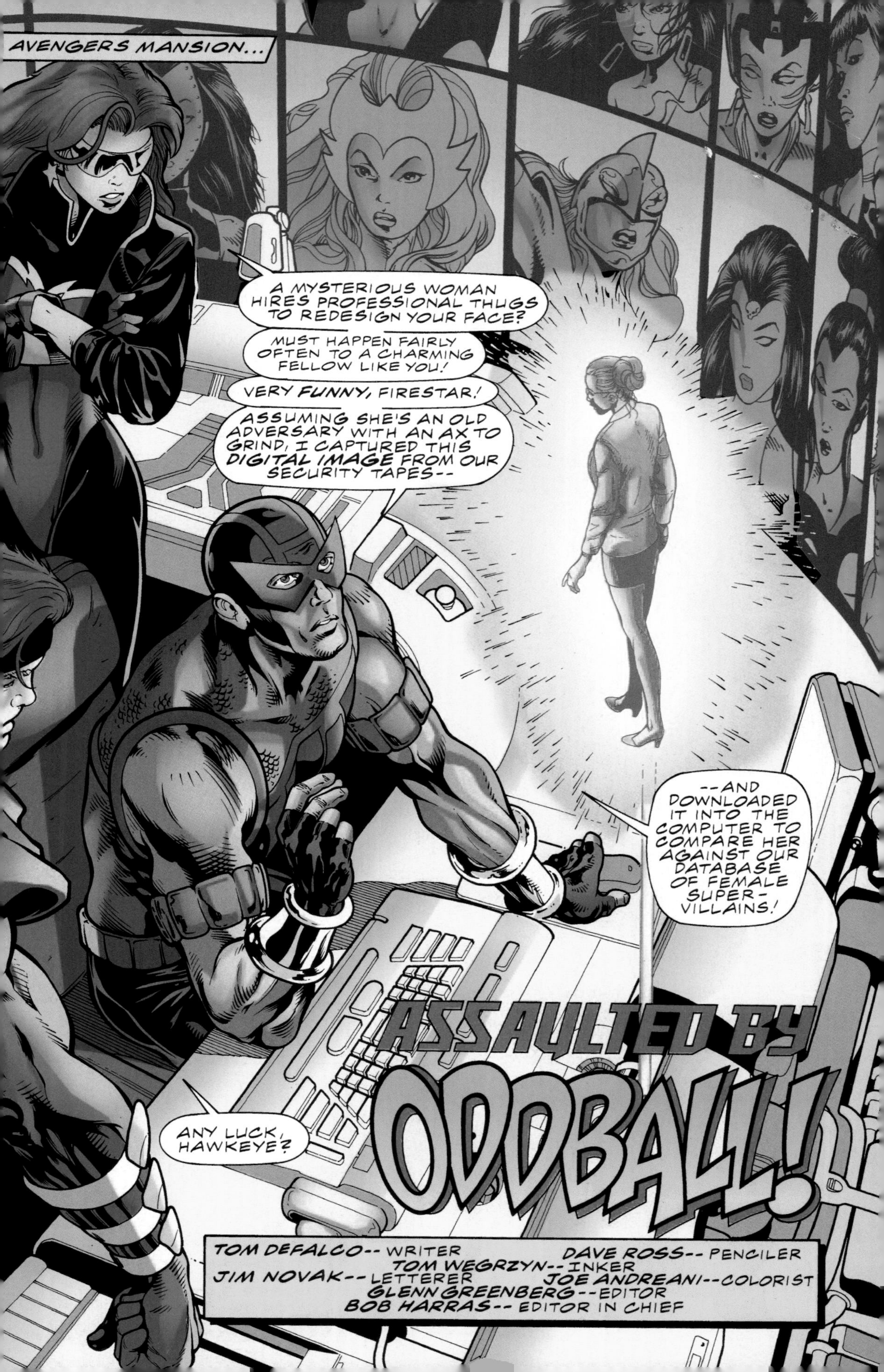
AVENGERS MANSION...
A MYSTERIOUS WOMAN HIRES PROFESSIONAL THUGS TO REDESIGN YOUR FACE?
MUST HAPPEN FAIRLY OFTEN TO A CHARMING FELLOW LIKE YOU!
VERY FUNNY, FIRESTAR!
ASSUMING SHE'S AN OLD ADVERSARY WITH AN AX TO GRIND, I CAPTURED THIS DIGITAL IMAGE FROM OUR SECURITY TAPES--
--AND DOWNLOADED IT INTO THE COMPUTER TO COMPARE HER AGAINST OUR DATABASE OF FEMALE SUPER-VILLAINS!
ANY LUCK, HAWKEYE?
ASSAULTED BY ODDBALL!
TOM DEFALCO-- WRITER
DAVE ROSS-- PENCILER
TOM WEGRZYN-- INKER
JIM NOVAK-- LETTERER
JOE ANDREANI--COLORIST
GLENN GREENBERG--EDITOR
BOB HARRAS-- EDITOR IN CHIEF

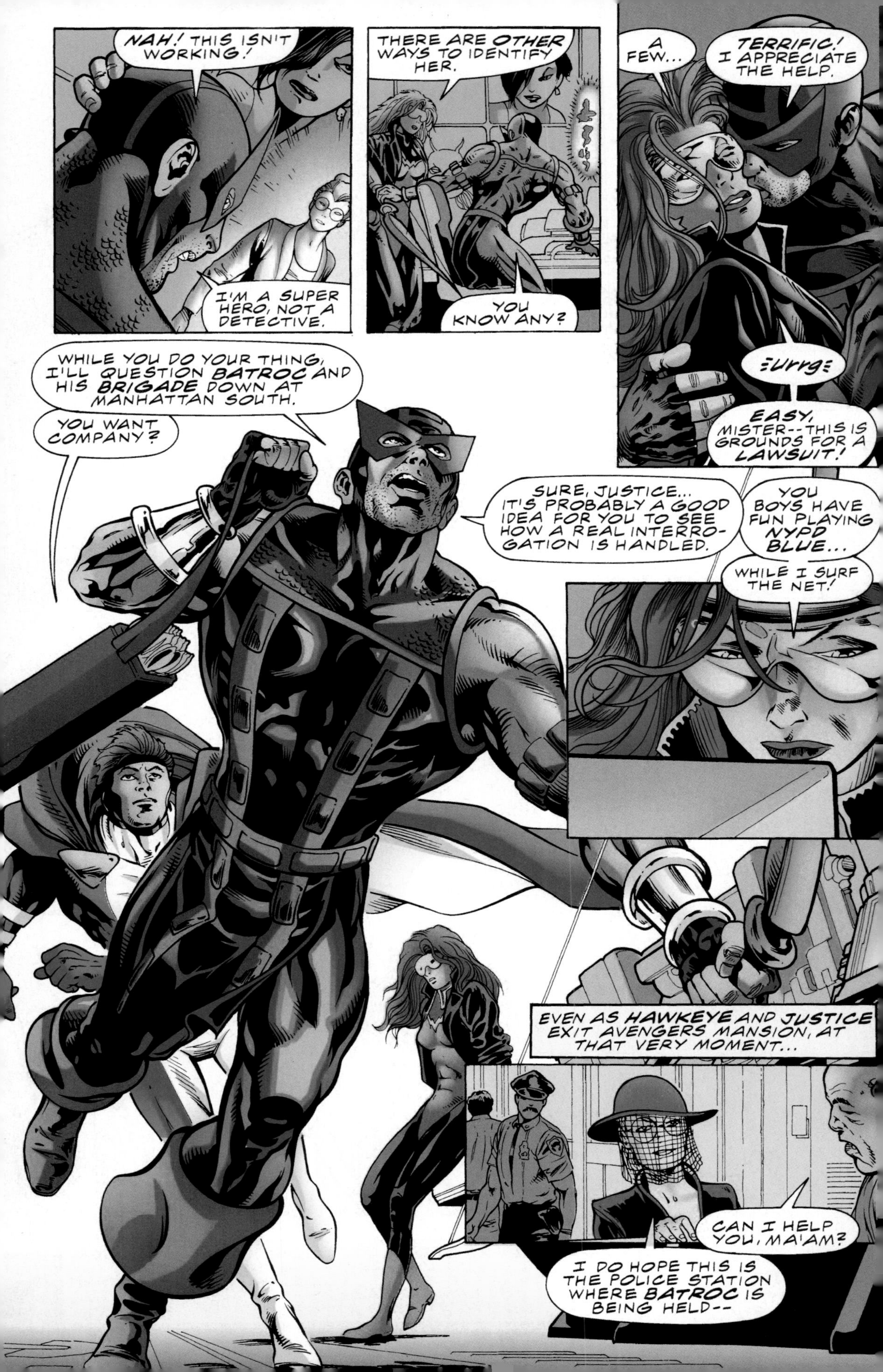
NAH! THIS ISN'T WORKING!
I'M A SUPER HERO, NOT A DETECTIVE.
THERE ARE OTHER WAYS TO IDENTIFY HER.
YOU KNOW ANY?
A FEW...
TERRIFIC! I APPRECIATE THE HELP.
URRG
EASY, MISTER--THIS IS GROUNDS FOR A LAWSUIT!
WHILE YOU DO YOUR THING, I'LL QUESTION BATROC AND HIS BRIGADE DOWN AT MANHATTAN SOUTH.
YOU WANT COMPANY?
SURE, JUSTICE... IT'S PROBABLY A GOOD IDEA FOR YOU TO SEE HOW A REAL INTERRO-GATION IS HANDLED.
YOU BOYS HAVE FUN PLAYING NYPD BLUE...
WHILE I SURF THE NET!
EVEN AS HAWKEYE AND JUSTICE EXIT AVENGERS MANSION, AT THAT VERY MOMENT...
CAN I HELP YOU, MA'AM?
I DO HOPE THIS IS THE POLICE STATION WHERE BATROC IS BEING HELD--

PWOOOM!

--OTHERWISE I'VE GONE TO A LOT OF TROUBLE FOR NOTHING!

THE AREA IS SECURE, GENTLEMEN.

YOU MAY NOW REMOVE YOUR GAS MASKS--AND CLEAR THE FLOOR OF UNCONSCIOUS BODIES.

YOU SURE WE HAVE ENOUGH TIME TO COMPLETE OUR MISSION BEFORE THESE COPS WAKE UP?

ABSOLUTELY! NOW, TAKE ME TO BATROC--!

AHHHHH, MA'MSELLE ALBINO--! EVERYTHING APPEARS TO BE GOING ACCORDING TO ZE PLAN.

OF COURSE!

AND YOU CAN DROP THE MA'MSELLE. I PREFER TO BE KNOWN ONLY AS THE ALBINO!

WHATEVER YOU WISH, MA PETITE... SO LONG AS I AM GRANTED ANOTHER OPPORTUNITY AT HAWKEYE!

THAT ISN'T IN THE CARDS, BATROC. YOUR PART IS DONE.

TAKE YOUR MEN AND GO!

IT IS UNTHINKABLE TO LEAVE WITHOUT COMPLETING OUR TASK!

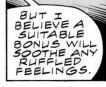

I UNDERSTAND YOUR NEED FOR REVENGE.

BUT I BELIEVE A SUITABLE BONUS WILL SOOTHE ANY RUFFLED FEELINGS.

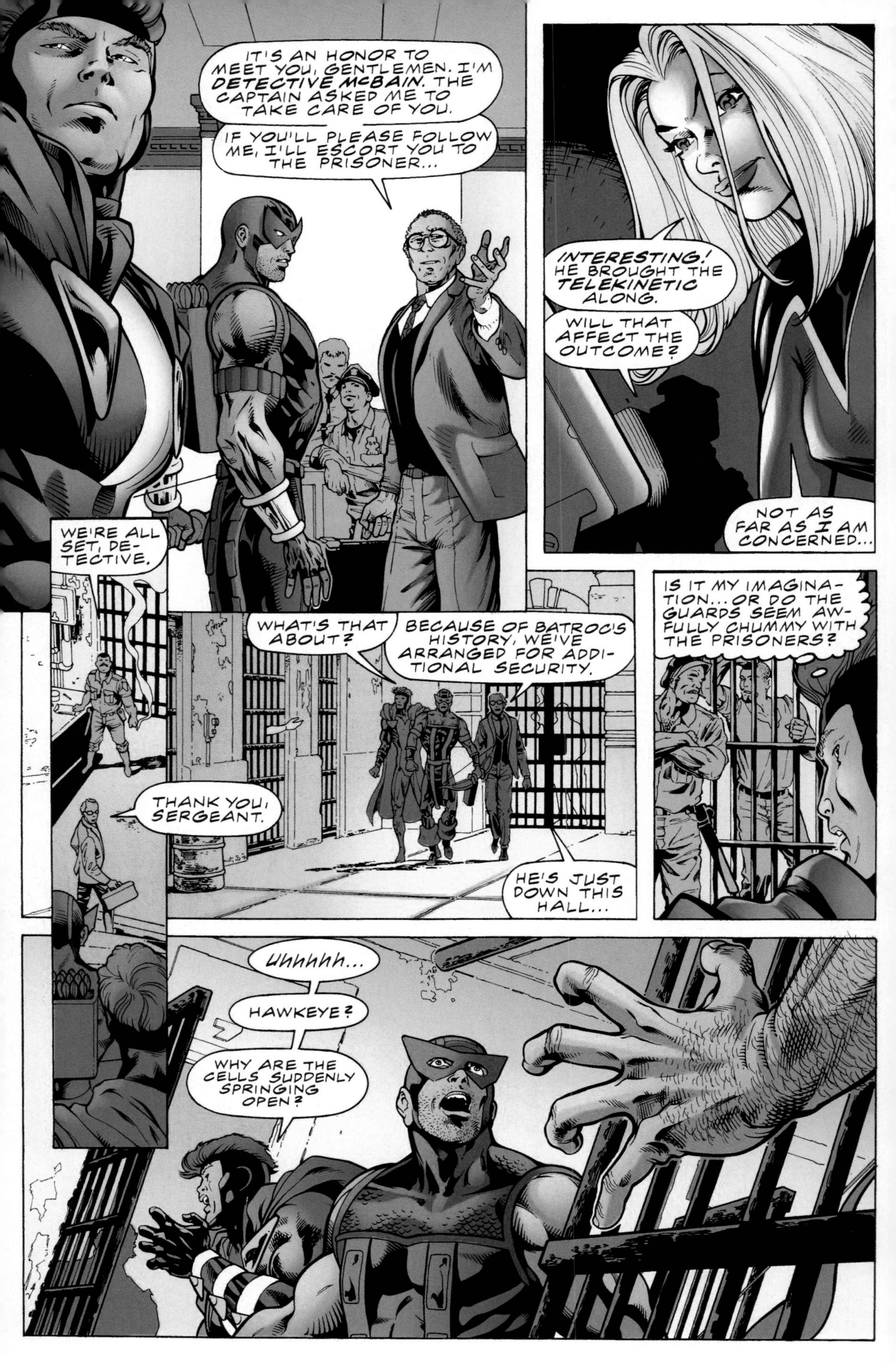
IT'S AN HONOR TO MEET YOU, GENTLEMEN. I'M DETECTIVE McBAIN. THE CAPTAIN ASKED ME TO TAKE CARE OF YOU.
IF YOU'LL PLEASE FOLLOW ME, I'LL ESCORT YOU TO THE PRISONER...
INTERESTING! HE BROUGHT THE TELEKINETIC ALONG.
WILL THAT AFFECT THE OUTCOME?
NOT AS FAR AS I AM CONCERNED...
WE'RE ALL SET, DETECTIVE.
THANK YOU, SERGEANT.
WHAT'S THAT ABOUT?
BECAUSE OF BATROC'S HISTORY, WE'VE ARRANGED FOR ADDITIONAL SECURITY.
HE'S JUST DOWN THIS HALL...
IS IT MY IMAGINATION... OR DO THE GUARDS SEEM AWFULLY CHUMMY WITH THE PRISONERS?
Uhhhhh...
HAWKEYE?
WHY ARE THE CELLS SUDDENLY SPRINGING OPEN?

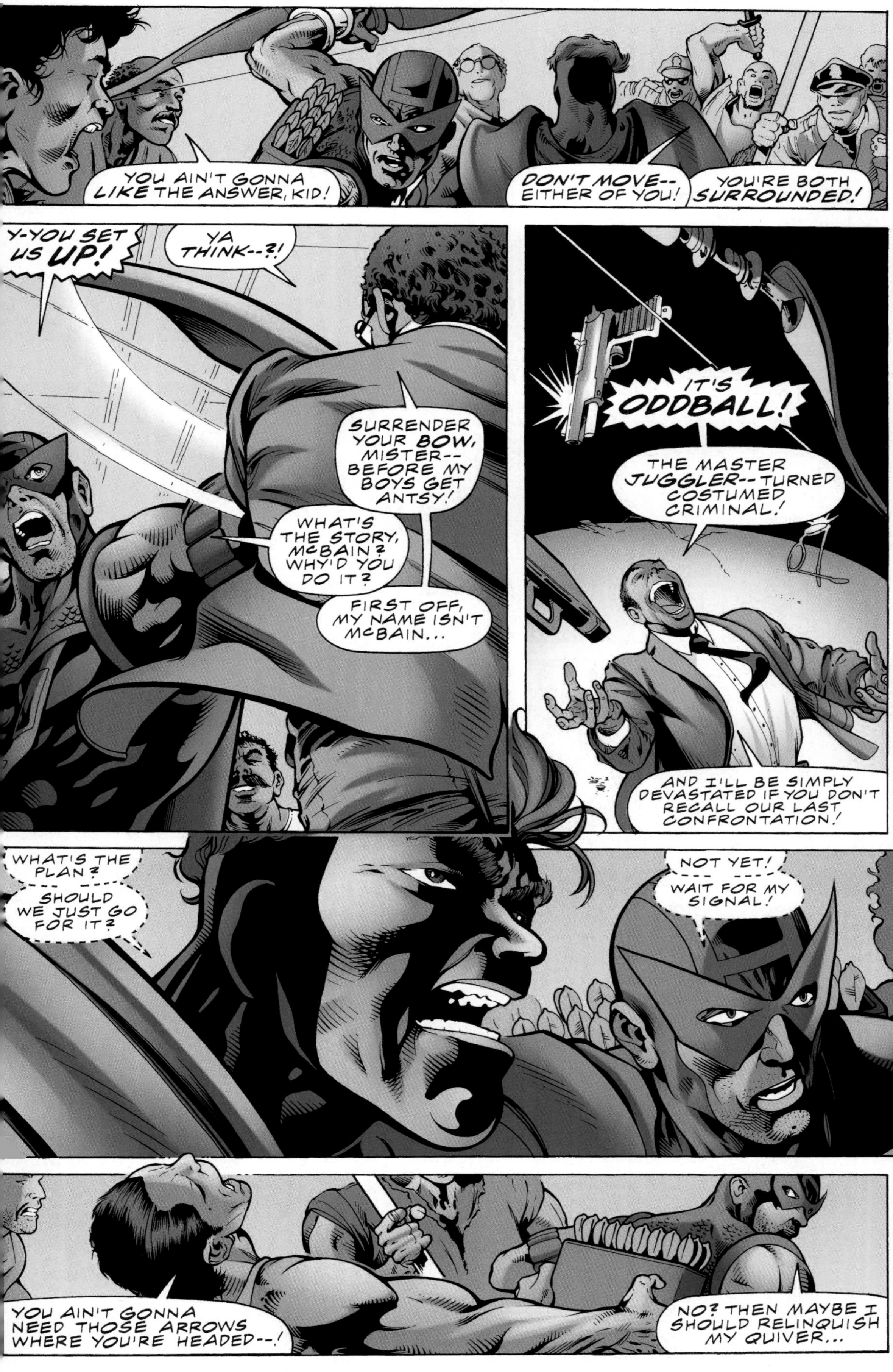
YOU AIN'T GONNA LIKE THE ANSWER, KID!
DON'T MOVE-- EITHER OF YOU!
YOU'RE BOTH SURROUNDED!
Y-YOU SET US UP!
YA THINK--?!
SURRENDER YOUR BOW, MISTER-- BEFORE MY BOYS GET ANTSY!
WHAT'S THE STORY, McBAIN? WHY'D YOU DO IT?
FIRST OFF, MY NAME ISN'T McBAIN...
IT'S ODDBALL!
THE MASTER JUGGLER-- TURNED COSTUMED CRIMINAL!
AND I'LL BE SIMPLY DEVASTATED IF YOU DON'T RECALL OUR LAST CONFRONTATION!
WHAT'S THE PLAN?
SHOULD WE JUST GO FOR IT?
NOT YET!
WAIT FOR MY SIGNAL!
YOU AIN'T GONNA NEED THOSE ARROWS WHERE YOU'RE HEADED--!
NO? THEN MAYBE I SHOULD RELINQUISH MY QUIVER...

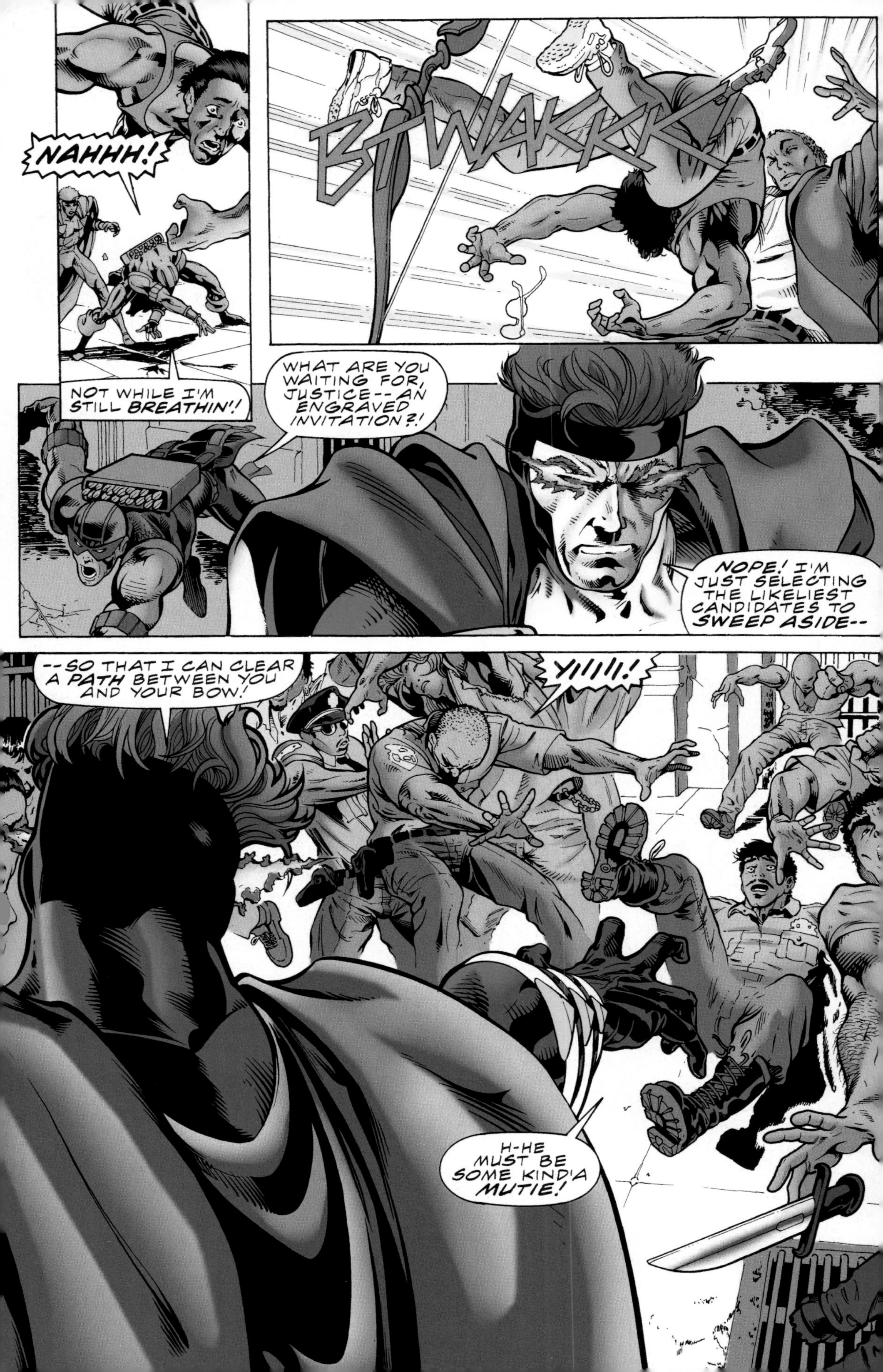
NAHHH!
NOT WHILE I'M STILL BREATHIN'!
BTWAKKK!
WHAT ARE YOU WAITING FOR, JUSTICE-- AN ENGRAVED INVITATION?!
NOPE! I'M JUST SELECTING THE LIKELIEST CANDIDATES TO SWEEP ASIDE--
--SO THAT I CAN CLEAR A PATH BETWEEN YOU AND YOUR BOW!
YIIIII!
H-HE MUST BE SOME KIND'A MUTIE!

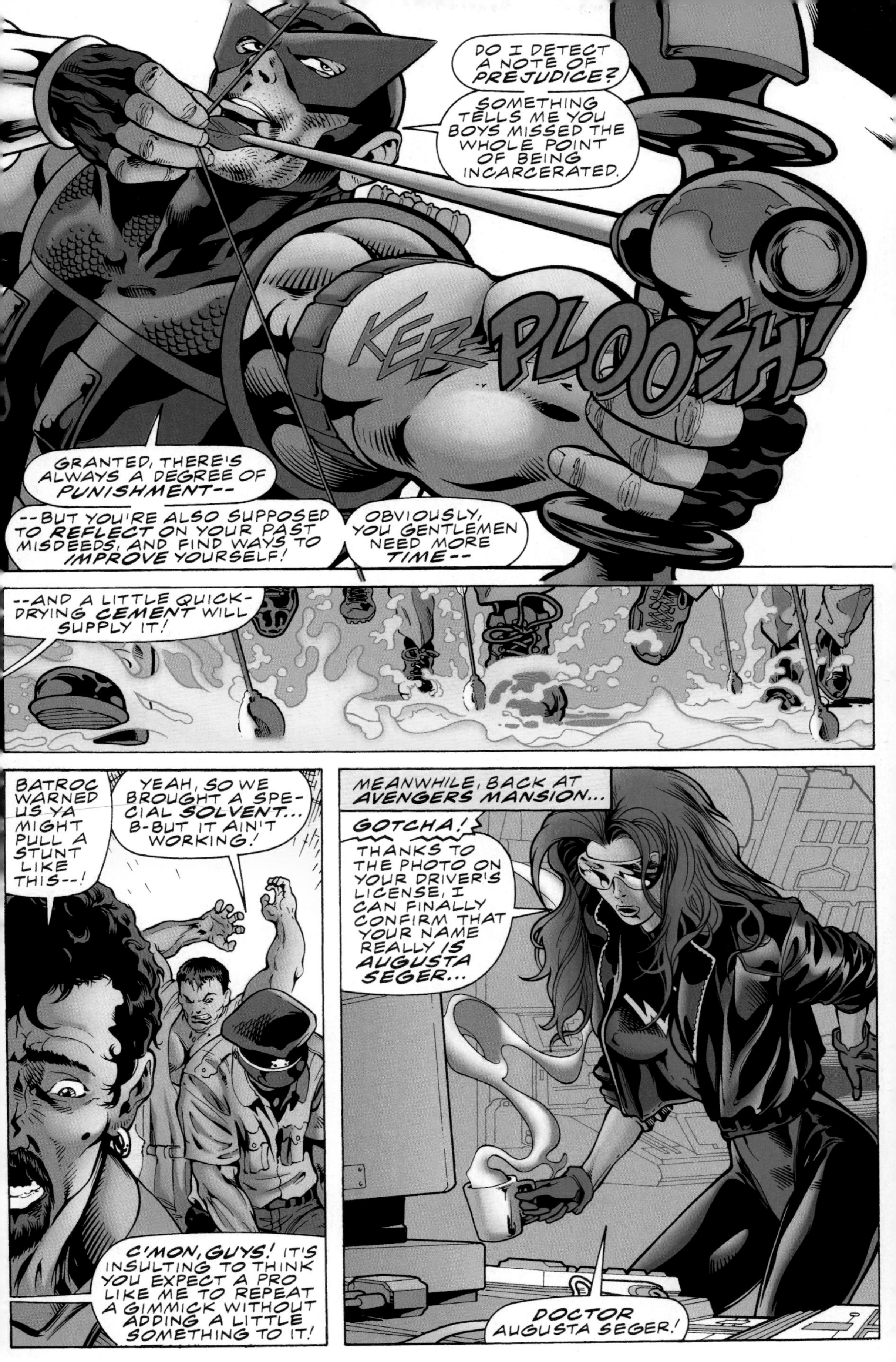
DO I DETECT A NOTE OF PREJUDICE?
SOMETHING TELLS ME YOU BOYS MISSED THE WHOLE POINT OF BEING INCARCERATED.
KER-PLOOSH!
GRANTED, THERE'S ALWAYS A DEGREE OF PUNISHMENT--
--BUT YOU'RE ALSO SUPPOSED TO REFLECT ON YOUR PAST MISDEEDS, AND FIND WAYS TO IMPROVE YOURSELF!
OBVIOUSLY, YOU GENTLEMEN NEED MORE TIME--
--AND A LITTLE QUICK-DRYING CEMENT WILL SUPPLY IT!
BATROC WARNED US YA MIGHT PULL A STUNT LIKE THIS--!
YEAH, SO WE BROUGHT A SPECIAL SOLVENT... B-BUT IT AIN'T WORKING!
C'MON, GUYS! IT'S INSULTING TO THINK YOU EXPECT A PRO LIKE ME TO REPEAT A GIMMICK WITHOUT ADDING A LITTLE SOMETHING TO IT!
MEANWHILE, BACK AT AVENGERS MANSION...
GOTCHA!
THANKS TO THE PHOTO ON YOUR DRIVER'S LICENSE, I CAN FINALLY CONFIRM THAT YOUR NAME REALLY IS AUGUSTA SEGER...
DOCTOR AUGUSTA SEGER!

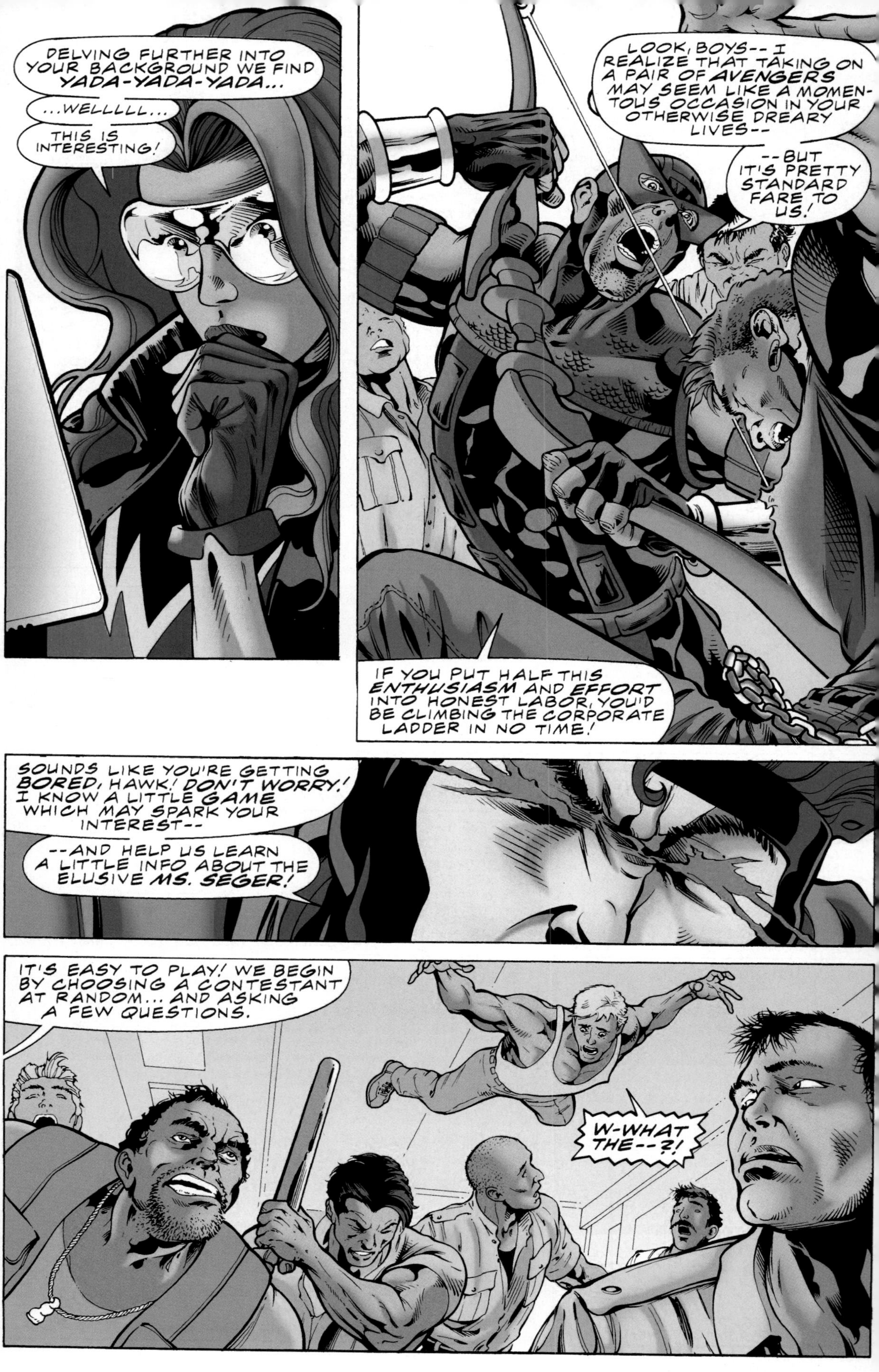
DELVING FURTHER INTO YOUR BACKGROUND WE FIND YADA-YADA-YADA...
...WELLLLL...
THIS IS INTERESTING!
LOOK, BOYS-- I REALIZE THAT TAKING ON A PAIR OF AVENGERS MAY SEEM LIKE A MOMENTOUS OCCASION IN YOUR OTHERWISE DREARY LIVES--
--BUT IT'S PRETTY STANDARD FARE TO US!
IF YOU PUT HALF THIS ENTHUSIASM AND EFFORT INTO HONEST LABOR, YOU'D BE CLIMBING THE CORPORATE LADDER IN NO TIME!
SOUNDS LIKE YOU'RE GETTING BORED, HAWK! DON'T WORRY! I KNOW A LITTLE GAME WHICH MAY SPARK YOUR INTEREST--
--AND HELP US LEARN A LITTLE INFO ABOUT THE ELUSIVE MS. SEGER!
IT'S EASY TO PLAY! WE BEGIN BY CHOOSING A CONTESTANT AT RANDOM... AND ASKING A FEW QUESTIONS.
W-WHAT THE--?!

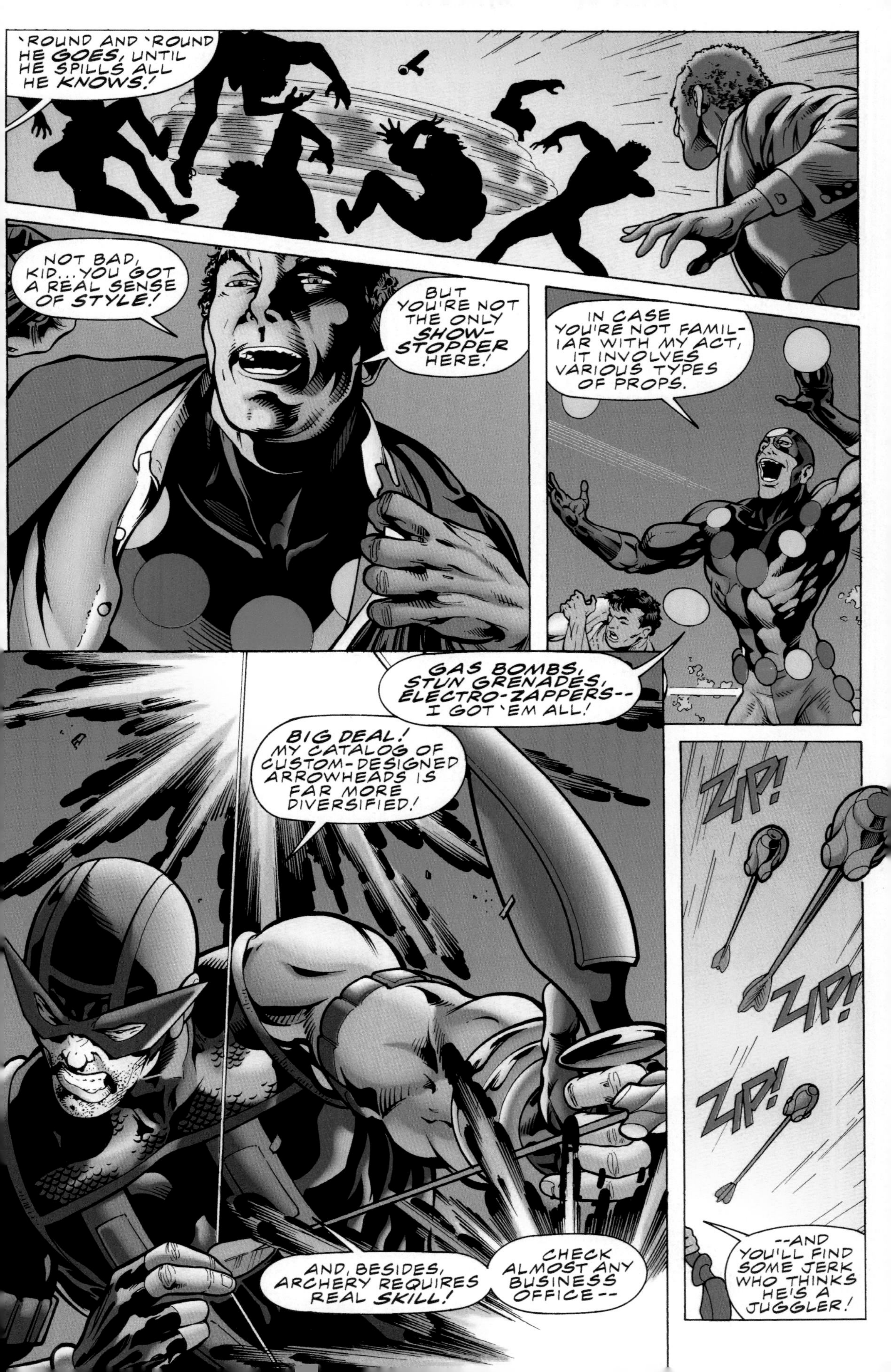
'ROUND AND 'ROUND HE GOES, UNTIL HE SPILLS ALL HE KNOWS!
NOT BAD, KID... YOU GOT A REAL SENSE OF STYLE!
BUT YOU'RE NOT THE ONLY SHOW-STOPPER HERE!
IN CASE YOU'RE NOT FAMILIAR WITH MY ACT, IT INVOLVES VARIOUS TYPES OF PROPS.
GAS BOMBS, STUN GRENADES, ELECTRO-ZAPPERS-- I GOT 'EM ALL!
BIG DEAL! MY CATALOG OF CUSTOM-DESIGNED ARROWHEADS IS FAR MORE DIVERSIFIED!
AND, BESIDES, ARCHERY REQUIRES REAL SKILL!
CHECK ALMOST ANY BUSINESS OFFICE--
ZIP!
ZIP!
ZIP!
--AND YOU'LL FIND SOME JERK WHO THINKS HE'S A JUGGLER!

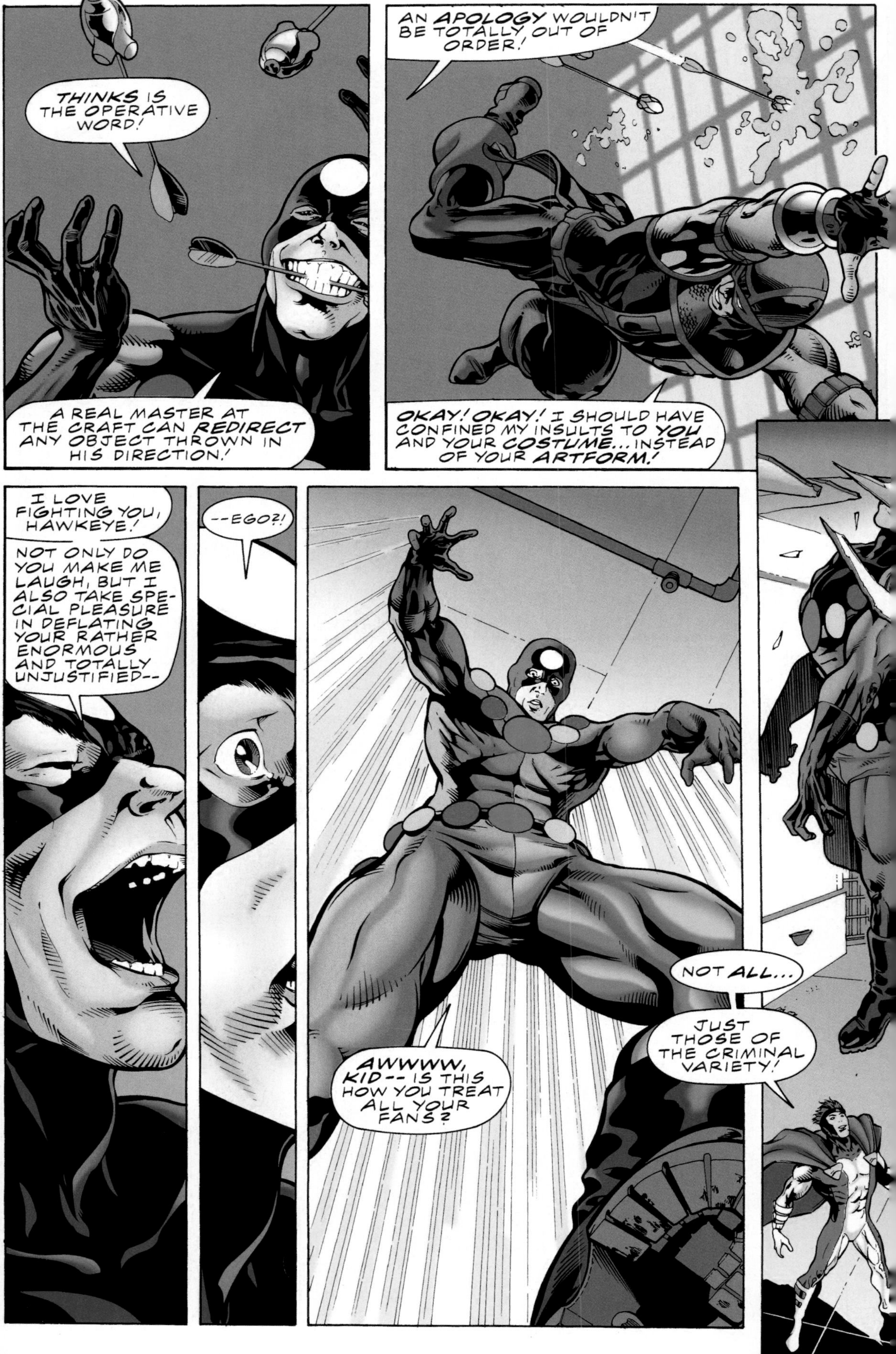
THINKS IS THE OPERATIVE WORD!
A REAL MASTER AT THE CRAFT CAN REDIRECT ANY OBJECT THROWN IN HIS DIRECTION!
AN APOLOGY WOULDN'T BE TOTALLY OUT OF ORDER!
OKAY! OKAY! I SHOULD HAVE CONFINED MY INSULTS TO YOU AND YOUR COSTUME... INSTEAD OF YOUR ARTFORM!
I LOVE FIGHTING YOU, HAWKEYE!
NOT ONLY DO YOU MAKE ME LAUGH, BUT I ALSO TAKE SPECIAL PLEASURE IN DEFLATING YOUR RATHER ENORMOUS AND TOTALLY UNJUSTIFIED--
--EGO?!
AWWWW, KID-- IS THIS HOW YOU TREAT ALL YOUR FANS?
NOT ALL...
JUST THOSE OF THE CRIMINAL VARIETY!

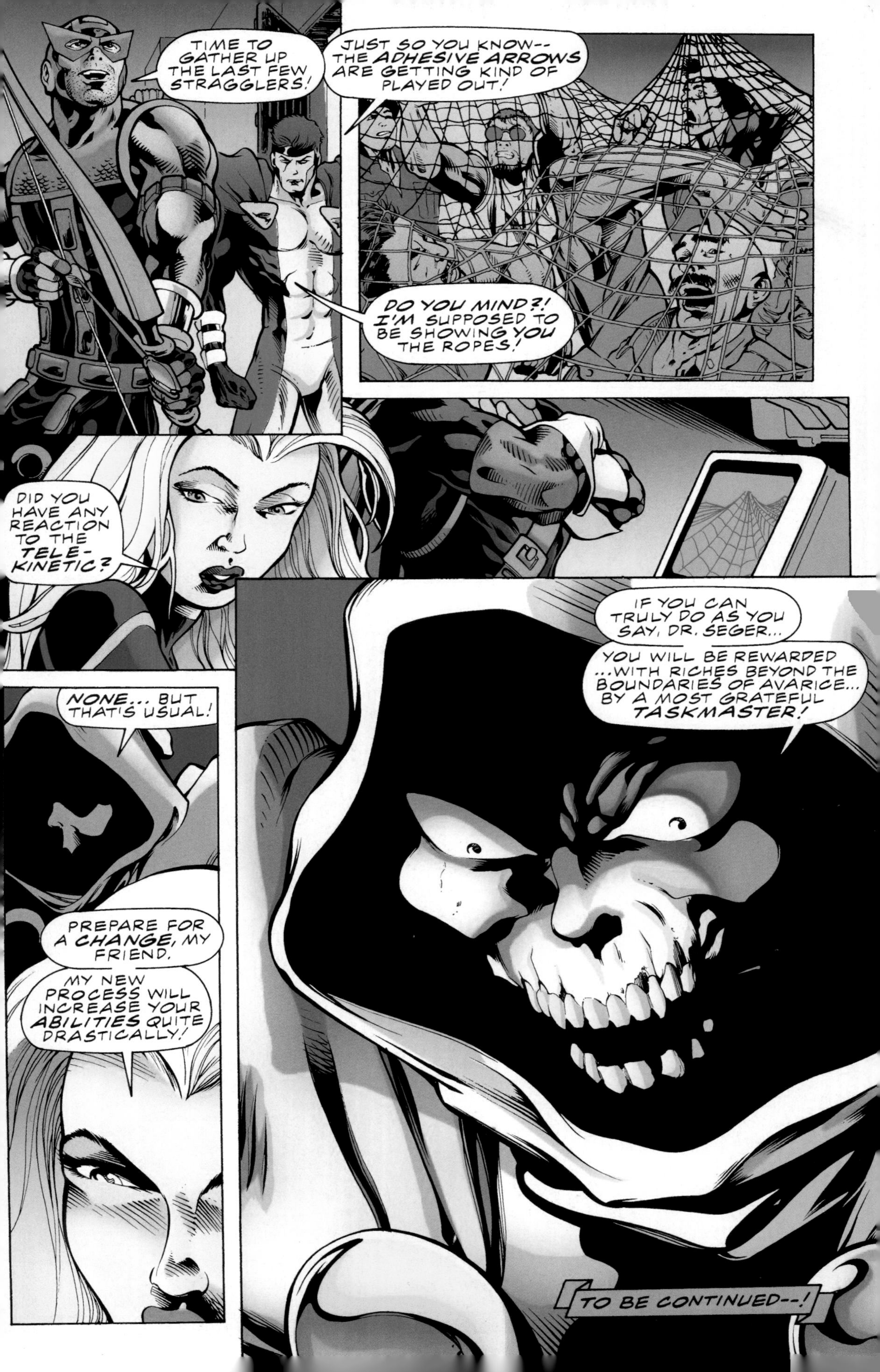
TIME TO GATHER UP THE LAST FEW STRAGGLERS!
JUST SO YOU KNOW-- THE ADHESIVE ARROWS ARE GETTING KIND OF PLAYED OUT!
DO YOU MIND?! I'M SUPPOSED TO BE SHOWING YOU THE ROPES!
DID YOU HAVE ANY REACTION TO THE TELE-KINETIC?
NONE... BUT THAT'S USUAL!
PREPARE FOR A CHANGE, MY FRIEND.
MY NEW PROCESS WILL INCREASE YOUR ABILITIES QUITE DRASTICALLY!
IF YOU CAN TRULY DO AS YOU SAY, DR. SEGER...
YOU WILL BE REWARDED ...WITH RICHES BEYOND THE BOUNDARIES OF AVARICE... BY A MOST GRATEFUL TASKMASTER!
TO BE CONTINUED--!

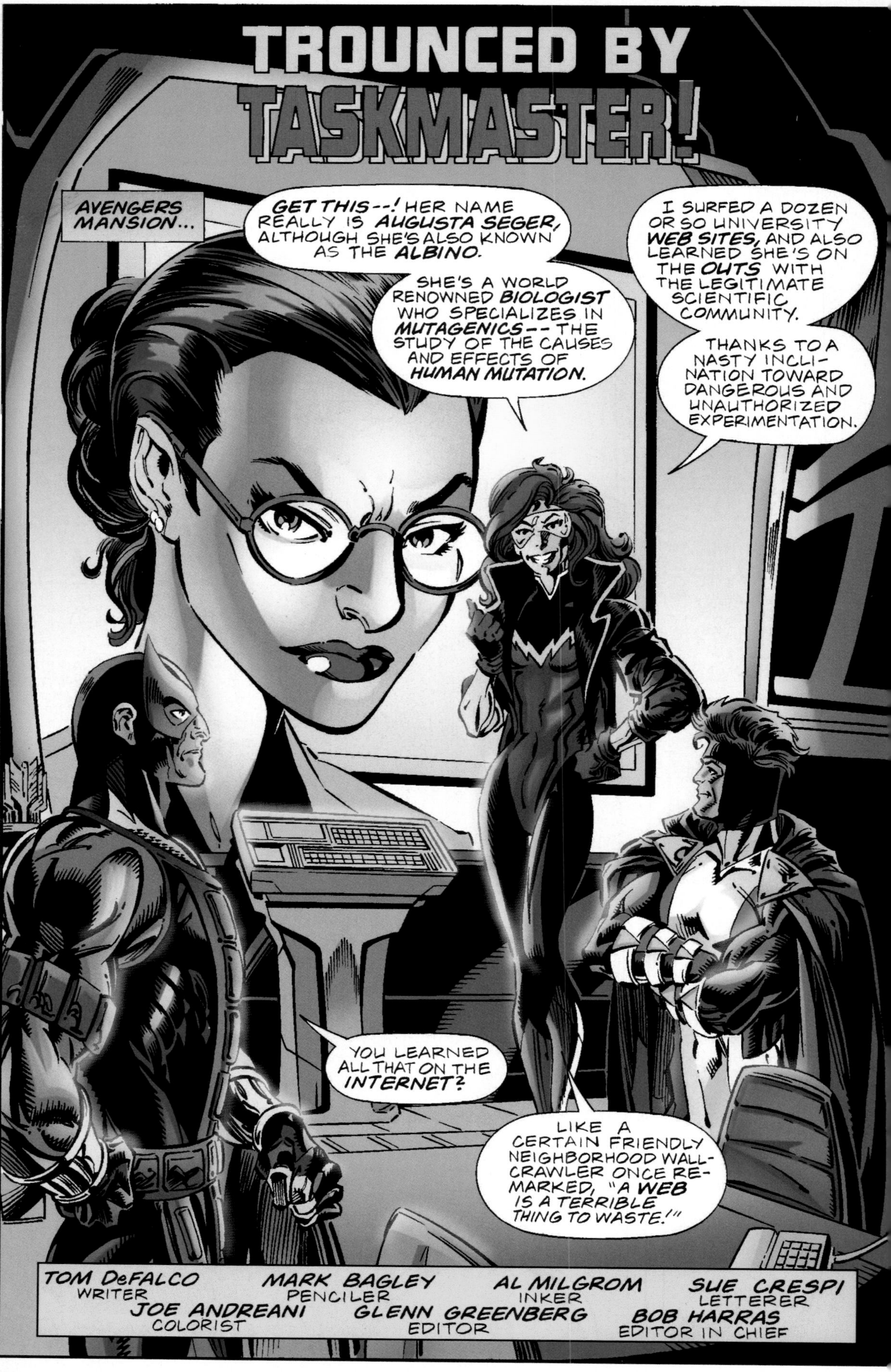
TROUNCED BY TASKMASTER!
AVENGERS MANSION...
GET THIS--! HER NAME REALLY IS AUGUSTA SEGER, ALTHOUGH SHE'S ALSO KNOWN AS THE ALBINO.
SHE'S A WORLD RENOWNED BIOLOGIST WHO SPECIALIZES IN MUTAGENICS-- THE STUDY OF THE CAUSES AND EFFECTS OF HUMAN MUTATION.
I SURFED A DOZEN OR SO UNIVERSITY WEB SITES, AND ALSO LEARNED SHE'S ON THE OUTS WITH THE LEGITIMATE SCIENTIFIC COMMUNITY.
THANKS TO A NASTY INCLI-NATION TOWARD DANGEROUS AND UNAUTHORIZED EXPERIMENTATION.
YOU LEARNED ALL THAT ON THE INTERNET?
LIKE A CERTAIN FRIENDLY NEIGHBORHOOD WALL-CRAWLER ONCE RE-MARKED, "A WEB IS A TERRIBLE THING TO WASTE!"
TOM DeFALCO WRITER
MARK BAGLEY PENCILER
AL MILGROM INKER
SUE CRESPI LETTERER
JOE ANDREANI COLORIST
GLENN GREENBERG EDITOR
BOB HARRAS EDITOR IN CHIEF

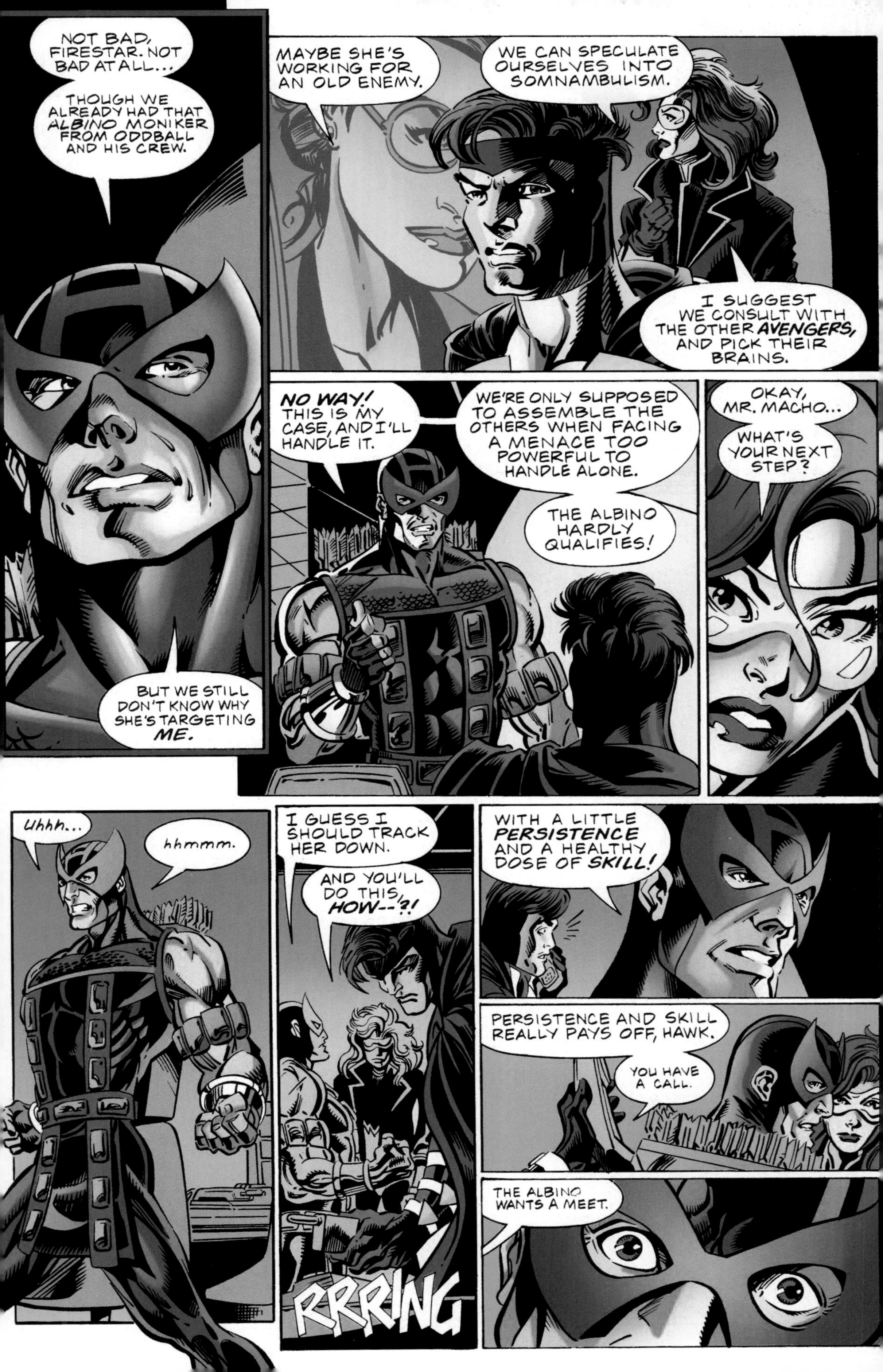
NOT BAD, FIRESTAR. NOT BAD AT ALL...
THOUGH WE ALREADY HAD THAT ALBINO MONIKER FROM ODDBALL AND HIS CREW.
BUT WE STILL DON'T KNOW WHY SHE'S TARGETING ME.
MAYBE SHE'S WORKING FOR AN OLD ENEMY.
WE CAN SPECULATE OURSELVES INTO SOMNAMBULISM.
I SUGGEST WE CONSULT WITH THE OTHER AVENGERS, AND PICK THEIR BRAINS.
NO WAY! THIS IS MY CASE, AND I'LL HANDLE IT.
WE'RE ONLY SUPPOSED TO ASSEMBLE THE OTHERS WHEN FACING A MENACE TOO POWERFUL TO HANDLE ALONE.
THE ALBINO HARDLY QUALIFIES!
OKAY, MR. MACHO...
WHAT'S YOUR NEXT STEP?
Uhhh...
hhmmm.
I GUESS I SHOULD TRACK HER DOWN.
AND YOU'LL DO THIS, HOW--?!
RRRING
WITH A LITTLE PERSISTENCE AND A HEALTHY DOSE OF SKILL!
PERSISTENCE AND SKILL REALLY PAYS OFF, HAWK.
YOU HAVE A CALL.
THE ALBINO WANTS A MEET.

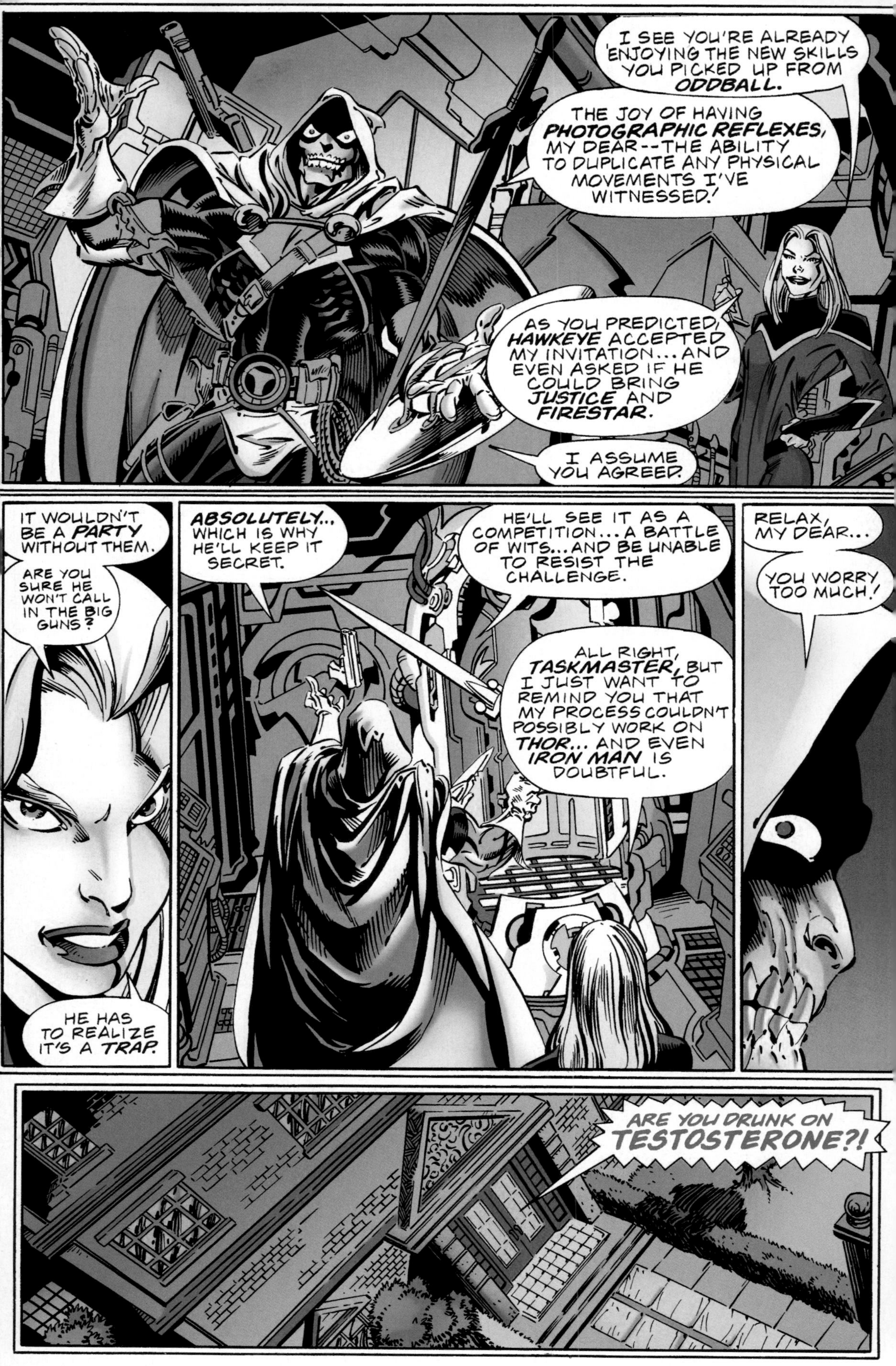
I SEE YOU'RE ALREADY ENJOYING THE NEW SKILLS YOU PICKED UP FROM ODDBALL.
THE JOY OF HAVING PHOTOGRAPHIC REFLEXES, MY DEAR--THE ABILITY TO DUPLICATE ANY PHYSICAL MOVEMENTS I'VE WITNESSED!
AS YOU PREDICTED, HAWKEYE ACCEPTED MY INVITATION... AND EVEN ASKED IF HE COULD BRING JUSTICE AND FIRESTAR.
I ASSUME YOU AGREED.
IT WOULDN'T BE A PARTY WITHOUT THEM.
ARE YOU SURE HE WON'T CALL IN THE BIG GUNS?
HE HAS TO REALIZE IT'S A TRAP.
ABSOLUTELY... WHICH IS WHY HE'LL KEEP IT SECRET.
HE'LL SEE IT AS A COMPETITION... A BATTLE OF WITS... AND BE UNABLE TO RESIST THE CHALLENGE.
ALL RIGHT, TASKMASTER, BUT I JUST WANT TO REMIND YOU THAT MY PROCESS COULDN'T POSSIBLY WORK ON THOR... AND EVEN IRON MAN IS DOUBTFUL.
RELAX, MY DEAR...
YOU WORRY TOO MUCH!
ARE YOU DRUNK ON TESTOSTERONE?!

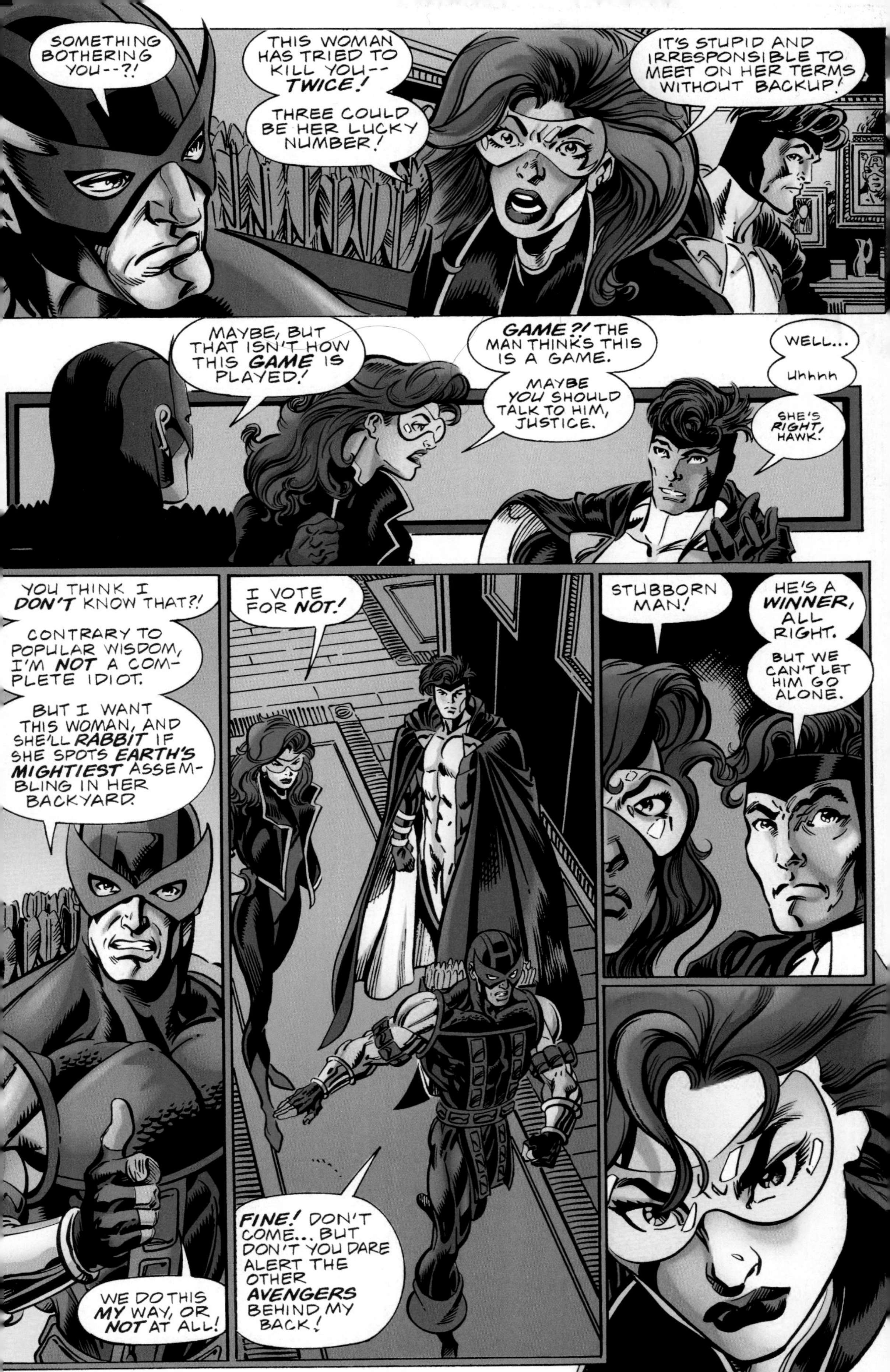
SOMETHING BOTHERING YOU--?!
THIS WOMAN HAS TRIED TO KILL YOU-- TWICE!
THREE COULD BE HER LUCKY NUMBER!
IT'S STUPID AND IRRESPONSIBLE TO MEET ON HER TERMS WITHOUT BACKUP!
MAYBE, BUT THAT ISN'T HOW THIS GAME IS PLAYED!
GAME?! THE MAN THINKS THIS IS A GAME.
MAYBE YOU SHOULD TALK TO HIM, JUSTICE.
WELL...
Uhhhh
SHE'S RIGHT, HAWK!
YOU THINK I DON'T KNOW THAT?!
CONTRARY TO POPULAR WISDOM, I'M NOT A COMPLETE IDIOT.
BUT I WANT THIS WOMAN, AND SHE'LL RABBIT IF SHE SPOTS EARTH'S MIGHTIEST ASSEMBLING IN HER BACKYARD.
WE DO THIS MY WAY, OR NOT AT ALL!
I VOTE FOR NOT!
FINE! DON'T COME... BUT DON'T YOU DARE ALERT THE OTHER AVENGERS BEHIND MY BACK!
STUBBORN MAN!
HE'S A WINNER, ALL RIGHT.
BUT WE CAN'T LET HIM GO ALONE.

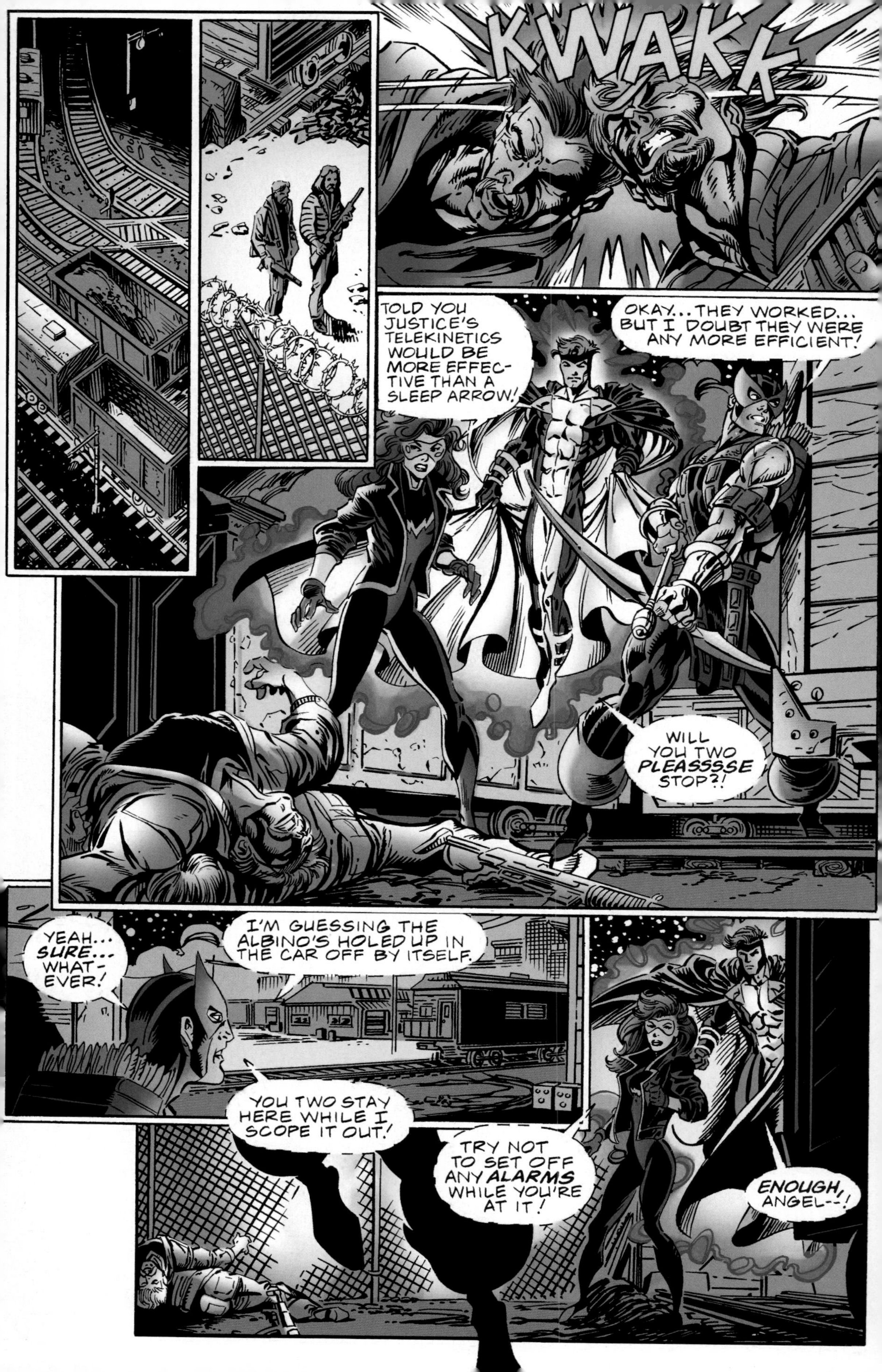
KWAKK
TOLD YOU JUSTICE'S TELEKINETICS WOULD BE MORE EFFEC-TIVE THAN A SLEEP ARROW!
OKAY... THEY WORKED... BUT I DOUBT THEY WERE ANY MORE EFFICIENT!
WILL YOU TWO PLEASSSSE STOP?!
YEAH... SURE... WHAT-EVER!
I'M GUESSING THE ALBINO'S HOLED UP IN THE CAR OFF BY ITSELF.
YOU TWO STAY HERE WHILE I SCOPE IT OUT!
TRY NOT TO SET OFF ANY ALARMS WHILE YOU'RE AT IT!
ENOUGH, ANGEL--!

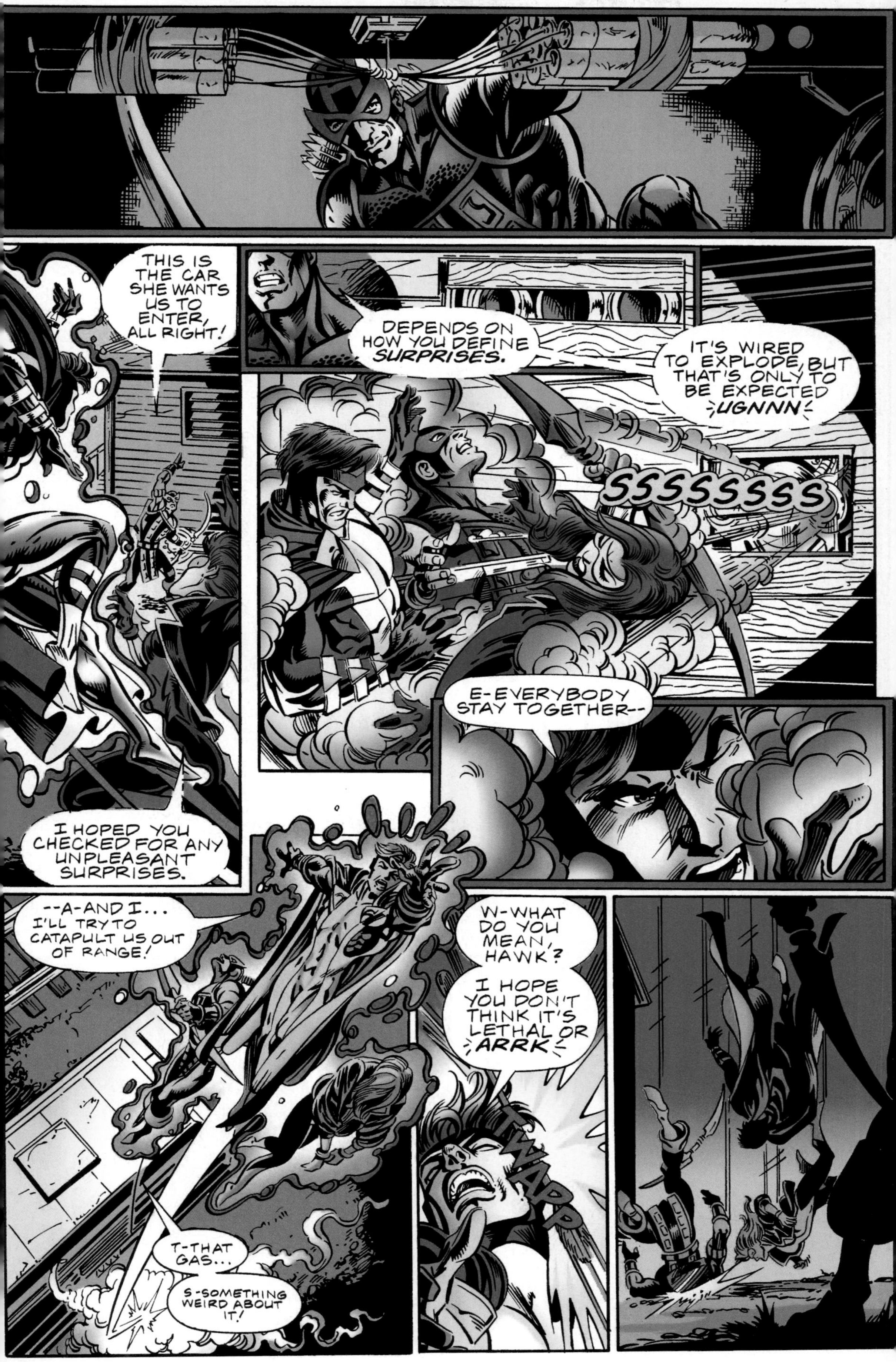
THIS IS THE CAR SHE WANTS US TO ENTER, ALL RIGHT!
I HOPED YOU CHECKED FOR ANY UNPLEASANT SURPRISES.
DEPENDS ON HOW YOU DEFINE SURPRISES.
IT'S WIRED TO EXPLODE, BUT THAT'S ONLY TO BE EXPECTED UGNNN
SSSSSSSSS
E-EVERYBODY STAY TOGETHER--
--A-AND I... I'LL TRY TO CATAPULT US OUT OF RANGE!
T-THAT GAS...
S-SOMETHING WEIRD ABOUT IT!
W-WHAT DO YOU MEAN, HAWK?
I HOPE YOU DON'T THINK IT'S LETHAL OR ARRK
THWAPP

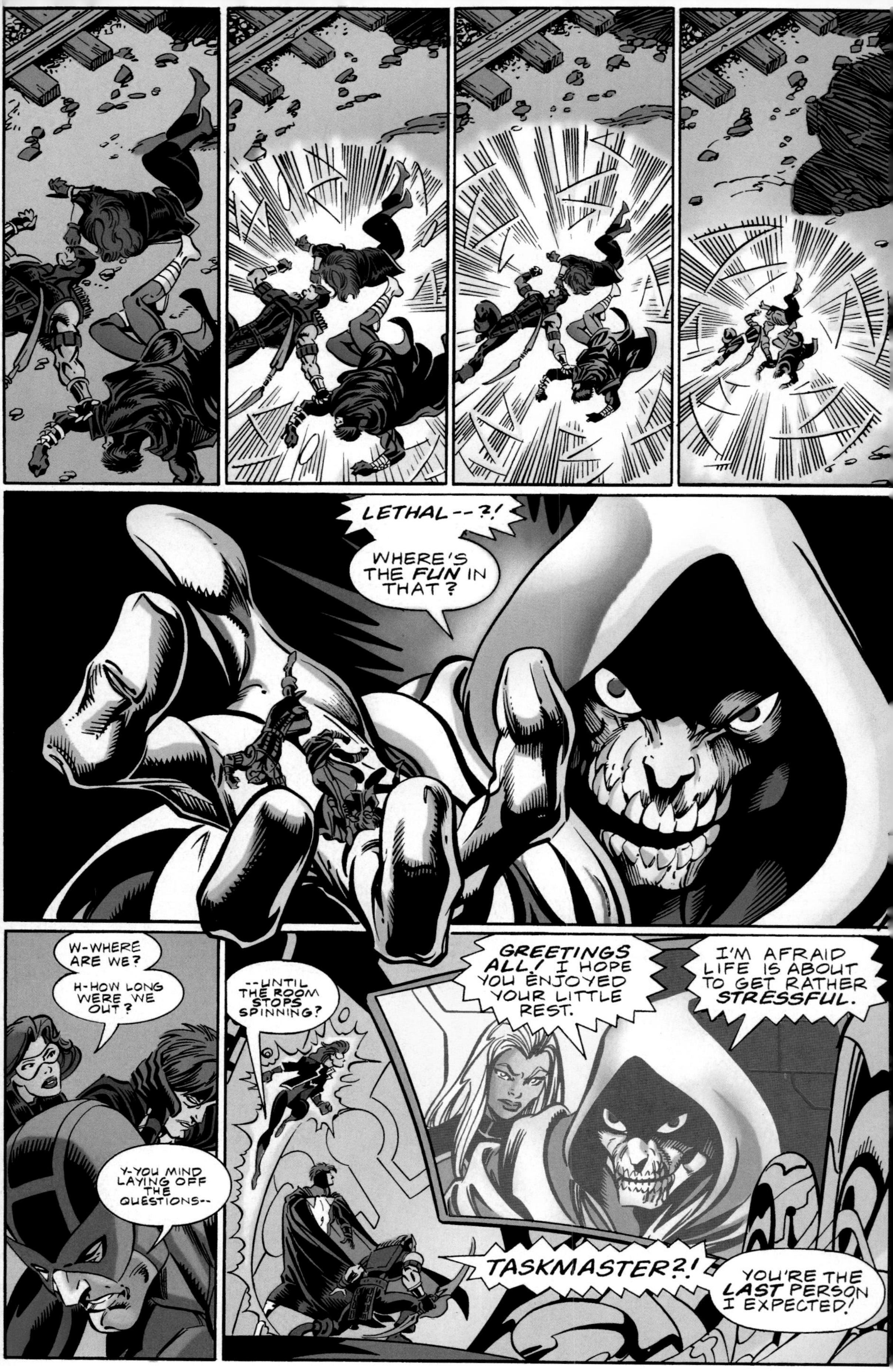
LETHAL--?!
WHERE'S THE FUN IN THAT?
W-WHERE ARE WE?
H-HOW LONG WERE WE OUT?
Y-YOU MIND LAYING OFF THE QUESTIONS--
--UNTIL THE ROOM STOPS SPINNING?
GREETINGS ALL! I HOPE YOU ENJOYED YOUR LITTLE REST.
I'M AFRAID LIFE IS ABOUT TO GET RATHER STRESSFUL.
TASKMASTER?!
YOU'RE THE LAST PERSON I EXPECTED!

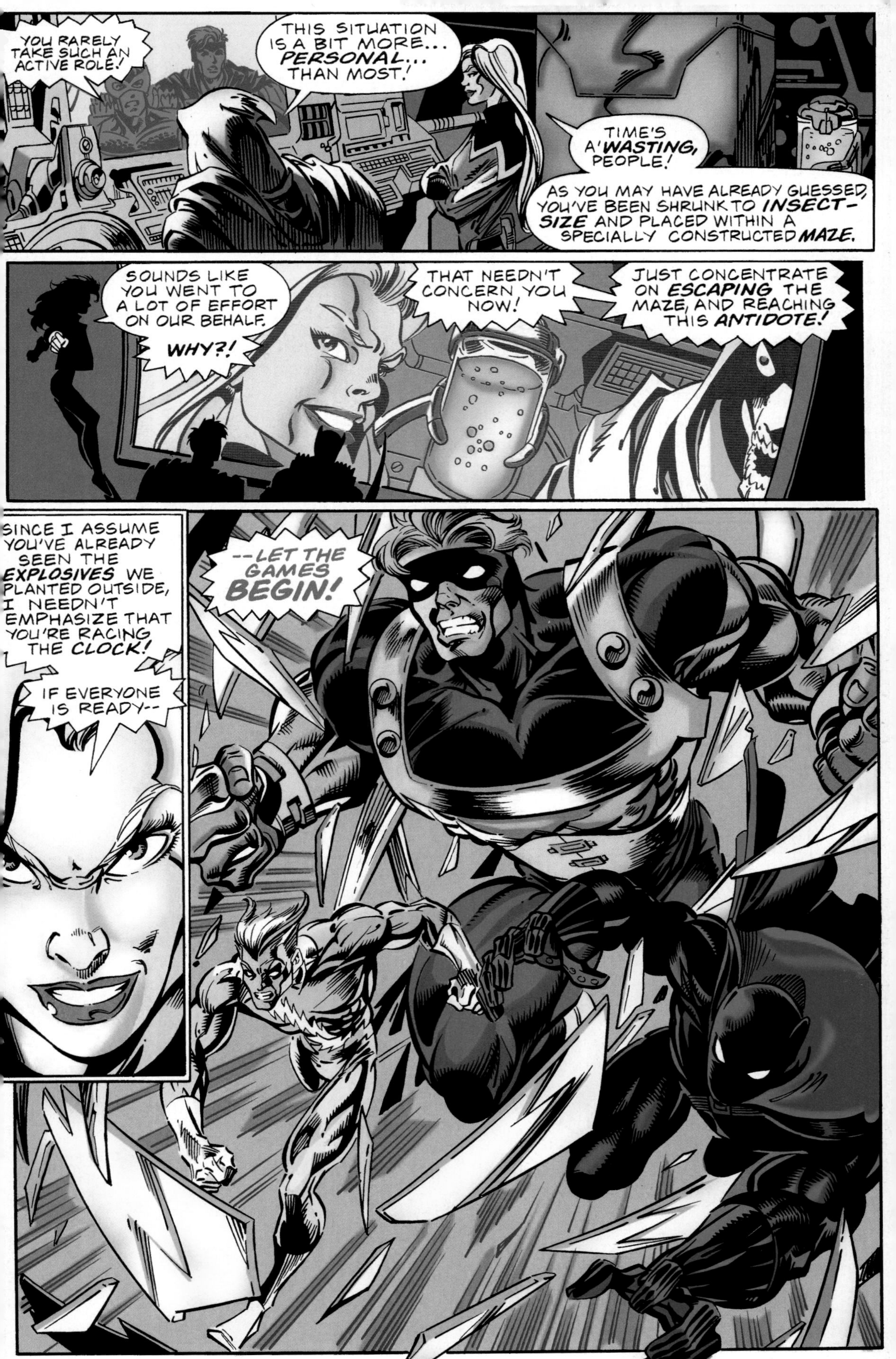

YOU RARELY TAKE SUCH AN ACTIVE ROLE!
THIS SITUATION IS A BIT MORE... PERSONAL... THAN MOST!
TIME'S A'WASTING, PEOPLE!
AS YOU MAY HAVE ALREADY GUESSED, YOU'VE BEEN SHRUNK TO INSECT-SIZE AND PLACED WITHIN A SPECIALLY CONSTRUCTED MAZE.
SOUNDS LIKE YOU WENT TO A LOT OF EFFORT ON OUR BEHALF.
WHY?!
THAT NEEDN'T CONCERN YOU NOW!
JUST CONCENTRATE ON ESCAPING THE MAZE, AND REACHING THIS ANTIDOTE!
SINCE I ASSUME YOU'VE ALREADY SEEN THE EXPLOSIVES WE PLANTED OUTSIDE, I NEEDN'T EMPHASIZE THAT YOU'RE RACING THE CLOCK!
IF EVERYONE IS READY--
--LET THE GAMES BEGIN!

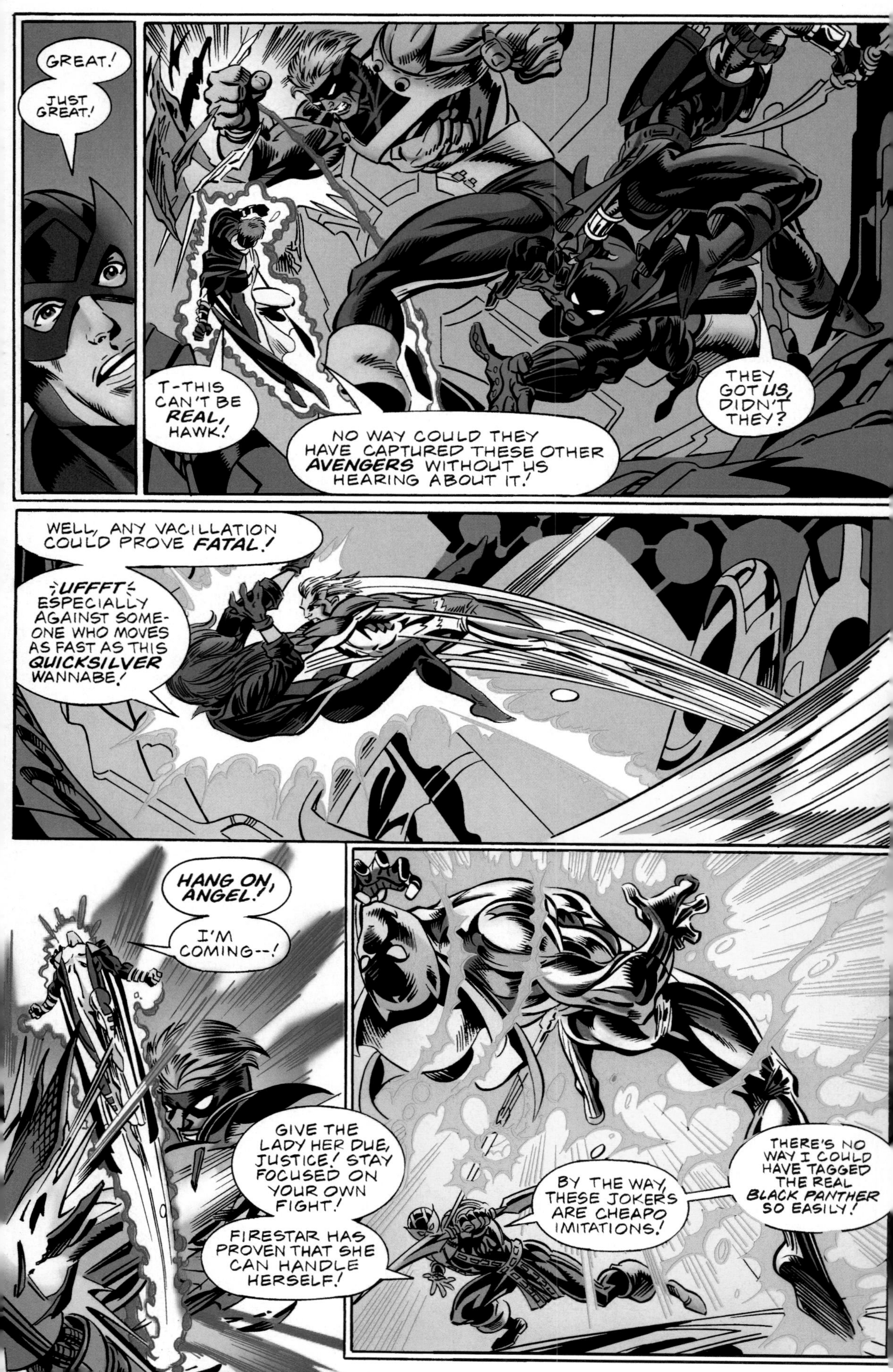
GREAT!
JUST GREAT!
T-THIS CAN'T BE REAL, HAWK!
NO WAY COULD THEY HAVE CAPTURED THESE OTHER AVENGERS WITHOUT US HEARING ABOUT IT!
THEY GOT US, DIDN'T THEY?
WELL, ANY VACILLATION COULD PROVE FATAL!
UFFFT ESPECIALLY AGAINST SOME-ONE WHO MOVES AS FAST AS THIS QUICKSILVER WANNABE!
HANG ON, ANGEL!
I'M COMING--!
GIVE THE LADY HER DUE, JUSTICE! STAY FOCUSED ON YOUR OWN FIGHT!
FIRESTAR HAS PROVEN THAT SHE CAN HANDLE HERSELF!
BY THE WAY, THESE JOKERS ARE CHEAPO IMITATIONS!
THERE'S NO WAY I COULD HAVE TAGGED THE REAL BLACK PANTHER SO EASILY!

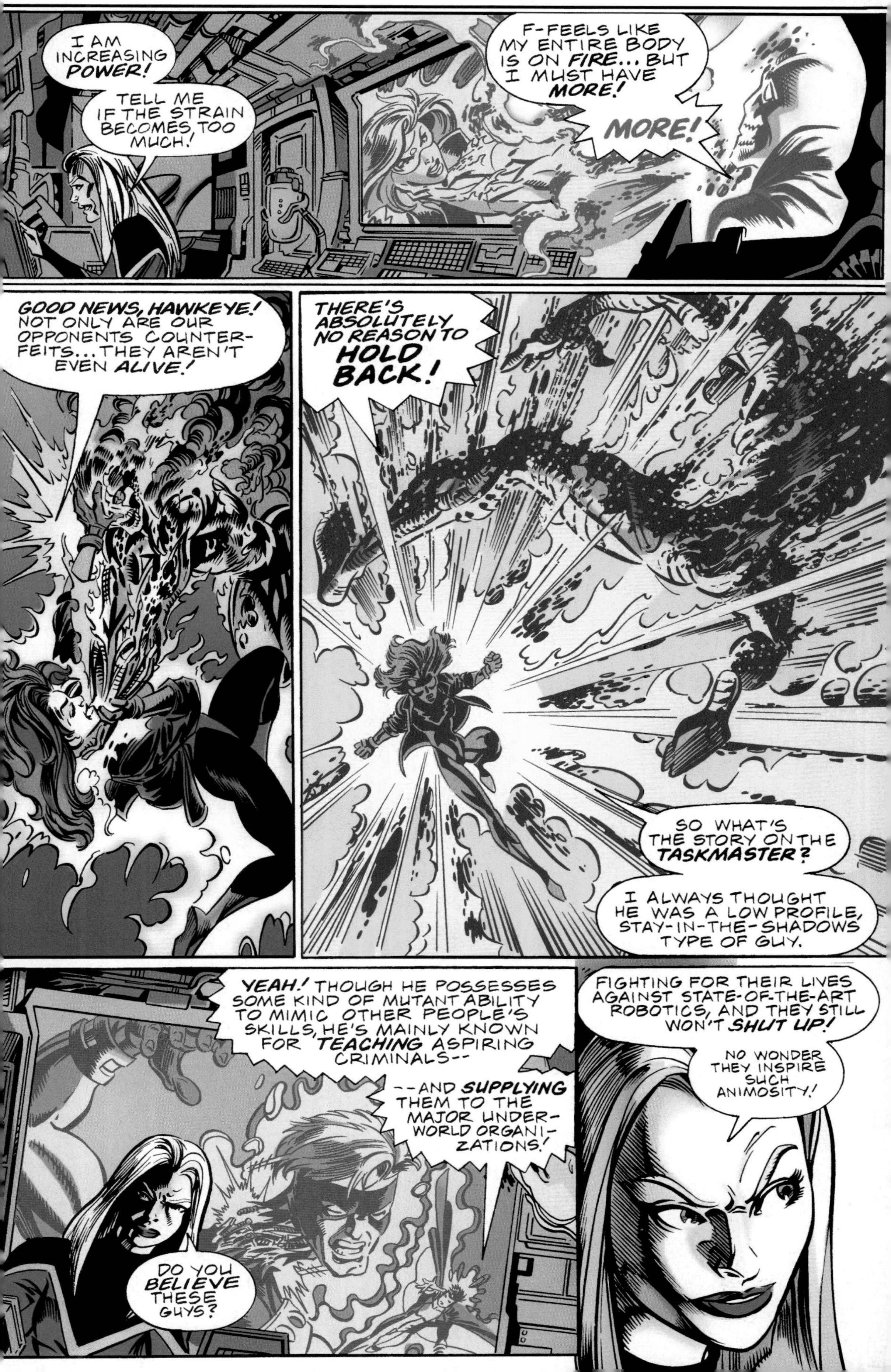
I AM INCREASING POWER!
TELL ME IF THE STRAIN BECOMES TOO MUCH!
F-FEELS LIKE MY ENTIRE BODY IS ON FIRE... BUT I MUST HAVE MORE!
MORE!
GOOD NEWS, HAWKEYE! NOT ONLY ARE OUR OPPONENTS COUNTERFEITS... THEY AREN'T EVEN ALIVE!
THERE'S ABSOLUTELY NO REASON TO HOLD BACK!
SO WHAT'S THE STORY ON THE TASKMASTER?
I ALWAYS THOUGHT HE WAS A LOW PROFILE, STAY-IN-THE-SHADOWS TYPE OF GUY.
YEAH! THOUGH HE POSSESSES SOME KIND OF MUTANT ABILITY TO MIMIC OTHER PEOPLE'S SKILLS, HE'S MAINLY KNOWN FOR TEACHING ASPIRING CRIMINALS--
--AND SUPPLYING THEM TO THE MAJOR UNDERWORLD ORGANIZATIONS!
DO YOU BELIEVE THESE GUYS?
FIGHTING FOR THEIR LIVES AGAINST STATE-OF-THE-ART ROBOTICS, AND THEY STILL WON'T SHUT UP!
NO WONDER THEY INSPIRE SUCH ANIMOSITY!

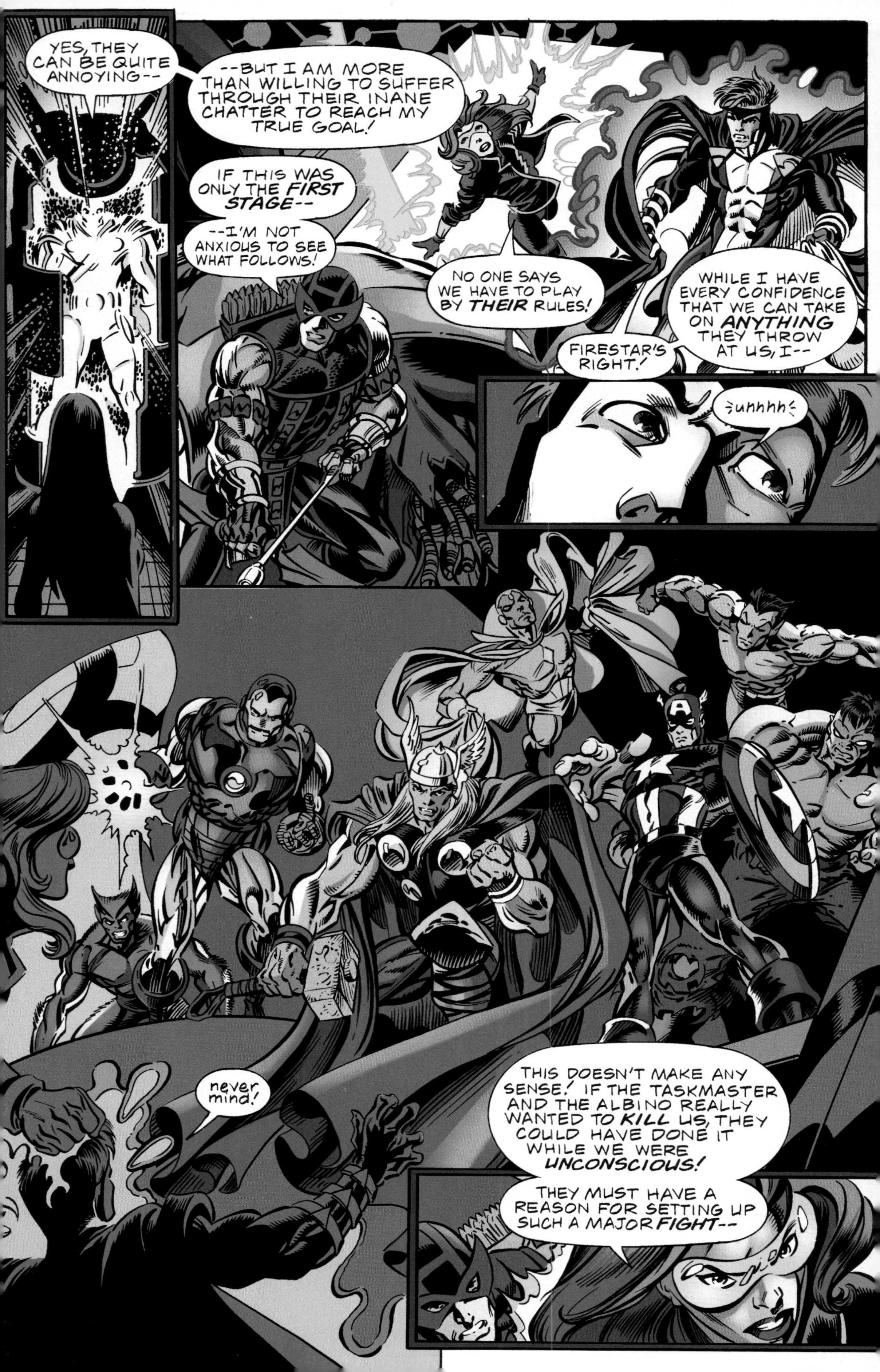
YES, THEY CAN BE QUITE ANNOYING--
--BUT I AM MORE THAN WILLING TO SUFFER THROUGH THEIR INANE CHATTER TO REACH MY TRUE GOAL!
IF THIS WAS ONLY THE FIRST STAGE--
--I'M NOT ANXIOUS TO SEE WHAT FOLLOWS!
NO ONE SAYS WE HAVE TO PLAY BY THEIR RULES!
FIRESTAR'S RIGHT!
WHILE I HAVE EVERY CONFIDENCE THAT WE CAN TAKE ON ANYTHING THEY THROW AT US, I--
unhhh
never mind!
THIS DOESN'T MAKE ANY SENSE! IF THE TASKMASTER AND THE ALBINO REALLY WANTED TO KILL US, THEY COULD HAVE DONE IT WHILE WE WERE UNCONSCIOUS!
THEY MUST HAVE A REASON FOR SETTING UP SUCH A MAJOR FIGHT--

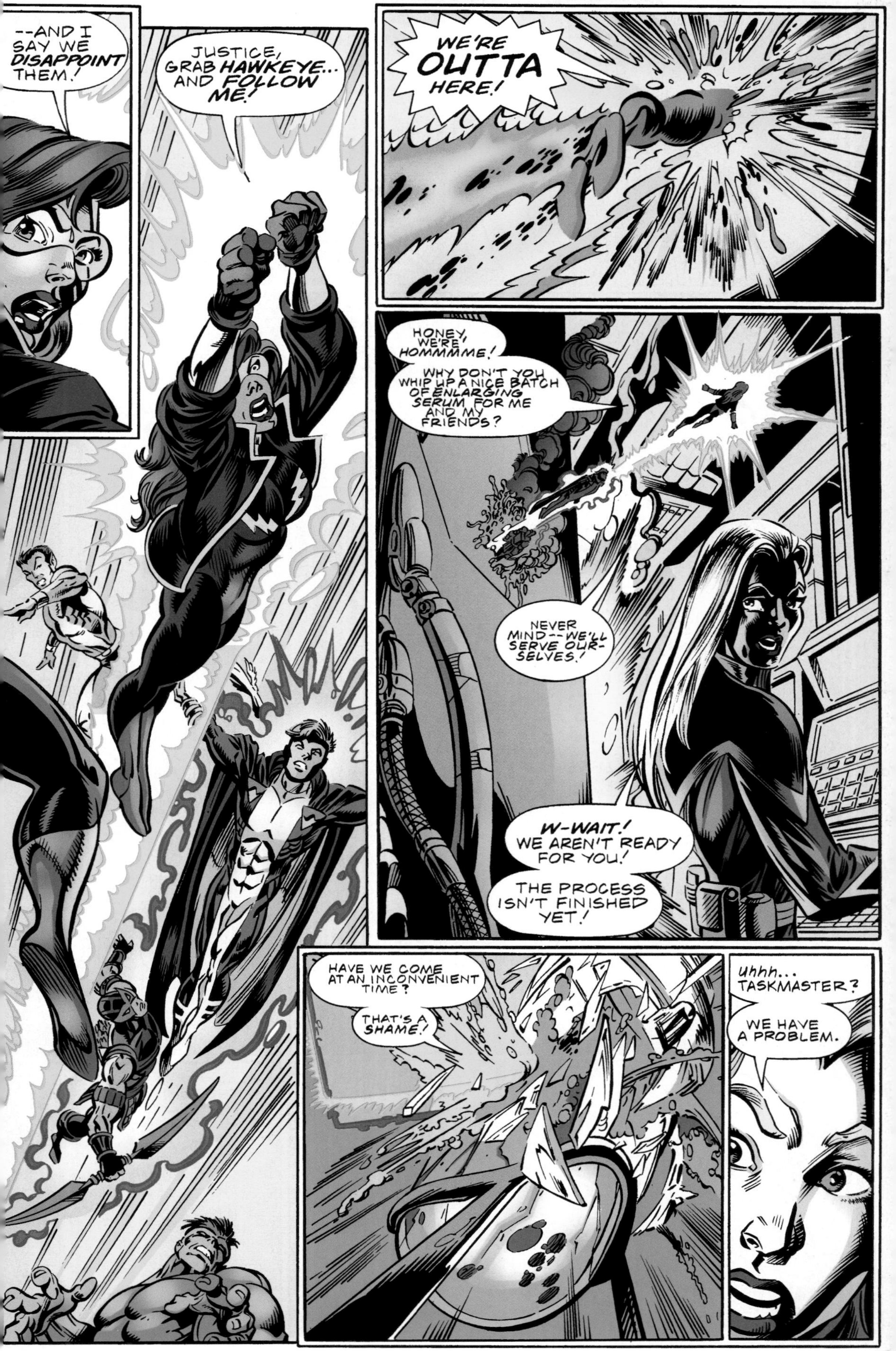
--AND I SAY WE DISAPPOINT THEM!
JUSTICE, GRAB HAWKEYE... AND FOLLOW ME!
WE'RE OUTTA HERE!
HONEY, WE'RE HOMMMME!
WHY DON'T YOU WHIP UP A NICE BATCH OF ENLARGING SERUM FOR ME AND MY FRIENDS?
NEVER MIND--WE'LL SERVE OUR-SELVES!
W-WAIT! WE AREN'T READY FOR YOU!
THE PROCESS ISN'T FINISHED YET!
HAVE WE COME AT AN INCONVENIENT TIME?
THAT'S A SHAME!
Uhhh... TASKMASTER?
WE HAVE A PROBLEM.

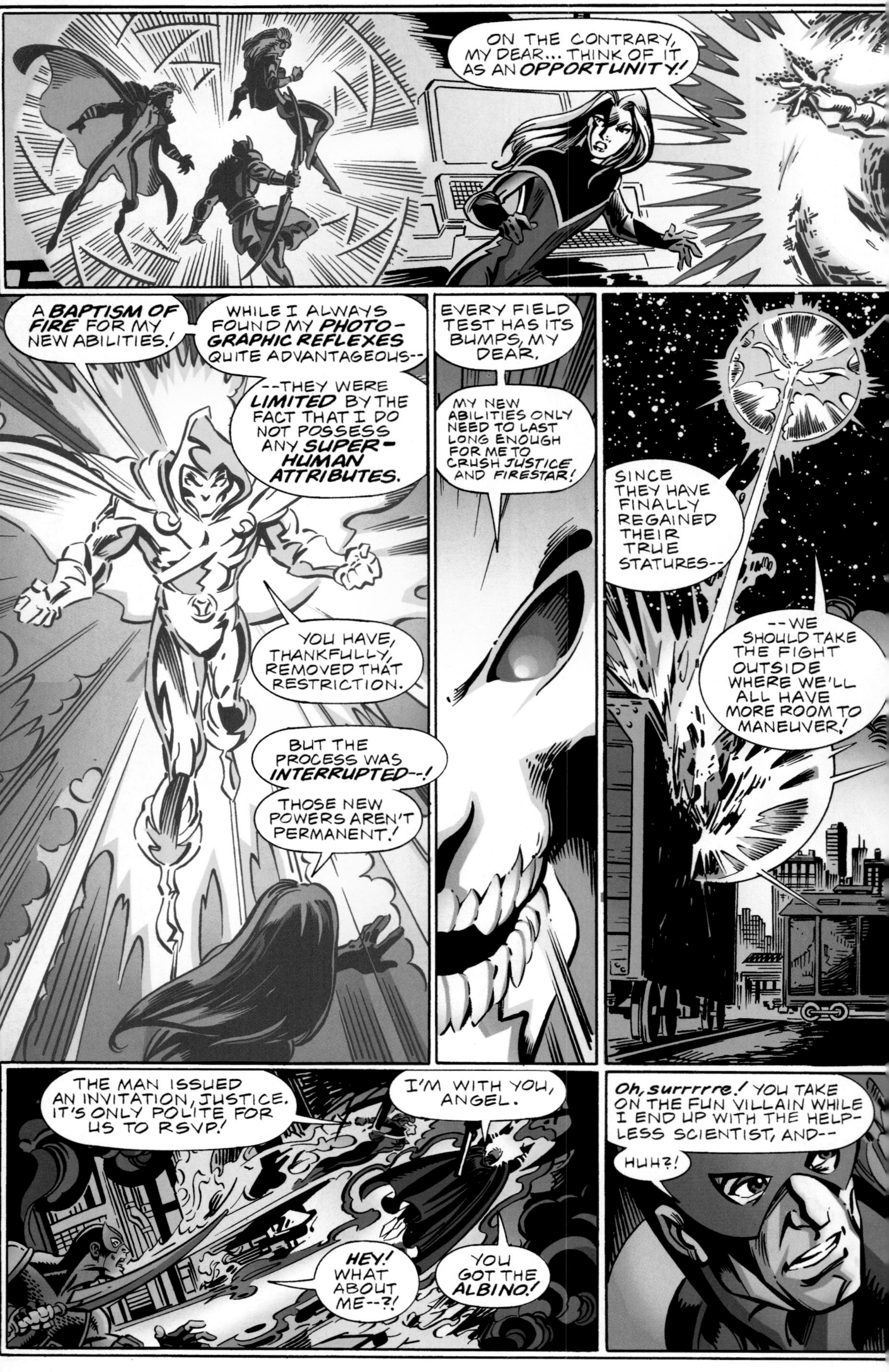

ON THE CONTRARY, MY DEAR... THINK OF IT AS AN OPPORTUNITY!
A BAPTISM OF FIRE FOR MY NEW ABILITIES!
WHILE I ALWAYS FOUND MY PHOTO-GRAPHIC REFLEXES QUITE ADVANTAGEOUS--
--THEY WERE LIMITED BY THE FACT THAT I DO NOT POSSESS ANY SUPER-HUMAN ATTRIBUTES.
YOU HAVE, THANKFULLY, REMOVED THAT RESTRICTION.
BUT THE PROCESS WAS INTERRUPTED--!
THOSE NEW POWERS AREN'T PERMANENT!
EVERY FIELD TEST HAS ITS BUMPS, MY DEAR.
MY NEW ABILITIES ONLY NEED TO LAST LONG ENOUGH FOR ME TO CRUSH JUSTICE AND FIRESTAR!
SINCE THEY HAVE FINALLY REGAINED THEIR TRUE STATURES--
--WE SHOULD TAKE THE FIGHT OUTSIDE WHERE WE'LL ALL HAVE MORE ROOM TO MANEUVER!
THE MAN ISSUED AN INVITATION, JUSTICE. IT'S ONLY POLITE FOR US TO RSVP!
I'M WITH YOU, ANGEL.
HEY! WHAT ABOUT ME--?!
YOU GOT THE ALBINO!
Oh, surrrrre! YOU TAKE ON THE FUN VILLAIN WHILE I END UP WITH THE HELP-LESS SCIENTIST, AND--
HUH?!

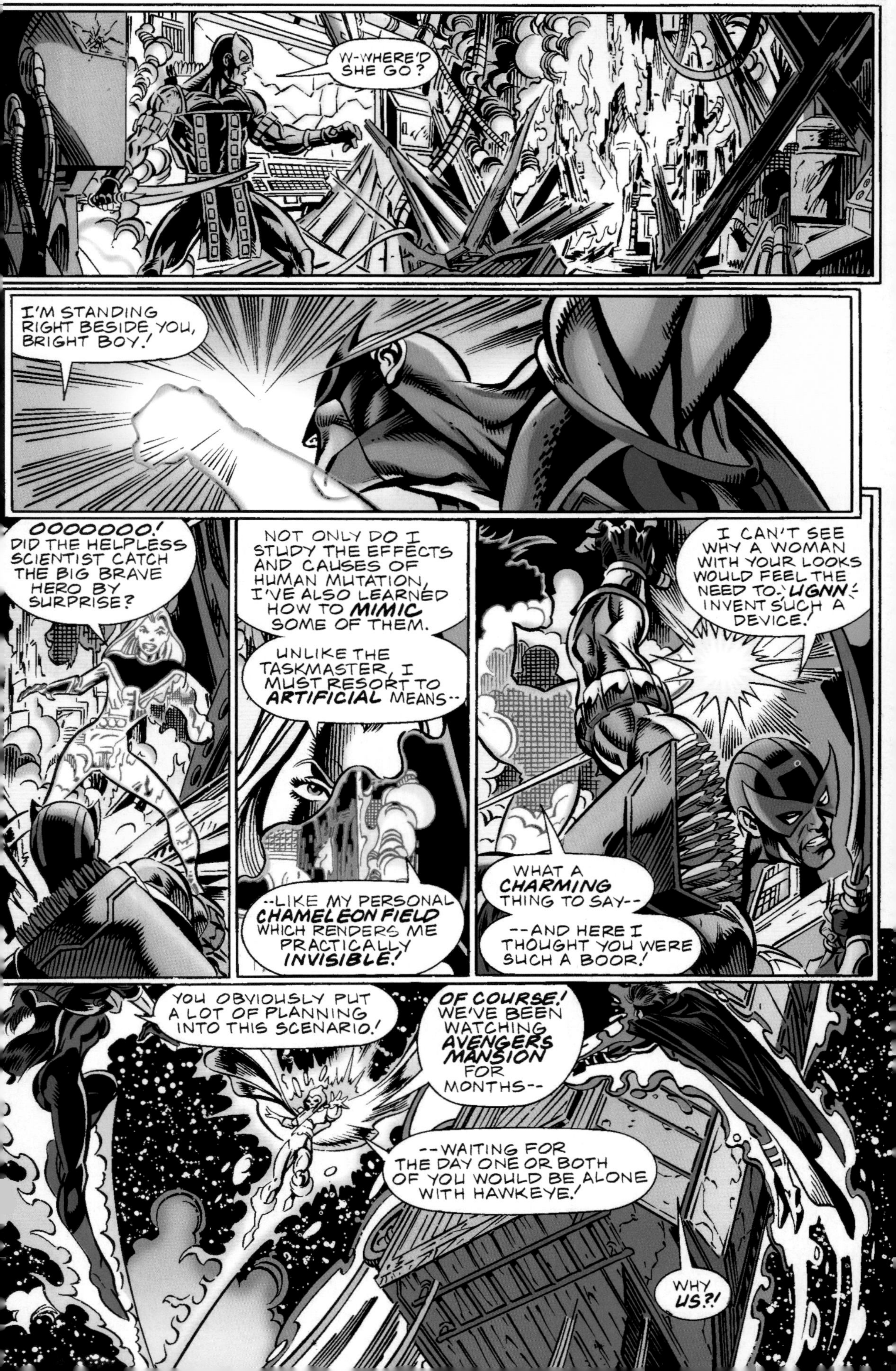

W-WHERE'D SHE GO?
I'M STANDING RIGHT BESIDE YOU, BRIGHT BOY!
OOOOOOO! DID THE HELPLESS SCIENTIST CATCH THE BIG BRAVE HERO BY SURPRISE?
NOT ONLY DO I STUDY THE EFFECTS AND CAUSES OF HUMAN MUTATION, I'VE ALSO LEARNED HOW TO MIMIC SOME OF THEM.
UNLIKE THE TASKMASTER, I MUST RESORT TO ARTIFICIAL MEANS--
--LIKE MY PERSONAL CHAMELEON FIELD WHICH RENDERS ME PRACTICALLY INVISIBLE!
I CAN'T SEE WHY A WOMAN WITH YOUR LOOKS WOULD FEEL THE NEED TO-UGNN-INVENT SUCH A DEVICE!
WHAT A CHARMING THING TO SAY--
--AND HERE I THOUGHT YOU WERE SUCH A BOOR!
YOU OBVIOUSLY PUT A LOT OF PLANNING INTO THIS SCENARIO!
OF COURSE! WE'VE BEEN WATCHING AVENGERS MANSION FOR MONTHS--
--WAITING FOR THE DAY ONE OR BOTH OF YOU WOULD BE ALONE WITH HAWKEYE!
WHY US?!

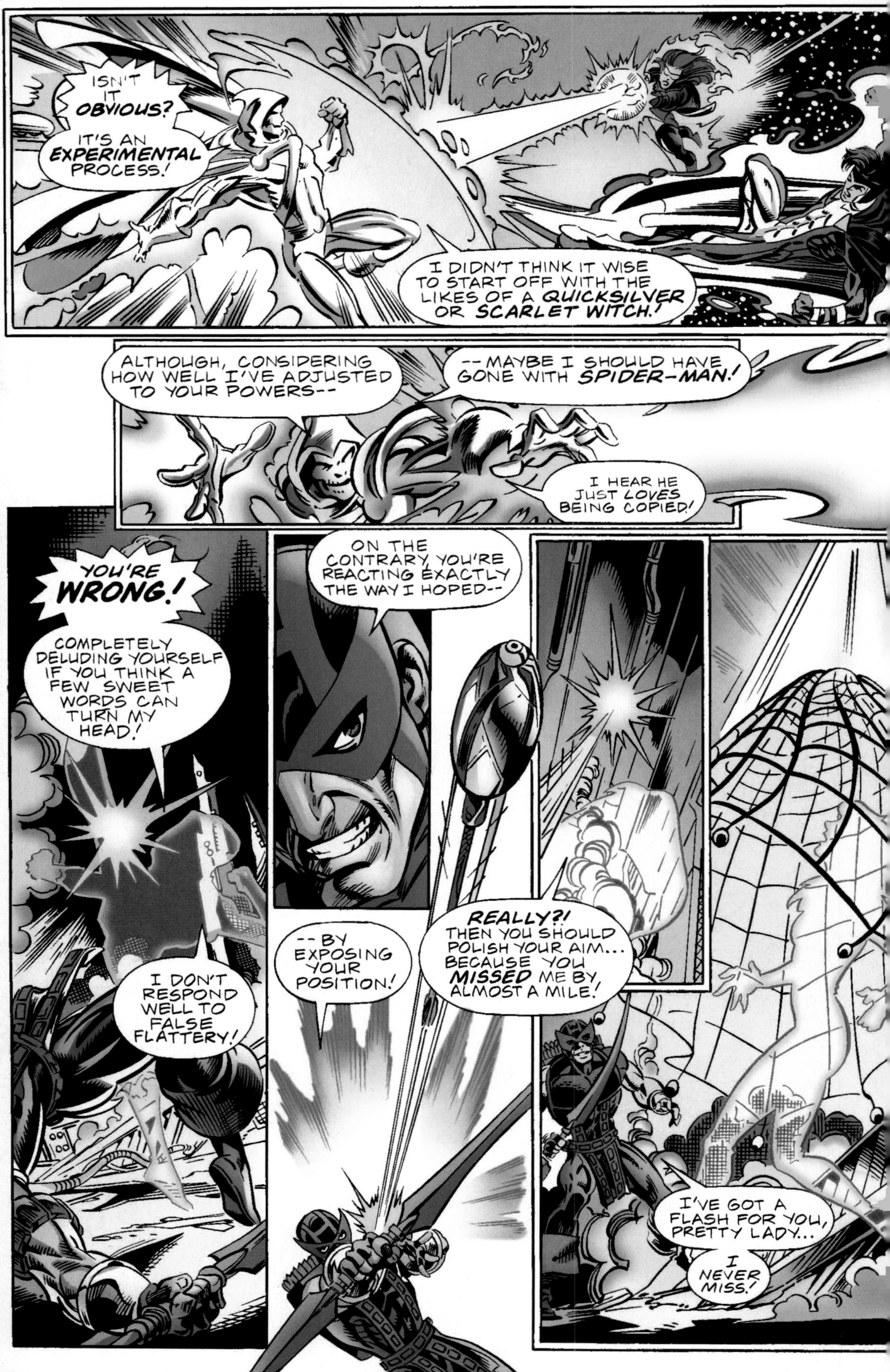
ISN'T IT OBVIOUS?
IT'S AN EXPERIMENTAL PROCESS!
I DIDN'T THINK IT WISE TO START OFF WITH THE LIKES OF A QUICKSILVER OR SCARLET WITCH!
ALTHOUGH, CONSIDERING HOW WELL I'VE ADJUSTED TO YOUR POWERS--
--MAYBE I SHOULD HAVE GONE WITH SPIDER-MAN!
I HEAR HE JUST LOVES BEING COPIED!
YOU'RE WRONG!
COMPLETELY DELUDING YOURSELF IF YOU THINK A FEW SWEET WORDS CAN TURN MY HEAD!
I DON'T RESPOND WELL TO FALSE FLATTERY!
ON THE CONTRARY, YOU'RE REACTING EXACTLY THE WAY I HOPED--
-- BY EXPOSING YOUR POSITION!
REALLY?! THEN YOU SHOULD POLISH YOUR AIM... BECAUSE YOU MISSED ME BY ALMOST A MILE!
I'VE GOT A FLASH FOR YOU, PRETTY LADY...
I NEVER MISS!

YOU THINK THIS IS OVER?

THE TASKMASTER WILL FREE ME AND FLASH-FRY YOU--

--AFTER HE'S FINISHED WITH YOUR FRIENDS!

A MOST POTENT COMBINATION...

I CAN HOLD YOU WITH JUSTICE'S TELEKINETICS WHILE BARBECUING YOU WITH FIRESTAR'S MICROWAVES!

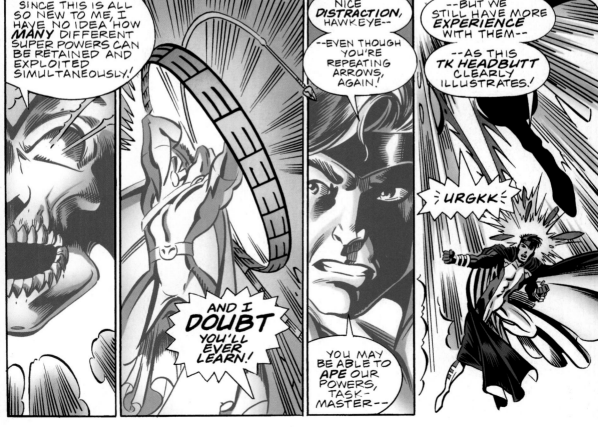

SINCE THIS IS ALL SO NEW TO ME, I HAVE NO IDEA HOW MANY DIFFERENT SUPER POWERS CAN BE RETAINED AND EXPLOITED SIMULTANEOUSLY!

AND I DOUBT YOU'LL EVER LEARN!

NICE DISTRACTION, HAWKEYE--

--EVEN THOUGH YOU'RE REPEATING ARROWS, AGAIN!

YOU MAY BE ABLE TO APE OUR POWERS, TASK-MASTER--

--BUT WE STILL HAVE MORE EXPERIENCE WITH THEM--

--AS THIS TK HEADBUTT CLEARLY ILLUSTRATES!

≥URGKK≥

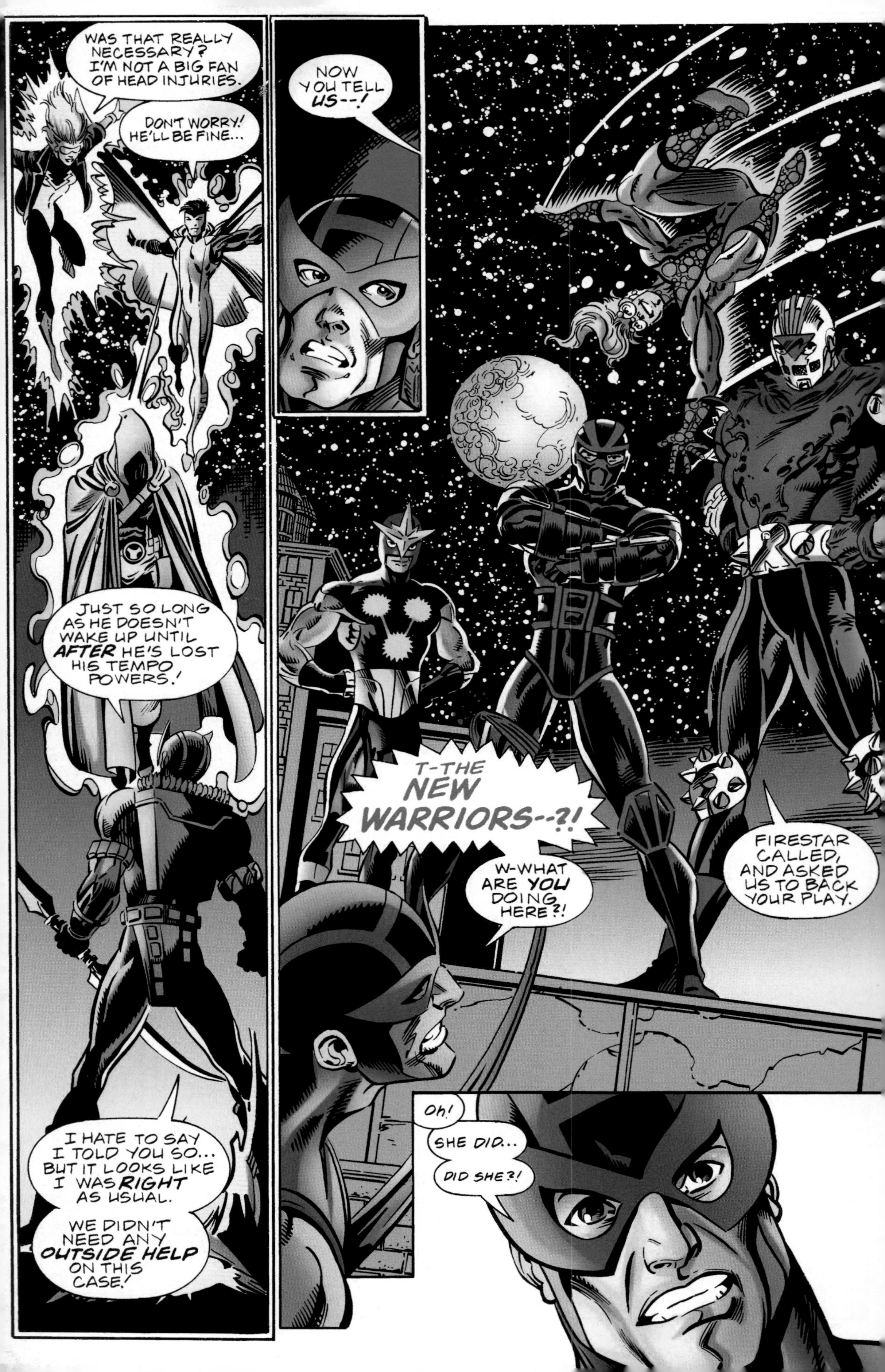

WAS THAT REALLY NECESSARY? I'M NOT A BIG FAN OF HEAD INJURIES.
DON'T WORRY! HE'LL BE FINE...
JUST SO LONG AS HE DOESN'T WAKE UP UNTIL AFTER HE'S LOST HIS TEMPO POWERS.!
I HATE TO SAY I TOLD YOU SO... BUT IT LOOKS LIKE I WAS RIGHT AS USUAL.
WE DIDN'T NEED ANY OUTSIDE HELP ON THIS CASE!
NOW YOU TELL US--!
T-THE NEW WARRIORS--?!
W-WHAT ARE YOU DOING HERE?!
FIRESTAR CALLED, AND ASKED US TO BACK YOUR PLAY.
Oh!
SHE DID...
DID SHE?!

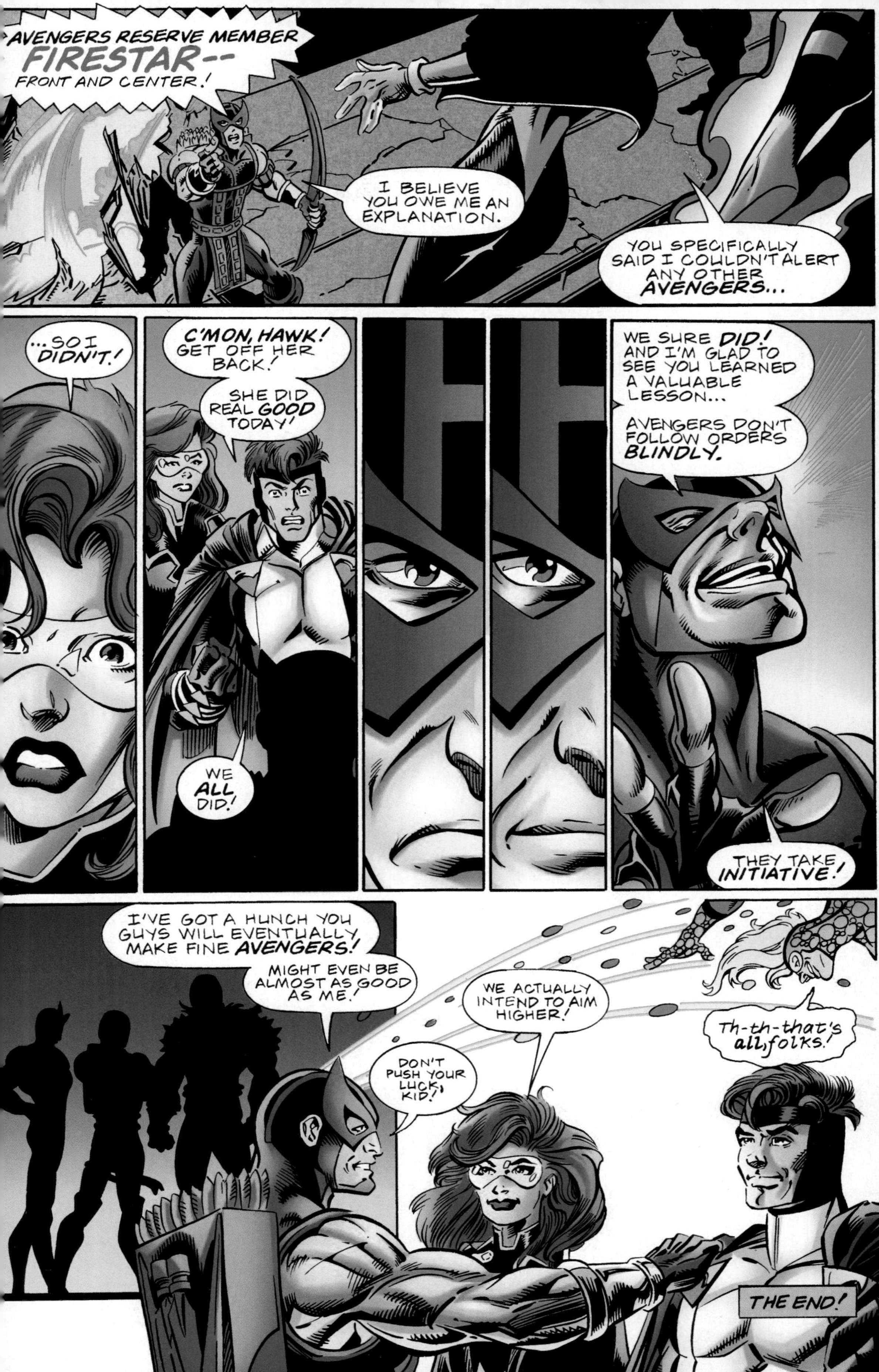
AVENGERS RESERVE MEMBER FIRESTAR-- FRONT AND CENTER!
I BELIEVE YOU OWE ME AN EXPLANATION.
YOU SPECIFICALLY SAID I COULDN'T ALERT ANY OTHER AVENGERS...
...SO I DIDN'T!
C'MON, HAWK! GET OFF HER BACK!
SHE DID REAL GOOD TODAY!
WE ALL DID!
WE SURE DID! AND I'M GLAD TO SEE YOU LEARNED A VALUABLE LESSON...
AVENGERS DON'T FOLLOW ORDERS BLINDLY.
THEY TAKE INITIATIVE!
I'VE GOT A HUNCH YOU GUYS WILL EVENTUALLY MAKE FINE AVENGERS!
MIGHT EVEN BE ALMOST AS GOOD AS ME!
DON'T PUSH YOUR LUCK, KID!
WE ACTUALLY INTEND TO AIM HIGHER!
Th-th-that's all, folks!
THE END!